Stacey Abbott is a Reader in Film and Television Studies at Roehampton University. An expert on sci-fi, horror, and cult TV, she is the author of *Angel* and *Celluloid Vampires*, the editor for the *Investigating Cult TV* series (U.K.), and has published on such favorite shows as *Buffy*, *Alias*, *Angel*, *Firefly*, *Lost*, and *Ultraviolet*.

The Cult TV Book

From Star Trek to Dexter,
New Approaches to TV Outside the Box

Edited by

Stacey Abbott

Soft Skull Press
New York

First published by I.B. Tauris & Co. Ltd. in the United Kingdom.

Library of Congress Cataloging-in-Publication Data is available.

ISBN: 978-1-59376-276-6

Cover design by John Yates
Printed and bound in the United States of America by Edwards Brothers, Inc.

Soft Skull Press
An Imprint of Counterpoint LLC
2117 Fourth Street
Suite D
Berkeley, CA 94710

www.softskull.com
www.counterpointpress.com

Distributed by Publishers Group West

10 9 8 7 6 5 4 3 2 1

To my super cyber sibs – Glenn, Les, Jeff, and Jo – with all my love.

Contents

Contents

Part 3 – Constructing Cult TV: The Broadcast Industry and Cult Television

Part 4 – The Cult in Cult TV: Audiences, Fans, and Fandom

Acknowledgments

This book has been a huge endeavour both in its conception and construction and I therefore owe the greatest of thanks to all of the contributors who have made this such an enjoyable and rewarding experience. They have each been a joy to work with, bringing enthusiasm and professionalism to the project in equal measures. The strength of this book lies in their expertise. I would also like to thank Philippa Brewster and everyone at I.B.Tauris who have supported this project alongside the *Investigating Cult TV series*. Philippa in particular has been an often invisible but significant presence, shaping the growing field of television studies. Her support of my work has been boundless and for that I am in her debt. To fellow TV scholars David Lavery, Rhonda Wilcox, Janet McCabe, Kim Akass, Deborah Jermyn, Lorna Jowett, and Bronwen Calvert, thank you for the many hours of enthusiastic debate and discussion. It has always been a joy. Of course, one of the greatest challenges in developing this book has been keeping up to date with the vast array of new cult programmes that have continued to appear on TV. I would therefore like to thank Stan Beeler for his generosity in recording and sending me DVDs of any new and interesting cult shows that came on the air in North America but had yet to be broadcast in the UK, the best of which included *Dexter, Pushing Daisies*, and *True Blood*. On a similar note, I would like to thank Denzell Richards and Susie Hyde for recording key cult programmes off Sky1 when I lost the channel during the Virgin-Sky feud. Each of you have ensured that my knowledge of cult TV remained as up to date as possible. Thank you for the hours of pleasurable TV viewing. To my friends Sergio Angelini and Miles Booy, I owe a debt for their enthusiasm and encouragement as they offered numerous suggestions as to what types of television programmes should be included in the book. While I may not have included everything you suggested (Miles, I'm sorry *Press Gang* didn't make the final cut), your knowledge and cult tastes are clearly felt in the final product and the book is better for it.

I, of course, owe the greatest debt to my husband and partner Simon Brown. He not only contributed two excellent chapters but offered unending support during the long hours, weeks, months, and years of the book's conception and birth – support which included watching hours of television, repeated discussions and debates over content and in the final days, practical and invaluable help compiling the Film and TV guide as well as editing the bibliography – not to mention repeatedly taking Max (our dog) out for walks while I finished my work (thanks to Max as well). I couldn't have done it without you both. As always, I owe a debt to my family for shaping the person I am and for their support over the years. My parents Stanley and Joan Abbott gave me the confidence to pursue my passion and it was from them that I gained my first-love, film. But it was with my siblings, Glenn, Leslie, Jeff, and Joanne, that I grew up watching and talking about television, from *Star Trek* to *Seinfeld* to *Desperate Housewives*. We haven't always watched the same programmes nor have we always shared the same opinions but our conversations have been a great environment in which to exchange ideas as well as a few laughs. You mean the world to me. For this reason I dedicate this book to you.

Contributors

Stacey Abbott is a Reader in Film Studies at Roehampton University. She is the author of *Celluloid Vampires* (University of Texas Press, 2007) and *Angel* (Wayne State University Press, 2009) and the Series Editor for the *Investigating Cult TV* series (I.B.Tauris) and has published on such favourite shows as *Buffy, Alias, Angel, Firefly, Lost,* and *Ultraviolet.*

Sergio Angelini's most recent publications include contributions to *Dizionario dei Registi del Cinema Mondiale* (Einaudi, 2005/2006), *The Reference Guide to British and Irish Film Directors* (BFI, 2006), *Investigating Alias* (I.B.Tauris, 2007), and the *screenonline* web resource. He is the television reviewer for *Sight & Sound* magazine and edits the educational quarterly *Viewfinder.*

Jes Battis is currently a postdoctoral research fellow at the City University of New York. He specialises in LGBT studies, fantasy literature, and popular culture and is the author of *Investigating Farscape* (I.B.Tauris, 2007).

Stan Beeler teaches Film and Television Studies in the English Department at the University of Northern British Columbia, Canada. His publications include *Reading Stargate SG-1* with Lisa Dickson, *Investigating Charmed: The Magic Power of TV* with Karin Beeler, and *Dance, Drugs and Escape: The Club Scene in Literature, Film and Television Since the Late 1980s.*

Miles Booy has a PhD in Film Studies from the University of East Anglia. He lives in Stafford with his wife and son. He is currently researching and writing a monograph on *Doctor Who* fandom.

Simon Brown is Senior Lecturer in Film Studies at Kingston University. He is a keen biker, the author of numerous articles on early and silent cinema, as well as co-editor of *Investigating Alias: Secrets and Spies* (I.B.Tauris, 2007).

Bronwen Calvert is an Associate Lecturer with the Open University in the North of England and Subject Area Leader in Literature at the Centre for Lifelong Learning in Newcastle upon Tyne, where she also teaches modern and contemporary fiction. Her research is on aspects of embodiment (especially kick-ass action heroines) in science fiction and fantasy narratives.

Jane Espenson has been a television writer for the last sixteen years, writing for shows attracting both cult and non-cult audiences. She was on the writing staff of shows including *Ellen, Gilmore Girls, The O.C.,* and *Tru Calling* and wrote a freelance episode of *Star Trek: Deep Space Nine.* She is especially proud of her work on Joss Whedon's *Buffy the Vampire Slayer, Angel,* and *Firefly,* and Ron Moore's *Battlestar Galactica.* Jane is currently writing and producing the *Battlestar Galactica* TV movie 'The Plan,' to air after the conclusion of the series.

Dick Fiddy is a TV Consultant working for the BFI. His TV work includes writing C4's epic exploration of the small screen, *TV Heaven*. He is the author of *Missing Believed Wiped: Searching for the Lost Heritage of British Television* and was the Consulting Editor on the BFI's *Television Handbook*.

Lincoln Geraghty is Principal Lecturer in Film Studies and Subject Leader for Media Studies in the School of Creative Arts, Film and Media at the University of Portsmouth. He is author of *Living with Star Trek: American Culture and the Star Trek Universe* (I.B.Tauris, 2007) and *American Science Fiction Film and Television* (Berg, forthcoming), and the editor of *The Influence of Star Trek on Television, Film and Culture* (McFarland, 2008).

Janet K. Halfyard is a Senior Lecturer at Birmingham Conservatoire (UK). Her publications focus on music in film and television, particularly in horror and fantasy genres, including *Danny Elfman's Batman : a film score guide* and several essays on music and performance in *Buffy the Vampire Slayer* and *Angel*.

Matt Hills is a Reader in Media and Cultural Studies at Cardiff University. He has published widely on cult media and fandom, and his most recent book on the subject is *Triumph of a Time Lord* (I.B.Tauris, 2009).

Nancy Holder is a *New York Times* bestselling author (for *Wicked: Witch and Curse*, with Debbie Viguie). She has written tie-in novels, short stories, and episode guides for *Buffy the Vampire Slayer, Angel, Smallville, Hellboy*, and other popular culture 'universes.' She lectures in the literature department of Eleanor Roosevelt College at the University of California and is a member of the Popular Fiction faculty for the Stonecoast MFA creative writing program at the University of Southern Maine.

Catherine Johnson is Senior Lecturer in Television at Royal Holloway, University of London. She is the author of *Telefantasy* (BFI, 2005) and the co-editor (with Rob Turnock) of ITV Cultures (Open University Press, 2005). She is currently researching the history of branding in US and UK television.

Lorna Jowett is a Senior Lecturer in Media and American Studies at the University of Northampton, UK, where she teaches some of her favourite things, including horror, science fiction, and television. She has published on gender and genre in horror and science fiction texts across television, film, and fiction.

Roz Kaveney is a writer, poet, and activist living in London. Her works include *From Alien to the Matrix*, *Teen Dreams*, and *Superheroes*; she edited *Reading the Vampire Slayer*.

Roberta Pearson is Professor of Film and Television Studies and Director of the Institute of Film and Television Studies at the University of Nottingham. She is the editor of *Reading Lost: Perspectives on a Hot Television Show* (I.B.Tauris, 2008) and author, co-author, and co-editor of numerous books and essays.

xiii

Denzell Richards lectures in Film at Roehampton University, where he is also completing his PhD thesis investigating texts on DVD and how audiences relate to and interact with the format.

Hillary Robson is an adjunct faculty member in the department of English at Middle Tennessee State University. Her areas of scholastic interest are fandom and fan culture, and popular culture studies. She is a co-author of the books *Saving the World: A Guide to Heroes, Lost's Buried Treasures*, and *Unlocking Battlestar Galactica* with David Lavery and Lynnette Porter, served as research assistant and contributor to *Unlocking the Meaning of Lost: An Unauthorized Guide*, and is co-editor of *Grace Under Pressure: Grey's Anatomy Uncovered.*

David Simmons has written and published material on a wide range of issues related to twentieth-century popular culture including the sixties' countercultural movement, H.P. Lovecraft, the American Horror film, and contemporary genre television. He is currently editing an upcoming collection on the television series *Heroes*.

Sharon Sutherland is Assistant Professor at the University of British Columbia Faculty of Law. She teaches mediation, negotiation, and contract law and practices as a child protection mediator. Sharon's current research examines applications of drama and theatre to conflict resolution pedagogy and practice.

Paul Sutton is Principal Lecturer in Film at Roehampton University. His research interests include film theory, the remake, and French and Italian cinema. He is currently writing a book for Blackwell *Remaking Film: In History, In Theory*.

Sarah Swan is a lawyer and a graduate of the University of British Columbia law faculty. She has collaborated with Sharon Sutherland on a variety of topics related to law and popular culture, including essays on *Angel*, *24*, and *Alias*.

Donato Totaro has been the editor of the online film journal *Offscreen* (www.offscreen.com) since its inception in 1997. Totaro received his PhD in Film and Television from the University of Warwick (UK) and is a part-time lecturer in Film Studies at Concordia University (Montreal, Canada). He has published on recent Asian cinema, the cinema of Andrei Tarkovsky, and the horror genre.

Rhonda V. Wilcox, professor of English, Gordon College, is editor of *Studies in Popular Culture;* co-editor of *Critical Studies in Television* and *Slayage*; author of *Why Buffy Matters: The Art of Buffy the Vampire Slayer* (2005); and co-editor of *Fighting the Forces: What's at Stake in Buffy the Vampire Slayer* (2002) and *Investigating Firefly and Serenity* (2008).

Tat Wood has a First from the University of Hertfordshire and an MA in Cultural Studies of University of East London. He spent fifteen years writing for news-stand magazines with 'TV' or 'Cult' in the title and a series of books for the US market. His most recent grown-up work was in *Time and Relative Dissertations in Space* (University of Manchester Press, 2007). His secret identity is an A-Level tutor.

Introduction: 'Never Give Up – Never Surrender!': The Resilience of Cult Television

Stacey Abbott

In a now infamous *Saturday Night Live* sketch, William Shatner, star of the classic cult TV series *Star Trek*, told his fans to 'get a life'. The humour of the sketch is based upon the fact that its depiction of the Trekkies/ers conformed to most people's expectations of the *Star Trek,* or cult TV, fan – socially inept, dressed in costume, obsessed with trivia and unable to distinguish fantasy from reality. In the 1999 film *Galaxy Quest* – an affectionate parody of *Star Trek,* its cast and fans – something, however, appears to have changed. Much of the film's humour continues to be derived from the overzealous fans who dress up like their favourite characters and know the inner workings and design of the show's space ship, not to mention the actors who have made a career out of making public appearances at conventions and store openings. The film's narrative surrounding a group of aliens who turn to the cast of the show for help against an alien aggressor, however, does serve to revalidate the cult TV fan and actor. Not only do the cast prove their worth by embracing the show's ethos – 'Never Give Up! Never Surrender' – and working together to save the alien race but also draw upon the help and expertise of their cult fans. What begins as a send up of the cult television phenomenon ends as a vindication of TV fandom.

This transformation captures a shifting attitude about cult television. Although cult TV was previously seen as the purview of socially awkward teenage boys (as portrayed by Justin Long in *Galaxy Quest* whose parents are just happy he has gone outside), it has now become an arena for a diverse range of audiences. Where once obsessive knowledge of a TV series' fictional universe was the reserve of the science fiction (SF) geek, now fans of *Seinfeld* memorise dialogue while fans of *Sex and the City* and *The Sopranos* go on organised location tours of Manhattan and New Jersey. Fan conventions used to be seen as 'freak shows' for 'has-been' actors but now they are a crucial market for the networks and studios to premiere new programmes and to garner fan loyalty while the shows are still on the air. Networks might hope for the large broadcast figures associated with mainstream television, but they also want their shows to generate the audience commitment associated with cult TV. Loyalty not only ensures that audiences tune in every week but also that they will buy the series DVDs, the tie-in CDs, the books, and fan magazines.

The nature of cult television has changed as well. While in the past, cult TV was largely synonymous with telefantasy – fantasy, horror, and science fiction – now it crosses generic boundaries to include animation, teen dramas, police series, comedy, and children's programming. Some would argue that cult TV has, of course, always been generically and culturally diverse. While the 'Trekkie' might be the stereotypical cult TV fan, fans of the 1960s series *Dark Shadows* (itself a generic hybrid – part soap/part horror) included middle-aged women and teenage boys and girls. While *The Simpsons* and *Southpark* may have set new standards for postmodern intertextuality, a popular characteristic of cult television, Hanna-Barbera's *The Flintstones* contained numerous intertextual references to Hollywood – note appearances by Cary Granite and Stoney Carmichael – to The Beatles in the form of 'Bug Music' and to television. *The Flintstones* offered their own parody of the popular horror sit-com *The Adams Family* when Fred and Wilma met their new neighbours – The Gruesomes. Children's television from *Sesame Street* and *The Clangers* to *SpongeBob SquarePants* has always had a loyal following among teenagers and adults. Finally, fans of *Monty Python's Flying Circus* and *Black Adder* take great pleasure in memorising and quoting dialogue. In fact, the cult of British comedy looms large in Canada and the United States and is made up of a niche but highly diverse audience who watch these programmes on specialised channels such as BBC World and PBS and who appreciate what makes British humour so distinct from more mainstream fare. Not all of these programmes are cult but they have over the years inspired cult practices and enthusiasm.

All of this is less about whether cult television has changed (although as some of the chapters in this book will demonstrate it clearly has) and more about how cult TV is perceived and understood. As a result we need a new way of thinking about it, one that considers how the evolving broadcast and communications landscape of the past fifty years has affected cult TV and its audiences. The aim of this book is to open up discussions of cult television and raise questions about how we define it. The contributors to this volume, therefore, offer not one shared definition but rather a range of definitions that embody the scholarly, journalistic, industrial, and fan perspectives on the subject. While some might suggest that a term 'that means everything means nothing' (Pearson in this volume), the reality is, as this book will demonstrate, that this term actually contains an array of precise meanings and functions dependant upon the context of its use.

To address this complexity, the book is broken up into four parts, each examining the different ways of defining and understanding cult TV both historically and within the contemporary media landscape. The first section lays the groundwork for defining cult television and considers the subject in the light of growing debates around quality TV, suggesting that the lines between 'Cult' and 'Quality' are increasingly blurred. The second examines the cult text itself asking how these niche, often marginal, shows have repeatedly served to redefine and challenge TV conventions by pushing the boundaries of what is acceptable stylistically, narratively, and thematically. The third section addresses the role that the industry plays in our understanding of cult TV and explores how media developments – from the expansion of different media formats through which television is consumed to the rise of niche/'cult' channels – have increasingly fostered a cult engagement with TV. The final section brings us back to the core aspect of cult television – its audience – by exploring the changing nature of fandom and its relationship to the industry. As a number of the authors in this volume suggest, the creators of our favourite programmes are themselves cult TV fans and that as a result the role of fandom has evolved. In tandem with these chapters, the book contains a series of brief case studies of individual TV shows. The choice of programmes is not designed to be a comprehensive history or canon but rather conceived to offer insight and understanding of cult television. All of the contributors to this volume have a scholarly or professional interest in cult television but they also share an enthusiasm for quality TV that captures their imagination and challenges our expectations, all of which is reflected in the chapters and arguments that follow.

While the popularity and commercial viability of cult programmes may fluctuate based upon the idiosyncrasies of the broadcast climate, cult TV persists. Not all programmes will rise to the heights of *The X-Files* or *Lost*. Some such as *Carnivale* will quietly persevere for a couple years, or perhaps only one like *Invasion,* before cancellation cuts them short. Others such as *Firefly* and *Wonderfalls* will come to an end all too quickly, if only to be rediscovered on DVD. What all of these programmes, like the writers who nurtured them and the fans who loved them, have in common, however, is a shared resilience to the capriciousness of network television. Cult television persists because the creators and the fans keep fighting for their little, original, often challenging shows, never forgetting to 'Never Give Up – Never Surrender!'

Part 1

Defining Cult TV:
History, Aesthetics, Discourses

1   Observations on Cult Television

Roberta Pearson

Defining Cult Television?

As the co-editor of a fairly recent book entitled *Cult Television,* I should have a ready definition of the term, but a term so universally applied both in and out of academia defies precise definition (Gwenllian-Jones and Pearson, 2004a). Many years ago, the faculty of Yale's Department of Political Science, doing their best to transform me into a hard-headed social scientist, taught me that a term that means everything means nothing. An all-inclusive definition, they told me, lacks analytic utility, making impossible the fine distinctions requisite to rigorous scholarly analysis. As a tribute to that early training, and in a spirit of sheer bloody-mindedness, I'm tempted to persuade the reader that academics should entirely abandon the useless concept of cult television. I'm even setting an example in my own work. My book on *Star Trek* as television, co-authored with Maire Messenger-Davies, replaces the term cult with genre, the industry's preferred term for science fiction and fantasy programmes. Unfortunately, abandoning the term 'cult' works for me, but not for others; it makes sense from an intellectual perspective, but not from a pragmatic one. The University of Minnesota Press wanted a readily recognisable and marketable title for my anthology as does I.B.Tauris for this very volume. It's not only publishers who love a succinct and catchy title; Brunel University has recently launched an MA in cult film and television and where Brunel has gone others may follow. As a quick Google will show, the term 'cult television' flourishes beyond the confines of academia in the virtual world and, by implication, in the 'real' world.

Such pragmatic considerations insuring that cult television will remain on the academic agenda for quite some time, it would be a good thing to have some vague idea of what we're all rabbiting on about. In our introduction, my co-editor, Sara Gwenllian-Jones, and I assayed a definition, although its inclusivity violates the social-science principle drilled into me in my youth: 'In the media, in common usage, and sometimes even in academia, "cult" is often loosely applied to any television programme that is considered offbeat or edgy, that draws a niche audience, that has a nostalgic appeal, that is considered emblematic of a particular subculture, or that is considered hip' (2004b: ix). This definition accorded with film studies' use of cult to refer to marginalised films that were perceived as trashy or, worse, offensive (due to violent or sexual content), that were hard to see (at least in pre-internet days), and that were treasured by a core group of aficionados who kept moving the goalposts to insure the rarity of what they valued. Cult film was pretty much what cult film fans said it was, film scholars had concluded. As I said in an article contrasting cult film with cult television,

> The common characteristic is found not in the texts but in their viewers; most commentators on cult cinema agree that the films elicit an excessive devotion which Mendek and Harper refer to as 'a ritualistic form of near obsession': 'The cult film draws on a (hard) core of audience interest and involvement which is not just the result of random, directionless entertainment-seeking, but rather a combination of intense physical and emotional involvement' (2000: 7). The mode of reception, rather than the mode of production or textual characteristics, seems best to define cult film. (Pearson, 2003)

Audiences, their activities, and the industry's exploitation thereof should be similarly central to any conception of cult television. A few pages after Gwenllian-Jones and I provided our all-purpose definition, we concluded that 'cult television ... caters to intense, interpretative audience practices' (2004: xvi). Focusing on audience practices, we believed, kept us from becoming mired in the endless subjective entanglements of interpretive analysis that a text-based definition would entail. Mark Jancovich and Nathan Hunt, in a book published the same year as ours, agreed that our understanding of cult television should be predicated on audience practices, not textual characteristics.

> Cult TV is defined not by any feature shared by the shows themselves, but rather by the ways in which they are appropriated by specific groups. There is no single quality that characterizes a cult text; rather, cult texts are defined through a process in which shows are positioned in opposition to the mainstream, a classification that is no more coherent as an object than the cult and is also a product of the same process of distinction that creates the opposed couplet mainstream/cult. (2004: 27)

Non-academic sources concur that audiences determine cult status. Take for example, Wikipedia, which, despite our deploring our students' use of it, acts as a handy indicator to the wisdom of crowds. 'Cult television ... attracts a band of aficionados or appreciators, known as a cult following, devoted to a specific television series or fictional universe.' The entry goes on to offer four more definitions; a series that has a 'strong loyal audience'; a series that 'encourages its viewers to do more than just sit and watch it'; 'any series that has achieved a moderate level of popularity, but not a large one'; and 'any unpopular or obscure series' (http://en.wikipedia.org/wiki/Cult_following).[1] One of the premiere cult television websites in the United Kingdom also points to audiences and their behaviours, telling us that cult shows 'attract a fanatical following. They have something that fascinates their acolytes who view favourite shows time after time without diminution of enjoyment' (http://fp.culttv.plus.com./ukcultv/whatis/html). Cult programmes are constructed in relationship to a putative, but never very well-defined, mainstream. Jancovich and Hunt state that audiences position their cult favourites 'in opposition to the mainstream.' In speaking of niche audiences and sub-cultures, Gwenllian-Jones and I implied the non-mainstream, as do the Wikipedia and cult TV website definitions. Brunel says that its cult film and television MA is 'taught by internationally recognised researchers in the field of alternative, oppositional and non-canonical screen cultures', in other words, the field of non-mainstream screen cultures.[2] Underpinning the mainstream/non-mainstream binary, at least for the academics, is Bourdieu's concept of distinction, a robust explanation for sub-cultural activities much utilised by scholars in their empirical investigations of cult television fandom (1984). Justified from both theoretical and empirical perspectives, scholars have predicated their understanding of the cult television phenomenon upon marginality; cult shows attract loyal fans but in fewer numbers than the more highly rated shows that constitute the mainstream.

Cult Television as Industry Bellwether

Recent developments, however, threaten this consensual agreement.[3] ABC languished at the bottom of the network league table until acquiring the mega-hit *Lost*, while NBC's flagging fortunes were boosted, if not reversed, with *Heroes* and HBO finally seems to have found its long-sought *Sopranos'* replacement in vampire-fest *True Blood*. Their complex narratives and elaborate mythologies resembling those of *The X-Files* or *Buffy the Vampire Slayer*, these shows may signal a fundamental reconfiguration of the American television industry – the mainstream as the new cult. Not having marginality as a defining criteria poses theoretical and empirical dilemmas for cult television scholars. In compensation, the mainstreaming of cult encourages a historical perspective, leading us to investigate the ways in which cult programmes have played major roles in industry transformations. Take, for example, the fount and origin of all things cult (at least in the United States), *Star Trek*.[4] The original series (*ST: TOS*) was, according to executive producer Herb Solow, 'not a big deal to NBC' (2005). In the classic network era, or TV1 (roughly the 1950s through the 1970s), sheer numbers determined a programme's fate, as each network sought to attract the one-third of the audience that ensured the stability of the network system. *ST: TOS* fell short of this mark and was cancelled but during its three years on air generated plenty of what would now be called audience buzz. In the first season 29,000 viewers, described by NBC as 'decision makers', wrote fan letters. When NBC threatened cancellation in

1967, 115,893 letters of protest deluged its mailrooms (Messenger-Davies and Pearson, 2007: 218). The younger, hipper viewers who had embraced *ST: TOS* were from the same demographically desirable audience segment that would later ensure the survival of other innovative, but relatively poorly rated, programmes such as *Hill Street Blues*. *ST: TOS* was a show before its time, presaging the niche broadcasting of the future TV2 (roughly the 1980s and the 1990s) that would also give rise to quality television, about which more below.

The letter writers were the Trekkers who kept *Star Trek* alive and who might be credited with initiating American cult television fandom. Paramount executives, impressed with the fans' dedication and, more importantly, with their disposable income, revived *Trek* in film form in 1979. The success of the film franchise, together with ongoing fan activities such as conventions, persuaded the studio to similarly resurrect *Trek* television in 1987. *The Next Generation*'s (*ST: TNG*) success in first-run syndication, that is, not going out in prime-time on ABC, CBS, or NBC, proved that a one-hour drama could flourish without support from the big three, a crucial step in the demise of the classic network era. *ST: TNG*'s success also led directly to three off-spring, *Deep Space Nine*, *Voyager,* and *Enterprise*. Like its parent, the middle child, *Voyager*, the flagship show on Paramount's 1995-launched United Paramount Network (UPN), helped to usher in the post-network TV2. By the time the youngest child, *Enterprise*, premiered in 2001, UPN was struggling to survive, the newest *Trek*'s dismal ratings performance not helping its chances. Having lowered the licence fee to keep *Enterprise* on life-support through the fourth season necessary to produce enough episodes for syndication, the studio finally pulled the plug in 2005. While NBC had considered *ST: TOS*'s cancellation no big deal, the death of *Enterprise*, the heart of what was by now a far-flung, multi-million dollar franchise encompassing everything from theme parks to novels, was a very big deal indeed for Paramount. Said a press release, 'All of us at Paramount warmly bid goodbye to *Enterprise* and we all look forward to a new chapter of this enduring franchise in the future' (2005). The most prominent new chapter took the form of a feature film, *Star Trek XI*, which garnered Paramount Pictures critical acclaim and box-office success in May 2009. A sequel has been green-lighted. CBS Paramount, which inherited the *Trek* television rights in the break up of media giant Paramount Viacom, is in the meantime seeking other profit points by adapting the franchise to the digital TV3 era; current developments include a site in Second Life and a massive multiplayer online role-playing game (see Geraghty on the *Star Trek* franchise in this volume).

Cult-like shows, with their capacity to proliferate revenue streams across multiple platforms, are of increasing value to studio and network executives dealing with the fragmented and fickle audiences of the TV3 environment.

Fan studies has established that cult fans are more likely to engage in repeat viewing and to purchase DVDs and licensed products, as J.J. Abrams' *Alias* has shown. Referring to the show as 'cult-fave spy-fi drama', the *Hollywood Reporter* said that it 'was among the first of a new breed of TV series that can be sustained for multiple seasons of modest primetime numbers on the strength of such ancillary businesses as DVD sales and video games' (Anon, 2005). *Alias*, a cult show, served as a bellwether of the television industry, as has *Lost*, Abrams' next project. But should *Lost*, despite its complex narrative and elaborate mythology, be called cult? In its first season, it attracted upward of 20 million plus viewers per episode, many more than the 'modest primetime numbers' of *Alias* or most other predecessors (Elber, 2007). In its seventh and last season (2002–2003), *Buffy*, for example, often ranked below 100th place and in 2003 achieved a highest rating of five, representing approximately five per cent of all households. But media commentators, not perplexed by the theoretical niceties that plague television scholars, do call *Lost* cult. The BBC referred to it as 'the cult US drama series' (Anon, 2006a). The ABC news website, commenting on the show's precipitous ratings drop, compared it to the undoubtedly cult *The X-Files*.

> The show was smart and intriguingly spiked with supernatural and sci-fi twists. It featured hot new stars who graced glossy magazine covers until the ratings tumbled. So much for 'The X-Files', which enjoyed a nine-year run before misguided plots and a time slot change eroded its appeal. Flash forward to today and you'll find its counterpart in 'Lost', another spooky, cerebral, sexy show which may end up killed off before its time. (Elber, 2007)

According to co-producer Damon Lindelof, the cultish elements identified by these and other media commentators are there by deliberate intent: 'We were aiming for that *Alias* type audience. We knew it was a little bit weird. It has a huge cast, it's serialised, and it requires the audiences' attention. It's everything procedural crime drama's aren't' (Armstrong, 2005: 30). From an industrial perspective, *Lost* is definitely cult, designed as such by its producers and recognised as such by industry insiders.

Like its more marginal predecessors, *Lost*, a mainstream hit with a cult sensibility, has been at the forefront of industry innovations.[5] Apple and Disney struck a deal to make *Lost* one of the first programmes available for downloading to the new visual i-Pod. *Television Week* reported, 'In one fell swoop, The Walt Disney Co. was transformed ... from the staid media company it had been known as under former Chairman and CEO Michael Eisner into a technologically innovative first mover under current CEO Robert Iger, according to many technology analysts'. Michael McGuire, research director at technology consulting firm Gartner, is quoted in the article as saying, 'This is an inkling of the steps of large media companies coming to grips with the issue of broadband distribution' (Sherman, 2005: 26). *Lost* has also been in the vanguard of what television scholars have dubbed trans-media storytelling, the expansion of a fictional universe across multiple platforms. In the summer of 2006, ABC launched *The Lost Experience*, an online, interactive, live role-playing game which the website said would take '*Lost* fans on an expansive, international Easter egg hunt through websites, commercials, emails, phone numbers, and more, in search of pieces to a larger puzzle, a puzzle which, when solved, will enlighten *Lost* fans to some of the show's deepest mysteries!' (www.thelostexperience.com/). In the autumn of 2007, *Lost* producers further expanded the fictional universe through a series of mobisodes, *Lost: Missing Pieces*, first made available via Verizon Wireless and then uploaded to the *Lost* website. Executive producer Carlton Cuse said that the mobisodes weren't a mini version of the show but instead provided viewers with additional information (cited in Gough, 2007). Since ABC did not broadcast any new episodes until the beginning of 2008, these mobisodes served to keep the audience engaged. Delaying its fourth season premiere to 2008 defied the previous rules of the American television industry, in which shows customarily begin in the autumn, as does producing only sixteen episodes per season and announcing the definitive end date, 2010, for the series.[6] *Lost*'s producers are highly attuned to the new and changing demands of TV3, as were *Star Trek*'s to those of TV2. Again, cult television makes television history.

Attracting much bigger audiences than cult hits such as *Buffy* while demonstrating the neat fit between a cult sensibility and the multiple profit points of TV3, *Lost* has dragged cult into the mainstream and motivated that imitation which is the sincerest form of flattery. Premiering in 2006, *Heroes*, a glossier version of cult favourite *The 4400*, achieved top ratings, encouraging in its turn the networks to commission more cult-like shows. Said *The New York Times*, 'The popularity of "Heroes" ... is widely thought to be the inspiration for the escapist trend for next season.' 'Almost a dozen' of the 'new shows will conjure up elements of science fiction, fantasy or the supernatural. The casts of characters include vampires, clairvoyants and immortals, some of whom can revive the dead or travel through time' (Elliot, 2007). Judging on past performance, even the undead may have little chance of surviving to a second season. Several *Lost*-inspired serialised dramas, including *The Nine*, *Kidnapped* and *Vanished*, premiered alongside *Heroes* but lasted only a single season. Said Kevin Downey in industry journal *Media Life*,

> The problem, say media buyers, is that dramas with ongoing storylines demand of viewers a much higher level of commitment, and it's turned out to be a level very few are willing to make. The thinking was that viewers, once hooked, would record shows they missed and visit the internet to learn what they missed. But

the hooking never took place. In place of serialized dramas, the networks will be rolling out an array of more traditional dramas, comedies and reality shows that neatly wrap up storylines in an hour or less. (Downey, 2007)

Lindelof and Abrams may have designed *Lost* to be 'everything procedural crime drama's aren't', but the networks are gambling that many viewers prefer storylines wrapped up in an hour or less to the intense, interpretive practices and dedication required by the cult-like *Lost* and *Heroes*. *Lost*'s shrinking audience numbers may confirm the networks' intuition. The show has not managed to sustain its initial buoyant ratings; from the high of 20 million plus in its first season it descended to a low of 12.8 million in February 2007. Veteran network executive Tom Nunan believes that 'whenever you get outside one of the big three franchises – cops, doctors or lawyers – and into the more high-concept shows, they tend to burn bright but burn out faster' (cited in Elber, 2007). *Heroes* too is in trouble, although media analyst John Rash attributes its difficulties to an industry-wide problem: 'A repeat of *Heroes* was the lowest rated show on the big four nets last night [August 20, 2007]. This is less of a reflection on TV's surprise smash last year and more indicative of how the two-episode business model for networks is just no longer tenable television strategy' (The Rash Report, 2007).[7] Like *Lost*, *Heroes* intended to experiment with new scheduling formats suited to TV3's viewing habits. *Lost* will offer fewer episodes in a curtailed season; *Heroes* intended to offer more episodes in an extended season. NBC's plan was to end *Heroes* 24-episode second season in mid-April 2008, before the May sweeps. The mini-series spin-off *Heroes: Origins* was meant to follow it in late April and May. *Origins* – which, according to *Heroes*' creator Tim Kring, is 'an anthology series, a rarity in modern broadcast network television' – would consist of six stand-alone episodes not tied to the series narrative arc, that is, more neatly wrapped up storylines (Ain't It Cool, 2007). NBC had commissioned *Origins*, hoping to offer viewers a total of 30 *Heroes* episodes in 2007–2008 as part of a new scheduling policy. Said NBC president Kevin Reilly, 'We've got something I call the "bulk-up challenge" for next year, which is trying to stay more consistent in our scheduling for the audience' (cited in Porter, 2007). But this plan, like many others, came a cropper as a result of the 2007–2008 writers' strike, which reduced *Lost*'s episodes from the planned 16 to 14 and put *Origins* on indefinite hold.

Despite the airing of fewer episodes than originally planned, *Lost* regained its favourable buzz in its fourth season, while *Heroes*' second season proved so disappointing that creator Tim Kring personally apologised to viewers. Maybe cult cycles in and out of the mainstream depending on the success of its current incarnations. Some would argue that *The X-Files* rivals *Lost*'s mainstream status. It was the first of the underdog Fox Network's shows to break into the

Nielsen top 25. Fourth season episodes averaged more than 19 million viewers and one episode attracted 29 million, higher than *Lost*'s best figure (although channel proliferation has generally depressed ratings per episode below those of the early 1990s) (*The X-Files Compilation*). Like *Lost*, the show generated huge media buzz and a host of imitators, which, like *Lost*'s, mostly failed. But, after *The X-Files*, cult once more retreated to the margins until *Lost* returned it to the media spotlight. Both *Heroes* and *Battlestar Galactica* became media phenomena while both Abrams' *Fringe* and Joss Whedon's *Dollhouse* have been renewed for a second season, despite the latter's low ratings. A theory of genre and the zeitgeist might explain cult as a cyclical phenomenon. Such speculation is beyond the remit of this chapter, but see Matt Hills in this volume for more on mainstream cult.

Cult Television and Quality

Lost's producers might prefer the show to be called quality rather than cult. Despite Lindelof's flaunting the show's cult credentials, some of his colleagues dislike the label. Said ABC Entertainment president Steve McPherson, 'I'm constantly telling [the producers] "Character, character, character." If you just had the machinations of the mythology it would be a cult show' (cited in Cotta Vaz, 2005: 32). Executive producer Carlton Cuse credits the show's wide appeal to the characters' backstories: 'The flashback stories are the emotional core of the series and give a much broader audience access. There's a genre audience that enjoys the mythology, but the broader audience wants to know more about the characters and the flashbacks and go back to the seminal events in their lives' (cited in Cotta Vaz, 55). These comments, made in the first season, in retrospect seem to anticipate the show's dramatic decline in audience numbers, as the ever-more elaborate machinations of the mythology not only frustrated the hard-core fans but also drove away more casual viewers. McPherson and Cuse know that producing a break-away hit in the fragmented audience environment of TV3 requires amalgamating audience segments; cult fans may sustain a show such as *Alias* by consuming its ancillary products but their numbers are too small to elevate a show to the top of the Nielsens. The president's and the producer's emphasis on character seemed aimed at the quality audience, which, although different, undoubtedly overlapped with the cult audience. The final section of this chapter explores the connections between cult and quality.

Quality is an even more elusive term than cult, inherently founded upon arbitrary taste judgments. The wisdom-of-crowds Wikipedia tells us that quality television is a 'term used by television scholars, television critics, and broadcasting advocacy groups to describe a genre or style of television programming that they argue is of higher quality, due to its subject matter or content' (http://en.wikipedia.org/wiki/Quality_television). Television critics and broadcasting advocacy groups may judge quality according to their own tastes, but television scholars need to rise above personal preferences and attend to industry and audience practices. Quality television began as a niche-broadcasting phenomenon aimed at the 'right' demographics, that is, viewers with the educational capital to respond to quality programmes' literary aesthetics and with the economic capital to purchase products offered by the sponsors. Quality audiences, like cult audiences, position their tastes outside a perceived mainstream and actively support their favourite shows. In 1983, when CBS cancelled *Cagney and Lacey*, its fans, like the Trekkers before them, staged a letter-writing campaign which persuaded the network to give the show another chance. This achievement inspired the 1984 founding of Viewers for Quality Television, which successfully fought to continue other low-rated quality shows. But by 2000, a decline in membership made the organisation no longer financially viable. Dorothy Collins Swanson, president of VQT, said that the internet had made the group redundant: 'There was a time when campaigning for a show had meaning, but because it can now be done with a click of a mouse it really has lost its specialness' (cited in 'Viewers for Quality Television Closes Shop'). But in an era when an entire network consciously opposed the mainstream in the famous slogan 'It's not TV, it's HBO', the increasing centrality of quality programming to industry strategy may also have rendered VQT superfluous to need. Like cult, quality has gone mainstream, a phenomenon commented on by numerous journalists including *The Observer*'s Paul Harris: 'In a medium often derided as Hollywood's less talented little brother, *mainstream US TV has suddenly been swamped by an unprecedented wave of critically acclaimed dramas. TV is now attracting Hollywood stars and directors to produce edgy and sophisticated programmes* that used to be the preserve of the movie studios' (2006).[8] Of course, many cult fans would assert that edginess and sophistication have long been the preserve of cult television; cult and quality are constructed through similar rhetoric.

This wave of critically acclaimed dramas to which Harris refers was the culmination of a trend that began in the 1970s, most conspicuously with the MTM Enterprises production company that gave the world *The Mary Tyler Moore Show, Hill Street Blues, St. Elsewhere,* and other critical hits (Feuer, Kerr, and Vahimagi, 1985). Cult programmes have played a role in the quality trend. The Academy of Television Arts and Sciences has never showered Emmys on cult shows (except in technical categories), but some taste arbiters have admitted the odd one into the quality canon.[9] VQT named *The X-Files* as the ninth best quality drama of the 1990s and bestowed its Founders Award upon *Buffy*. In 2005, *Time Magazine* proclaimed *Battlestar Galactica* the television show of the year: 'The writing and performances are first-class, especially Edward James Olmos as the noble but authoritarian commander in charge of saving the last remnants of humanity. Laugh if you want, but this story of enemies within is dead serious, and seriously good' (Poniewozik, 2005). Scholars have argued that some cult programmes bear quality hallmarks. *Twin Peaks*, the first show deliberately designed to appeal to the cult audience, came trailing clouds of quality associated with the cinematic auteur David Lynch and the televisual auteur Mark Frost, who had worked on *Hill Street Blues*. Linda Ruth Williams points to the show's 'textual thickness' and its 'endlessly interpretable text', attributes often seen as characteristic of quality (Williams, 2005: 43). Catherine Johnson argues that *The X-Files* 'can be understood as a new kind of quality television that emerges in the early 1990s – "quality/cult" television' (Johnson, 2005b: 56). She continues, 'the series' sophisticated scripts, complex multi-layered narratives, and visually expressive cinematography, combined with its exploration of contemporary anxieties concerning late capitalism [are] characteristic of quality television' (61).

Cult television fans position themselves against the mainstream partly by arguing for the quality of their programmes. At the Cult TV Weekender organised by Britain's Cult TV website, topics for debate in the nightly discussion group have included 'In Search of Quality Television'.[10] Academics have commented on cult fans' embrace of the signifiers of traditional literary quality. Jancovich and Hunt tell us that 'cult fandom ... often employs reading strategies that are specifically based on the privileging of form over function that distinguishes bourgeois taste' (2004: 28). Among these reading strategies are privileging 'ideas, characters, and the arc story lines of television series over special effects', (33–34) which 'places an emphasis on the literary values associated with legitimate culture' also associated with 'the tracing of literary reference and origins' (35). Petra Kuppers makes similar observations about *Babylon 5* fans (2004: 45–60). Matt Hills argues that episode guides 'construct a corpus of canonical televised episodes, allowing for comparative aesthetic evaluations and the attribution of discourses of "quality" to cult TV series' (2005b: 192). The implication of a show meriting an episode guide is that it 'displays culturally valued criteria of aesthetic development, complexity and coherence' (193). Fan fiction, far from being oppositional or resistant, caters to reading strategies that value canonicity, characterisation, and coherence.

Conclusion

This chapter began by arguing that cult television is best understood from an industry/audience rather than from a textualist perspective. The previous section has shown that quality television can be understood in precisely the same terms. Both cult and quality serve as marketing brands to attract particularly desirable audience segments and both are central to industry strategy in the ever-shifting TV3 environment. Audience taste patterns have been organised to ensure producers' maximum profits. Academics inclined to celebrate the plethora of 'good' television now available to us should attend to this very pragmatic bottom line as well as remember that we ourselves are at the heart of the cult and quality demographics. As Deborah L. Jaramillo implies in her discussion of *The Sopranos*, HBO, and branding, the comfortable fit between television producers and academic viewers has caused the latter sometimes to forget that quality television – and, by extension, cult TV – is just another element of the cultural logic of capitalism: 'What better way to conceal the fact that Time Warner has its hands in every possible prized demographic in every possible tier than by creating a landscape in which the creativity of auteurs is compromised by such a crassly commercial tier as broadcast television?'(2002: 62). That being said, I've now got to stop writing, go check my *Radio Times* and set Sky Plus to record *The Sopranos* and *The 4400* while I'm on holiday. They're such good shows!

Recommended Reading

Gwenllian-Jones, Sara and Roberta E. Pearson (eds) (2004) *Cult Television*. Minneapolis: University of Minnesota Press.

Jancovich, Mark and Nathan Hunt (2004) 'The Mainstream, Distinction, and Cult TV', in Gwenllian-Jones and Pearson (eds), 27–44.

Johnson, Catherine (2005) 'Quality/Cult Television: *The X-Files* and Television History', in Hammond and Mazdon (eds), *The Contemporary Television Series*. Edinburgh: Edinburgh University Press: 57–51.

Notes

1. It is, of course, possible that academics have contributed to this definition.
2. For more information, see http://www.brunel.ac.uk/courses/pg/cdata/c/cult+film+and+tv+ma/full+details
3. While the chapters in this volume deal with both US and UK television, here I focus solely on the latter, the complexities of which are more than enough for my allotted 5,000 words.
4. For a fuller account, see Messenger-Davies and Pearson, 2007: 209–223.
5. For a fuller account, see Pearson, 2007: 239–256.
6. For announcement, see http://www.hollywoodreporter.com/hr/content_display/television/news/e3i40c53e11c19e214eb627b388db788b37
7. The two-episode business model refers to the practice of an original airing during the regular season and a repeat-airing during the summer.
8. Emphasis in original.
9. *The X-Files*, for example, garnered 16 Emmys but of these 13 were in the technical categories, with one for writing and two for acting.
10. See http://www.cult.tv/index.php?cm_id=427&cm_type=article

2   Members Only: Cult TV from Margins to Mainstream

Sergio Angelini and Miles Booy

Cult television isn't what it used to be. It emerged as a response by television programmers to the exigencies of the baby boom generation; now it is an integral branding component of cross-platform marketing strategies in a multimedia age. What follows is a brief overview of these two models of cult television, and a brief account of the history of the transition from one to the other.

Umberto Eco in his seminal essay on the cult phenomenon suggested that for a text to become a bona fide cult it would have to fulfil three criteria: it must be perceived as an authorless 'living textuality'; it must provide a 'completely furnished world' that can be totally inhabited by its adepts; and finally it must also be composed of segments that can be detached and enjoyed, 'irrespective of their original relationship with the whole' (1987: 198). Eco was writing before home video, but he is nonetheless describing the immersive experience most enthusiasts of cult television would recognise as crucial parts of their experience as fans.

Finding Your Audience

...obviously, [you are] working so hard on The Twilight Zone that, in essence, for the time being and for the foreseeable future, you've given up on writing anything important for television, right?

Mike Wallace interviewing Rod Serling in 1959[1]

When cults first emerged around television shows, the appeal was to a minority audience who took content and form seriously and who came to believe that within a select number of broadcasts material was being effectively smuggled in, providing viewers with something new, different, and perhaps even subversive/ dangerous. Rod Serling, hitherto a writer of highly praised naturalistic dramas such as *Patterns* and *Requiem for a Heavyweight*, turned to the science fiction and fantasy genre in the late 1950s to escape from the censorship and interference of the networks and sponsors. The enormously influential anthology series *The Twilight Zone* switched from week to week from space opera to supernatural horror, from comedy to drama. The show's broad generic spectrum meant that it could deal with issues such as racism and alcoholism and, for the most part, get under the censor's radar. It could even creatively tackle current events, such as its story about Fidel Castro ('The Mirror', 3:6) and what became one of, if not the first, dramatic series to refer to the Vietnam War ('In Praise of Pip', 5:1). The symbolic and allegorical subtext of *The Twilight Zone*'s stories was often apparent only after attentive viewers had successfully unpeeled the narrative layers and got past their delight in the snap of the twist endings (see Beeler on *The Twilight Zone* in this volume).

Other writers followed Serling's use of allegory in SF anthology shows such as *The Outer Limits*. Most famously, Gene Roddenbury used it in *Star Trek*. Even *Doctor Who*, made under radically different conditions and not created for such subversive purposes, soon developed the knack. Its second story, *The Daleks* (tx. 21 December 1963–01 February 1964), dealt with the rise of the paranoid xenophobic Daleks after a nuclear war on the planet Skaro. Whilst dealing with the aftermath of atomic holocaust, it is constructive to contrast this programme's huge popular success (the programme's ratings shot up, the Daleks were a mid-sixties craze in England) with that of Peter Watkins' *The War Game*, made a year later. That film realistically detailed the consequences of a nuclear strike but would not be transmitted by the BBC for 20 years. Whilst many taboos have been broken since the sixties and a wide range of issues are now more commonly raised on primetime television, the SF allegory remains an alluring vehicle for successfully getting contentious material to a receptive audience. Thus, whilst Chris Gerolmo and Steven Bochco's *Over There*, a continuing drama about U.S. soldiers in Iraq, was cancelled after 13 episodes, the revamped *Battlestar Galactica*, which treated the same subject less literally, was more successfully received, allowing the show to become more upfront and transgressive as it progressed over the years. If science-fiction programmes have seemed so often to be cult programmes, it is not just because of the world's never-failing supply of unattached young men ready to take these shows to their hearts, but because the genre's marginal status has so often made it the refuge for writers seeking to say obliquely what they cannot say upfront.

However, the 'furnished world' which Eco suggests that the cult text must create is not reducible to purely allegorical readings. Nor is it merely the details of the story and the world in which it happens, though these are important and constitute a starting point. *Star Trek* invites the viewer to an imagined reality with its own codes of practice, décor, character types, catch-phrases, and a narrative continuity which builds up as consecutive episodes visit previously unseen parts of the U.S.S. Enterprise, invoke different articles of the Federation constitution, allude to family members or past lives of the regulars, and encounter new alien species. Sharing these details of a series' surface is one way in which fans bond, but the trajectory of fan appreciation, as can be measured from the fanzines and websites of long-lasting cults, has often shifted away from detail and minutiae to some deeper meaning. Thus, modern *Star Trek* fans are more likely to talk about the programme's much-vaunted liberalism as the source of their allegiance rather than the details of the Federation/Klingon conflict, and what appeals about the diverse sketches of *Monty Python* isn't narrative continuity – there isn't any – but a shared sense of absurd humour.

Trek, of course, debuted in the 1966–1967 U.S. TV season, living perpetually on the brink of cancellation and generating a letter-writing campaign to keep it on the air in an 'adult' timeslot. This is as good a candidate as any if one is trying to provide a date for when a cult appreciation of a television programme became an organised movement seeking genuine clout in the destiny and direction of its object of adoration. If *Trek* was a science fiction show in the Serling mode – in that the meaning was clear if you had ears to hear it – *The Prisoner* was altogether stranger. If it sometimes seems like the cult show par excellence, that may be because, with whatever degree of consciousness, it dramatises the whole process of cult narrative by having the protagonist literally inhabit a world of stylised construction, odd props, and oblique meanings. Its conclusion satisfyingly revealed the limitations of most episodic drama by undermining the heroic stature of its protagonist, literally (and figuratively) dismantling the show's physical environment and deliberately choosing plot discontinuity and fragmentation in a deflating finale that explained nothing at the level of story or character, the standard by which the popular but formulaic output of its production company ITC had hitherto always been measured (and never found wanting). In its place it provided such derisory plot 'resolutions' as to make clear that whatever was at stake in the programme it was not the manifest plot but something that had meaning and resonance only when stripped of its generic protuberances and brilliantly marshalled attack on the conventions of the ITC action adventure drama, a club of which it was a clearly very unwilling member. For devotees of cult television, part of the appeal is the way in which such shows bring something new to one's appreciation of genre and the syntax of television itself. A certain self-reflexivity would seem almost inherent in this model of cult television, built as it is on an unwritten compact about non-manifest meaning between the producers and at least part of the audience.

That part of the audience needn't be large, of course. Any number of programmes we now regard as cult (*Blake's 7*; *Doctor Who*; *The Prisoner*) retained, at least for much of their run, decent viewing figures at a time when audience sizes were larger than now. Cult readings of *The Daleks*, if they existed at the time, were lost in a flood of toys and comic strips, which filleted the creatures down to croaking robots in bright primary colours suitable for children to play with. Even as unlikely a project as P.J. Hammond's impenetrably dark but vividly imagined *Sapphire & Steel* – in which time is envisaged as a corridor with weak spots, and the eponymous otherworldly agents enter our world to deal with the things which leak through – was broadcast on the United Kingdom's main commercial channel at seven in the evening as mainstream family entertainment.

These British examples are important because fans value 'authored' series, such as *The Prisoner,* which promise a consistent identity and personal point of view. Post-war British broadcasting shared that valuation and has been historically marked by shorter production cycles to allow it. It thus offers rich pickings in term of cult television. Philip Martin's *Gangsters*, for instance, began as a one-off violent thriller about Birmingham criminals, but the subsequent series incorporated references aimed squarely at film buffs and employed parodic elements (episodes end with exaggerated cliff-hangers followed by a 'To be continued' title card) to Brechtian effect. In the second series, Martin himself appears, typing out pages of a script describing events as they unfold onscreen. He also plays a hired killer who dresses and speaks like WC Fields, and who dispatches the series' hero simply by touching him, mocking the elaborate attempts previously made on his life. The final episode concludes with the leading lady throwing her hands up in despair and walking off the set as the camera pulls back to show the whole studio crew standing around as she leaves.

Thus cult television, as Eco would understand it (i.e., a grass-roots pop culture phenomenon in which fans 'find' a show with genuine subtext and a strong personality and read it in a way that is one step removed from the larger audience), can be more or less dated from the mid-sixties on either side of the Atlantic. Nearly 20 years later, when the U.S. networks shifted away from simple Nielsen ratings to a more demographics-centred approach, the role of niche audiences would change, and with them the definition of the cult television text.

The crucial event is the renewal of the medical drama *St. Elsewhere,* a poor ratings performer that, to everyone's surprise, was not cancelled. Unlike its clear artistic progenitor *Hill Street Blues* (also produced by the MTM production company), which saw its ratings slowly improve as its first season progressed, *St. Elsewhere* just did not seem to be catching on despite its similarly dark humour, large cast of eccentric characters, and overlapping story arcs. 'TV Guide' explained,

> The show had good comp. Which meant that *St Elsewhere* had good audience composition; it attracted a large number of viewers from TV's prime advertising audience, those between the ages of 18 and 49 with sizeable incomes and an instinct for buying ... Perhaps in the end that will be *St Elsewhere*'s legacy: that a show ... managed to

survive because of the shape of its audience. (Leahy cited in Feuer, Kerr, and Vahimigi: 1984, 269)

The television world post-*St. Elsewhere* was certainly one of smaller audiences, but it was not a shift towards cult aesthetics so much as an economic prioritisation of educated urbanites with disposable income, those viewers most desired by advertisers. Its largest consequence was the rise of 'quality' television of the *ER* or *The West Wing* type, though it is certainly true that these programmes prominently feature many of the characteristics of the cult text: story arcs within which weekly narrative units could be placed, visual stylisation, ambiguity, and a playful (but not necessarily critical) attitude towards generic and televisual conventions. The 'audience' became 'audiences', a coalition of different groups who viewed a text for diverse, possibly contradictory, reasons. Cult readings would flourish in the 25 years since *St. Elsewhere*'s renewal, but if the chosen show was to survive, they would still have to co-exist with more mainstream practices.

The case of *Twin Peaks* demonstrates how tentatively 'cult' TV exists in network television. Launched in 1990, *Peaks* burnt brightly, but briefly. Its critically acclaimed first season of eight episodes was followed by a full season of 22 parts, during which the programme spluttered and died. In shows like *Trek,* a cult/fan reading emerged, unexpectedly, within a programme aimed at the mainstream. With film director David Lynch on board as co-creator, *Peaks* was packaged as cult before anyone had even seen it. If *Trek* had developed a world ripe for both immersion and appropriation more or less without realising it, the town of Twin Peaks, where characters speak in instantly quotable dialogue and come complete with props (the log, the Dictaphone, Nadine's eye-patch), seems consciously built for such a purpose.

Twin Peaks was dense, allusive, and complexly plotted, but it did not last. More sustained success was met by those shows which adapted its themes and innovations into more conventional series. Thus, FBI agents specialising in weird cases was the premise of *The X-Files*, and quirky community policing became the basis of *Picket Fences*. *Northern Exposure* used Pacific Northwest landscapes, just as *Peaks* did, but dispensed with its dark vision of murderous spirits in the woods and substituted instead a benevolent pastoralism of sporadic pagan connotations. By the end of the nineties, the networks were adrift in the supernatural imagery that *Peaks* had flirted with (*Buffy; Angel; Charmed*). These programmes all contained cult material and found fan bases which generated cult readings. These were geared, as Sara Gwenllian-Jones puts it, towards

the consumption habits of fans [which] have helped ensure that niche audiences which include high quotas of avid viewers have become a highly desirable market for an increasingly intermedial culture industry. (Gwenllian-Jones: 2003, 166)

So far, so cult, but it is noticeable too that all those programmes (*Buffy, X-Files* etc.) had replaced the abrasive edges of *Twin Peaks* with more conventional formats and plotting. All were more obviously heroic and were made up, for the most part, of episodes containing beginning, middle, and end with a climax and resolution in the traditional places. All of these more successful shows weren't just shows at all, of course, but massive franchises spun off into books, soundtracks, comic strips, and other merchandise. The whole notion of a 'mainstream' has been enthusiastically declared dead in recent years by many. However, the evidence of these more mainstream programmes finding greater success than *Twin Peaks* would question this wisdom, suggesting that something of a mainstream aesthetic survives. How cult television works within it is the question we now turn to.[2]

Members Only

A prime example of how cult television series have changed in their audience positioning is the new version of *Battlestar Galactica*. Whilst the programme retains its male-friendly world of a war-ravaged race fleeing in starships, the dynamics of the show are now based on male-female confrontation, with the women usually given the upper hand. The primary representative of the Cylons is now a lusty and sexy blonde dominating the mind and actions of the feeble Baltar (Fig. 2.1); cocky cigar-chomping flyer Starbuck is also now female, the president elect is female and constantly butts heads with the still male General Adama, who usually bows to her political savvy. Boomer

Fig. 2.1   Sexy Cylon dominates feeble Baltar in Battlestar Galactica

has also become female and has not only gone from being the token African American to being the token Asian American in the cast but also become a sleeper Cylon, initially unaware of her own alien nature. Such a refit is also apparent in such varied action adventure shows as *Buffy, Xena: Warrior Princess, La Femme Nikita, Alias*, and *Terminator: The Sarah Connor Chronicles* that focus entirely around strong women. These programmes and others like them are marked by the degree to which seriality and other soap opera elements have been embraced as an organising principle and as a strategy to strengthen viewer loyalty, something once anathema to Network schedulers but now the norm.

In a world where programming looks like this, cult appeal is often demarcated along a very fine line. *Remington Steele* was a humorous detective show with a romantic 'will-they-won't-they?' subplot around its leads. It featured cinematic in-jokes in every episode, was a mainstream hit, and made a star of Pierce Brosnan. One of its original writers, Glenn Gordon Caron, left and used the same format for *Moonlighting*, which plays like the cult version of the same show with mere references to other movies replaced by full-on genre pastiches (as in the film noir homage 'The Dream Sequence Always Rings Twice' [2:4], set in the forties and shot in black and white) and direct-to-camera addresses. Part of the cult experience is to be in on the jokes at such self-referential moments, and they pepper the contemporary niche-marketed text, often reaching a crescendo at the series' conclusion. Cult shows tend to depart with grand, undercutting gestures. *St. Elsewhere, The Prisoner, Gangsters,* and even *Roseanne* concluded in such as a way as to emphasise the artificiality of the form, whilst *Magnum P.I.* and *Life on Mars* end with the viewer's television set being switched off. When Rob Lowe was promoting the U.K. screening of his abruptly cancelled legal drama *The Lyon's Den*, he sold it on the strength of its finale, stating that the show had 'the most outrageous ending of any TV series you've ever seen' (cited in Rackham: 2004, 57) (Lowe's hero unexpectedly and suddenly turned out to be a murderous psychotic). The final episode of *Star Trek: Enterprise*, set several years in the show's future, took the form of a holodeck presentation in which characters from another *Star Trek* spin-off, *Star Trek: The Next Generation* (*ST: TNG*), navigate the story by freeze framing, pausing, and fast-forwarding. Thus, the *ST: TNG* characters become viewer proxies and *Enterprise* itself acts as a futuristic cult TV show. This notion of setting a concluding episode decades in the future was pioneered by J. Michael Straczynski's *Babylon 5*. It allows for the creation of stories set between the penultimate and final parts and thus encourages fans to fill in the narrative blanks through fan fiction or home-made sequels/prequels and was adopted for the grand finales of series as diverse as the ironic teen soap *The O.C.* and the morbidly comic *Six Feet Under.*

It's hard to avoid consistently citing *Babylon 5* when considering the modern cult text. Designed to tell a giant story across five seasons, *B5* pushed the limits of how far a cult-orientated series could go in terms of narrative strategy. It's difficult to see how *24*, *Lost*, or *Prison Break* could exist without its example, though such shows would probably balk at some of *B5*'s more ambitious narrative twists. The episode 'Babylon Squared' (1:20), for instance, constitutes the first part of a story crucial to the understanding of the whole history of its universe, but the second half was not told until 'War Without End' (3:16/17), a couple of seasons later. Standalone episodes were initially created to try and hold the interest of more casual viewers, but *Babylon 5*'s essentially uncompromising stance could make only so many concessions to any but the truly faithful fan. Straczynski also scripted most episodes himself, paving the way for the current generation of television auteurs such as David Kelley and Aaron Sorkin, whose prodigious output of 15 or more scripts per year for shows which they created imbued series such as *Ally McBeal* and *The West Wing* with the aura of the 'authored' text.

Our use of the word 'aura' is not meant to imply that the authorship signatures of 'showrunners' such as Kelley, Sorkin, or anyone else are not genuinely present, that the creativity they represent is not valuable, or that their freedom was not hard-won. We use such terms to emphasise that authorship signatures, however genuine, are deployed as elements in a text's marketing and are intended to take specific effect during its reception. This industrial approach is particularly apt if one considers the case of HBO (Home Box Office). The company behind such varied successes as *Sex and the City*, *Deadwood*, *The Sopranos*, *The Wire,* and *The Larry Sanders Show* truly is the house that cult television built. Delivered on subscription by cable, it is perceived as being creatively freer since its content, particularly with regards to language and nudity, is largely uncensored. As such, it is a brand that has come to signify content made for an exclusive and adult viewership with shows that freely embrace subcultures and which promote an anti-establishment viewpoint as a way to differentiate itself from the main networks.

We have sought in this brief chapter to outline some of the features of the cult text from its initially innocent emergence through to the more calculated positioning and reception of the modern niche-driven text. We use the word *reception* specifically, rejecting the alternative term *consumption* (as used by Sara Gwenllian-Jones above). What finally defines the truly cult text is that it is the point where the consumption metaphor breaks down. The cult text is never consumed (i.e., destroyed or used up) in its reading. It is always available, complete, and undiminished, bristling with new moments to be activated. If you smile as you read the words 'No! Not the mind probe!' we recognise you not just as a *Doctor Who* fan, but as one who has gone far beyond a consideration of the plot, the theme, or any part of the manifest or symbolic content. You now take pleasure in a particularly strangely delivered line by a minor guest-star in an episode screened 25 years ago.[3] You almost certainly also take pleasure from the fact that when, in another *Who* story, the omnipotent Sutekh finally rises from the chair in which he has been paralysed and imprisoned for centuries, the hand of a BBC technician is clearly seen keeping the cushion in place.[4] We salute you – and your scarf – for this is cult reading at its best, so slippery they'll never catch it, let alone niche-market it, so full of love and laughter it could be a romantic comedy.

Even if *Doctor Who* had never returned, the show would never be over for the many who practice the readings cited above. There are endless moments, invisible to the non-initiate, to be activated and become the next round of in-jokes, and that remains true of shows with a much shorter history than *Doctor Who*. The cult text appears either innocently or by calculation, but it finds final form only as the locus for continuing, inexhaustible readings.

Recommended Reading

Eco, Umberto (1987) '*Casablanca*: Cult Movies and Intertextual Collage', in U. Eco *Travels in Hyperreality*, trans. by William Weaver. London: Picador: 197–211.

Twin Peaks

(ABC, 1990–1991)

Miles Booy

Co-created by David Lynch and Mark Frost, *Twin Peaks* debuted as an eight-episode (including the pilot) series in 1990. The discovery of the corpse of local high school girl Laura Palmer was our entry point into the goings on in Twin Peaks, a north-western town five miles south of the Canadian border (liminal metaphors abound). The forests around the town seem to offer entry to a dark spiritual realm, The Black Lodge, the domain of a baleful spirit, Bob. Other, less supernatural plotlines, proliferated, notably an ownership battle over the local sawmill. Re-commissioned for a second season of 22 episodes, the programme struggled to retain its initial intensity, and to find a similarly engaging plotline once the murder had been resolved. A scheduling shift, in the United States, from Thursday to Saturday, at that point regarded ratings wise as a dead-end, certainly did not help, and the programme was cancelled at the end of the 90/91 season.

Elsewhere in this book, Sergio Angelini and I suggest that the cult-ness of *Twin Peaks* appears to have been constructed at the outset. That hardly seems remarkable now, but this is the point of the sea-change when a cult audience became something which, rather than emerging unexpectedly through viewer response, could be factored in during production. It had quotable dialogue, quirky characters with visual motifs, and a certain amount of visually impressive cinematography which drew attention to itself. 'Twin Peaks is a long way from the world,' says Sheriff Truman, and it certainly seems like a fantasy environment readily constructed for fans to vanish into.

Advance publicity for *Twin Peaks* claimed it would 'change television'. And to a certain extent, it did. Prior to *Peaks*, 'cinematic' was the ultimate accolade a TV drama could attain, but it was rarely awarded by critics or viewers. *Peaks*, recruiting cast and crew from America's newly vibrant and suddenly visible Independent sector, made the relationship between the two seem more casual, and the barriers between them were suddenly permeable. It is easy to overstate this, because much of *Peaks* looks like conventional television drama, especially in the second season. However, the program offered high-profile exposure to independent directors prepared to grab the moment with some eye-catching camerawork. Fan favourite Tim Hunter (previously the director of *River's Edge*

[U.S., 1986] which also centres on a female corpse) is the obvious example, but in the years following the program's cancellation a good number of its directors, along with the younger cast members, played in a multiplex near you. In the same period, Hollywood A-listers such as Barry Levinson and Oliver Stone brought projects to the small screen (Stone's title, *Wild Palms*, seemed eerily similar).

A book like this one inevitably emphasises the elements which fans engaged with: the quirkiness, the supernatural elements, and the visual stylisation. But if *Peaks* refused to place its mysteries in a 'weekly monster/villain' template, it did attempt to mix them into a soap opera format. A different entry in a different book might have begun by outlining the complex web of romantic relationships around town. Upon discovering Laura's corpse, we also find that one of her boyfriends, James Hurley, has fallen for her best friend, Donna. James, his parents absent, lives with an uncle, who is unhappily married to Nadine and is having an affair with his lifelong sweetheart, Norma, the owner of the local diner. Norma nervously awaits the release of her own husband, Hank, from jail... and so on.

'Soap noir' was how co-creator Mark Frost described this heady mixture, and the two genres are reflected in various ways. Differing mise-en-scènes are used around different characters, so that Agent Cooper, participating in a piece of detective gothic, wanders the forest, whilst Catherine Martell, whose storylines turn on a battle for ownership of the local sawmill, inhabits an interior world of offices, bedrooms, and hotels.

The two genres are also incarnated in the form of the two (major) investigations into Laura's death. When, in the pilot, Cooper asserts his suspicion that a white powder found in Laura's safe deposit box might be cocaine, the local sheriff is shocked: 'Mr. Cooper, you didn't know Laura Palmer.' That, of course, is the point, for the detective genre prioritises the outside view which deduces according to the evidence. Four episodes later, the teenage couple James and Donna assert an opposing interpretive strategy: 'The police didn't love Laura. Nobody loved her but us'. Their soap opera model prioritises knowledge that isn't neutrally produced by deductive reasoning, but that which is derived from emotional involvement and personal experience. The two discourses fuse at various points, most spectacularly in the revelation of Laura's killer, the dual figure of her father and the mysterious Bob – but is Bob a gothic spirit who inhabits Leland Palmer and forces him to commit atrocities, or is he simply Laura's own creation, the mental mask she places on her attacker to deny who it really is that climbs into her bed at night? Sustaining the ambiguity even when a ratings crisis forced the production crew to bring Bob back was a considerable achievement.

Did *Peaks,* cancelled after its second season, really 'change television'? The number of programs which rushed into the space that it opened up for cult shows suggests it did. One way or another *The X-Files, Northern Exposure*, and countless others owe something to the strangeness and bold visual styling of *Twin Peaks*. They took from it the lesson that a fan culture could be a useful component of a larger audience, but they found that larger audience – larger, that is, than *Twin Peaks'* – by softening the program's harder edges. Thus, *Buffy*'s over-arching plotlines could safely be assured of resolutions in the season finale. *The X-Files* kept a few things ambiguous forever, but much of the output of these shows was 'monster of the week' stuff – very good 'monster of the week' stuff, but generically familiar and narratively conventional.

Peaks itself went out on a hard-edged bang, concluding with a badly received prequel movie, *Fire Walk With Me* (David Lynch, U.S., 1992), which was critically lambasted as incoherent, violent, and noisy. That last word seems key to me. The film is largely set in Laura's head. Its several lengthy scenes featuring extreme background noise nearly obliterating the dialogue represent her split consciousness, her knowing, but also denying, the identity of her abuser. Not an easy movie, but as good as anything in the series.

Notes

1. From *The Mike Wallace Interview* show (ABC, tx. 22 September 1959) as cited in Zicree, 1982, 3. The 25-minute interview can be seen in the Panasonic DVD release 'Treasures of *The Twilight Zone*'.
2. There is no space to discuss it here, but generalisations about the state of the mainstream certainly require qualification with reference to national conditions. On Christmas Day 2007, the seasonal episode of *Doctor Who* was viewed on its initial transmission alone by over 13 million people. This is a viewing figure far above those achieved by domestic audiences for most U.S. dramas in a nation with a population several times larger than that of the United Kingdom. U.K. theorists may well have reason to be wary of American claims of the complete disintegration of the aesthetic centre.
3. The story in question is 'The Five Doctors' (tx. 25 November 1983)
4. 'Pyramids of Mars' (13:3)

3   The Aesthetics of Cult Television

Rhonda V. Wilcox

As a girl in the 1960s, I watched, enthralled, as the vampire Barnabas Collins (Jonathan Frid) swept through a graveyard in the television series *Dark Shadows*. When a twirl of his cape knocked over a tombstone (cardboard? styrofoam?), I was briefly shocked, more briefly dismayed, and then amused, as I was thrown out of the fictional world I had been inhabiting. This sort of defamiliarisation and disillusionment is typical of the sort of pleasure to be found in cult cinema, but far from typical of the aesthetic pleasures of cult TV. Certainly there are elements of enjoyable unbelievability in some series: the Daleks of *Doctor Who* come to mind, and the cheerful anachronisms of *Xena: Warrior Princess*. But these textual disruptions are less and less present; the noteworthy aesthetic elements of cult television are very different from those of cult film.

Cult TV typically has been excluded from the academy, quite literally: the Academy of Television Arts and Sciences has rarely given awards to cult TV makers; and yet those makers do not identify themselves as creating schlock or trash. In his *Screen* article on the cult film 'Trashing the Academy', Jeffrey Sconce notes that the celebration of cult film can be seen as a reaction to 'the social construction of taste', with implicit class issues (1995: 371). Sconce points out that critics from Lester Bangs to Pierre Bourdieu believe taste to be defined by the rejection of Others' views. Nonetheless, I propose that an aesthetic of cult television can be based on the embracing of certain elements (mainly textual) rather than on a set of rejections deriving, in effect, from sociopolitical competition. My attempt may be no more successful than Lawrence Kohlberg's poignant post-World War II attempt to find a rational basis for virtue (indeed, the comparison is hubristic). But the attempt will be based on empirical observation, however subjective the assessment must ultimately be. I will leave it for others to define cult television; here I will simply describe [gloss] some of its aesthetic elements. However, I will begin by saying that, by definition, cult television is television which has an *intently* attentive audience. Sconce and others have identified cult film as characterised by textual excess; I would say that cult TV can instead be characterised by textual plenitude: Cult TV shows support aesthetic analysis. If that were not the case, fans and scholars would not have chewed over them so long. Sara Gwenllian-Jones and Roberta E. Pearson, in the introduction to their collection *Cult Television*, argue that 'an understanding and definition of cult television must be predicated on the full circuit of communication, that is, texts, production/distribution, and audiences, rather than an overvaluation of any one or two of these three factors' (2004b: x). My discussion of the aesthetics of cult TV will focus mainly on the text, but with the awareness that the audiences for these texts are unusual in their attentiveness, and that the makers seem to create their work in the hope (or sometimes expectation) of having such audiences (see Espenson in this volume). Cult TV audiences do recognise themselves as different; this attentiveness to the text is one of the qualities that constitute the difference and forms one basis for understanding the nature of the aesthetics of cult TV.

Music and sound have been too often omitted from serious aesthetic discussions of television. First in the television episode, of course, is its musical theme. A memorable television series will have a memorable theme song; I cannot call to mind any exceptions. (Does this mean that the composer was inspired by the material, or that a good composer was hired along with good writers, or that we as audience never bothered to attend to a show that started with a bad theme?) The theme song is particularly important in cult television, however, because it is the doorway through which we enter the special world of the cult show. As Umberto Eco has said in discussing cult film, the cult creation 'provide[s] a completely furnished world' (1987: 198); and as Gwenllian-Jones and Pearson add, 'cult series usually – though not exclusively – belong to one or another of the fantastic genres of science fiction, fantasy, horror, or speculative fiction' (2004b: xii). In the summer of 2007, the music played outside Buckingham Palace as part of the ceremony of the changing of the guard included not only standard military marches but also the fanfare from *Star Trek*. One might argue that a military band's performance was appropriate for some of the themes of the series. But I still remember being entranced by the elements of the theme that came before the fanfare. In an era when the boisterousness of the *Bonanza* theme was more typical, *Star Trek* started not immediately with the fanfare but with four very quiet notes, presented with a visual backdrop of nothing but stars in the blackness of space. Then came the voice of William Shatner as Captain Kirk: 'Space – the final frontier.' The combination of the quiet music and the interweaving of the spoken word brought a viewer (or we might say listener) to an unexpected place. Or consider the significance of Angelo Badalamenti's theme for *Twin Peaks*: its solemn, slow beauty signals the depth of emotion below a sometimes quirky surface. The contrapuntal rhythms of the *Doctor Who* theme, with its mixture of fast, driving background and longer notes in the fronted melody, are only too appropriate for a story of time travel. Mark Snow's memorable *The X-Files* theme, whistling in the dark, suggests the mystery of that series' world (see Halfyard in this volume for a further discussion of music and cult television).

It would be easy to cite more, but it could also be argued that these are simply extreme examples of doing what all good TV theme songs do: drawing the audience into the world of the series. If nothing else, it is important to note that cult television music is among the best television music. But it can also offer special pleasures because of the audience's attentiveness. Janet Halfyard, in an article analysing the theme songs of *Buffy* and its spinoff *Angel*, notes that the two are melodically linked: in very different presentations (for instance, rock guitar in *Buffy* but cello in *Angel*), the songs open with the same notes (Halfyard, 2001). Listeners may subconsciously recognise the relationship between the titular characters. What Gwenllian-Jones and Pearson refer to as 'dense intertextuality' (2004b: xvi) applies to the music of these series as well as to the narrative and language. Or consider the distorted chord which serves as the brief theme for *Lost*; it echoes a segment of the theme song of *The Twilight Zone*, its distant antecedent, and thus cues viewers to the kind of content to come. *Lost* may have started with a plane crash, but it moved from apparent realism to the kind of paranormal and science fiction events that could easily have happened in *The Twilight Zone*. This kind of richness of reference can be not only intertextual but also intratextual in the long course of a television series. An oft-cited case occurs in *Buffy*: when Buffy's mother Joyce dies, her mentor Giles is shown sitting alone, listening to the Cream song 'Tales of Brave Ulysses' ('The Body', 5:16); long-term viewers knew that years before in the series, the same song played before Joyce and Giles made love.

The series may play with music in more obvious ways as well. *Northern Exposure* created a memorable exposure of gender representation when it presented protagonist Joel Fleischman, in a dream sequence, taking the role of a popular male singer in a music video, surrounded by scantily clad dancing women, but then deleted the music and had the women keep dancing. Defamiliarisation has rarely been funnier. *Northern Exposure* also made good use of the musical soundtrack provided by DJ 'Chris in the Morning' as an accompaniment to the philosophical issues explored on the series and (as with the *Star Trek* theme) interwove spoken word: As the town listened to the radio station, the viewers/listeners were provided with a voiceover by the philosophical Chris, combining ideological with musical themes. (*Angel* on occasion made use of a green demon emcee to something of the same effect). *Northern Exposure* also offered an episode that focused on the nature of communication by having one of its regulars (Shelly) sing, rather than speak, throughout the episode. Other cult series, such as *Xena* and *Buffy*, have provided entire musical episodes. While occasionally non-cult series will 'put on a show' musically, the cult series musicals use the experiment with form to advance the narrative in serious ways (see Helford; Wilcox). If we explored further, the *Buffy* musical also might lead us into curious extratextual territory, since it was taken on tour for interactive display in movie theatres around the United States (cf. the quintessential cult movie *The Rocky Horror Picture Show* [Jim Sharman, UK/US, 1975]) during the years after the series was cancelled.

Other experiments include *Buffy*'s 'The Body', in which the solemnity of death is accentuated by the lack of television's usually pervasive non-diegetic music, and 'Hush' (4:10), in which the characters are unable to speak for the majority of the episode, and thus explore the theme of communication. In sum, the music and sound of cult series can take advantage of a playful complexity supported by the audience's attentiveness and willingness to see themselves and their art object as different.

Literal seeing – the visual element of a series – has traditionally been foregrounded for film, although much television has been visually formulaic. But I have heard more than one person say that it is possible to instantly spot an episode of *The X-Files* when flipping across television channels. This visual recognisability is due in large part to the work of director of photography John Bartley, who made the series visually extraordinarily dark in response to its narrative themes. Another remarkably dark series is *Angel* (D.P. Herb Davis), which I have described as making use of chiaroscuro – darkness made visible by touches of light (both visual and thematic). Light can be used in very different ways as well. Watching the first episode of *Roswell*, I remember thinking that it used brightness (to the point that it was hard to see) in the same way that *The X-Files* used darkness and did so for the same purpose: for an effect of mystery. I was delighted to discover that Bartley was the D.P. for both series. He also worked on *Lost*, a series that mixes colourfully bright scenes with rarer scenes of darkness, again to mysterious effect. A recurrent visual motif of *Lost* exemplifies another element of camera work: the extreme close-up of the eye of the character from whose point of view most of the episode will be shown (varying from week to week). Or consider *Twin Peaks'* Agent Dale Cooper's detective techniques in investigating a murder through the reflection in a videotaped eye (Fig. 3.1). Such visuals have left far behind the medium close-up reverse shot clichés of standard television. The new *Battlestar Galactica* uses a handheld camera to suggest a documentary effect, perhaps particularly significant for a science fiction text. In all of his shows, Whedon makes purposeful use of long, uncut shots (e.g., following Buffy as she moves through her home upon discovering her mother's body). Tammy A. Kinsey has explained the surprisingly dense visual content of the flash transitions of *Angel*, comparing them to experimental cinema (2005).

The significant elements include not only the representational choices of lighting and camera work but also the visual content provided by production design/art direction, costumes, and make-up. Barbara Maio has written at length about the generic and cultural hybridity of *Firefly* – a hybridity which is part of the message of a series in a future where China and the United States are the remaining superpowers. *Beauty and the Beast* literally gave viewers an underworld as an essential part of the series – a gentler place than the city above. *The Prisoner* is still appreciated for the sardonic setting of its pristine, openly artificial village streets, which served as the ultimate entrapment (the

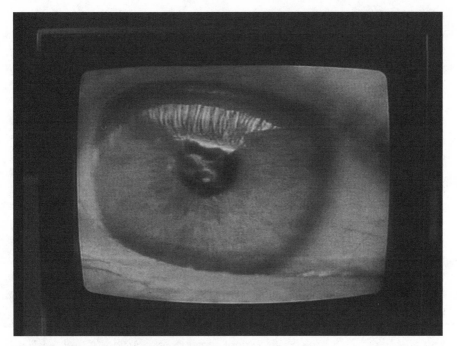

Fig. 3.1   Reflected evidence in Twin Peaks

real Welsh location of Portmeiron having been chosen for its unreal effect). More recently, *Heroes* has interwoven diegetic comic-book drawings of some of its characters with camera shots of those characters posed to echo the drawings – thus providing a pleasurable consciousness of the varied levels of reality contemplated in the series. More challenging, over the years, has been the make-up for aliens, vampires, and other otherworldly creatures. These have not generally constituted an aesthetic strength for the series; unlike cult film, cult TV series do not usually flaunt the unbelievability of their creatures but rather depend on the audience's willingness to suspend disbelief. How long does it take to accommodate the appearance of some of the regulars of *Farscape*? Despite the blue makeup and muppet-style puppetry involved in some of the characters, audience members assert that the suspension of disbelief happens. One of the most brilliant episodes of *Angel* used a muppet-style puppet version of the hero to mock television itself, but the effect may have been to make the regular characters seem more real in comparison to the puppets ('Smile Time', 5:14). Certainly techniques have improved over the years (contrast the Klingons of *Star Trek* and *Star Trek: The Next Generation*); and some series (such as *The X-Files*) make discreet use of lighting to blur the view of monstrous makeup. In many good shows, creative contributions are encouraged from all the makers, including those who work in make-up/prosthetics – and the same can be said for costuming, which can also certainly have purposeful relevance to content. *Alias* highlights questions of identity and performance in the famous wigs and costumes of its protagonist (Abbott and Brown, 2007). For *Buffy*, Cynthia Bergstrom not only designed costumes to indicate character but also, for example, discussed the use of colour as reflecting character relationships in the musical episode (Wilcox *Why Buffy Matters*, 2005; cf. Abbott, 2005c 337–338). The colour palette too can be used more broadly: many episodes of *Smallville* (a series which is stronger visually than narratively) highlight the red, yellow, and blue colours favoured by Superman. This intertextual visual allusion is hardly unique. Both *Xena* and *Buffy* provide cruciform death scenes. And, again, there are intratextual visual allusions as well. David Lynch and Mark Frost presumably expected viewers to recognise the red-curtained 'Other Place' from episode 3 when Agent Dale Cooper returned to it in the last episode of the series. In the fourth-season all-dream finale of *Buffy* ('Restless', 4: 22), Whedon expected viewers to recognise a costume recalling one worn in the first episode. Once more, the visual elements of these series are particularly dense with meaning, and makers can build the potential for self-reference over the years, counting on the attention of those who will not only view but also re-view.

A fair number of cult series are not particularly notable linguistically. However, some of them invite viewer enjoyment through recognition of a specialised vocabulary (e.g., *Star Trek*). Others are particularly admirable for the wit and grace of their language – for example, that of Joshua Brand and John Falsey and the other writers of *Northern Exposure*, and Joss Whedon and his company of writers in *Buffy*, *Angel*, *Firefly*, and *Dollhouse*. Michael Adams' *Slayer Slang* demonstrates that Whedon plays not only with vocabulary but also with the form of words in creating a witty heroic language suited to his protagonists; the breaks in linguistic form recreate the characters' breaks from societal tradition (2003). In this sense they are suited to the cultic valuing of difference. As for the use of language to quote or allude to earlier works of literature, some critics worry that discussing these elements of cult television is little more than an attempt to gain cultural capital – to curry cultural favour. Petra Kuppers, for instance, refers to *Star Trek: The Next Generation*'s 'Shakespeare complex' (2004: 50). I would argue instead that allusions to earlier literature are neither more nor less valid in television than they are in any other cultural product which incorporates language. Their value depends on their aptness and their effectiveness in illuminating the text at hand. But to completely omit recognition of the element of language (including allusion – not to mention other figures of speech) from among television aesthetics would seem a curious lacuna. In any case, as noted, cult series language does sometimes reinforce the sense of the 'completely furnished world.'

Character and narrative are the aesthetic elements most often discussed by critics and fans of cult television. Gwenllian-Jones and Pearson identify narrative seriality as characteristic of cult television series (2004b: xi–xii). As long ago as Fiske and Hartley's *Reading Television* and Newcomb's *TV: The Popular Art*, critics have been comparing television to serially published multi-part Victorian novels. One of the most distinctive elements of television as a medium is, of course, its length; film is the short story to television's novel. Many television series in the past, despite having continuing characters, have presented plots encapsulated within separate episodes. A series which advances a story through episode after episode runs the risk of not being able to engage viewers who come late to the series. A cult show – a show with an intent audience – is more likely to be serial (or is it that a serial show is more likely to be cult?). Shows which lose audience numbers are sometimes pressured to become more episodic, less complex. Earlier cult series such as *The Avengers* and *Star Trek* were more likely to be mainly episodic, but even they had a glacial, incremental forward movement; we learned of Spock's parents or Mrs. Peel's rediscovered husband as the series progressed. For the most part, cult series provide audiences with some closure at the end of most episodes, besides some through-story, thus engaging the potential for long-term development available in the many hours of television. *Twin Peaks* and *Roswell* carried a major narrative through 16 or 17 episodes and then (less successfully) changed focus. Henrik Ornebring argues that for *Alias*, 'several narratives are always resolved or taken in an unexpected direction around the middle of the season (episodes 10–13)' (2007: 20). Whedon planned season-long arcs, as did Rob Thomas for the first two seasons of *Veronica Mars*. An overriding arc can be seen running through the seven years of *Buffy*. And then there is *Babylon 5*: J.M. Straczynski wrote five seasons carrying out his planned narrative. Writers such as these have been able to provide attentive viewers with the pleasures of foreshadowing as well as long-term character growth. And the greater attention to continuity given to most cult series has allowed richer development of both character and narrative.

Depth can be seen in both the x and the y axis of these series. Many cult series are purposefully symbolic, and the symbolism is often culturally significant. Of course, the teens in Roswell are aliens – unable to fit into their world. Of course, Buffy's boyfriend became a monster after she slept with him. Of course, Whoopi Goldberg's Guinan explains that the android Data is being treated as 'property' in *Star Trek: The Next Generation*. From *The Twilight Zone* on, certain television series have followed in the Science Fiction/ Fantasy tradition of slipping in the social meaning through the symbolism. The fact that symbolic meaning requires an extra level of 'reading' means that it is particularly suited for the cult series and attentive cult audiences, who generally enjoy the prowess of careful reading. Not only symbol but also myth can be seen in many of the cult series. Paul Zinder argues that *Alias*' Sydney Bristow fits the Campbellian hero monomyth, and many critics make the same case for Buffy. Mark Gelineau believes that *Firefly*'s Captain Mal Reynolds is a trickster figure, and a similar case could be made for *Doctor Who* (2008). Jana Riess argues that Angel has some qualities of a bodhisattva – and the examples could continue (2004). It would be harder to find a cult series without mythic elements than with.

Further explorations can also be provided by parallel universes and time distortions. Gwenllian-Jones and Pearson write, 'Seriality, textual density, and perhaps most especially, the nonlinearity of multiple time frames and settings that create the potentially infinitely large metatext of a cult television text create the space for fans to revel in the development of characters and long, complex narrative arcs' (2004b: xvii). Like symbolism, parallel universes and time shifts offer the opportunity to consider another interpretation. *Star Trek*'s 'Mirror, Mirror' (2:4) provides a parallel universe in which characters discover hidden qualities in their second selves: would a harsher world erode the idealism of these people, or could they instead seed change in that harsher realm? George Takei appears both in this episode and, decades later, in *Heroes* – in which the 'Five Years Gone' episode (1:20) displays a post-apocalyptic world to a time traveller, not only motivating much of the urgency of the rest of the plot but also forcing characters to consider dark moral choices. *Northern Exposure* travels through time simply by visiting history in the episode 'Cicely' (3:23), which plays with the relationships of the regular characters by having their actors play different parts (Rob Morrow, instead of Dr. Joel Fleischman, plays a visiting Franz Kafka) and also provides an origins story based on one of television's first respectful presentations of a lesbian couple: though they are not regulars, the characters are presented as the founders of the town which plays so large a part in the series. *Buffy* may have provided the most metatextually unnerving of the parallel universes. In 'Normal Again' (6:17), we see a world in which Buffy Summers is a mental patient with delusions of being a superhero (How crazy is it to carry the struggle against evil to such extremes?). To the combined fascination and dismay of fans, the episode's ending left uncertain which of the worlds was 'real': it closed with one version of Buffy reclaiming her status as warrior for the right, but then – as the last shot – the other Buffy psychotically withdrawn in the asylum. The whole world of the show was thus cast in doubt. And such variations are not limited to interpretations within one text. Many of the texts have more and more pleasurably complex interrelationships. *Star Trek*'s Spock appears in *Star Trek: The Next Generation*. *Buffy* and *Angel* run back-to-back hour-long episodes with *Rashomon*-like perspective changes. *Heroes* runs graphic novels on the internet with backstories of the characters.

With internet graphic novels, of course, we have moved outside the television text per se. Cult television fans vehemently discuss the nature of 'canon' – meaning not the traditional literary/artistic term referring to those cultural products which are granted cultural capital and are to be passed on, but that the fans discourse on the nature of the primary source itself, which is no longer as clear-cut as it once was. Are the *Heroes* graphic novels canonical? What about the work of vidders, assembling clips of the series with musical accompaniment to create a new text? Is some fan fiction more canonical than other fan fiction? There are, it seems, degrees of canonicity. (See my *Northern Exposure* essay's postscript on canonicity.) It would not be possible for me to discuss here the aesthetic qualities of these various creations, though their very existence attests to the cultic nature of the series which inspired them. It is, however, worth noting another textual variant. A number of cult series (e.g., *The Avengers*, *Star Trek*, *Star Trek: The Next Generation*, *The X-Files*, and *Firefly*) have been followed by film sequels – most of which are lesser works than their television originals. Comparing these films to the cult TV series on which they are based may be one way of clarifying the aesthetics of cult television.

There are, then, aesthetic elements characteristic of cult series. But perhaps the difference most noteworthy is not in the kind but in the degree. This brief introduction has, I hope, suggested that there is a plenitude of material worthy of attention not just as sociological artefact but as aesthetic choice in cult TV. Many of the aesthetic techniques of which television is capable are more fully used in cult series, the series with audiences that are willing to watch again and again.

Recommended Reading

Abbott, Stacey (2005). 'Kicking Ass and Singing Mandy: A Vampire in LA', in Abbott (ed.) *Reading Angel: The TV Spin-off with a Soul*. London and New York: I.B.Tauris, 1–13.

Gwenllian-Jones, Sara and Roberta E. Pearson (eds) (2004) Introduction. *Cult Television*. Minneapolis, London: University of Minneapolis Press, ix–xx.

Lavery, David (1995) 'The Semiotics of Cobbler: *Twin Peaks*' Interpretive Community', in Lavery (ed.) *Full of Secrets: Critical Approaches to Twin Peaks*. Detroit: Wayne State University Press, 1–26.

Wilcox, Rhonda V. (2005) *Why Buffy Matters: The Art of Buffy the Vampire Slayer*. London and New York: I.B.Tauris.

Wilcox, Rhonda V., and Tanya R. Cochran (2005) ' "Good Myth": Joss Whedon's Further Worlds', in Wilcox and Cochran (eds) *Investigating Firefly and Serenity: Science Fiction on the Frontier*. London and New York: I.B.Tauris, 1–11.

4   *Babylon 5*
(PTEN, 1994–1997; TNT 1998)

Sergio Angelini

With the notable exception of the revived *Doctor Who*, television science fiction seems destined to remain a genre forever relegated to the fringes of the mainstream, one designed to appeal only to a small but dedicated band of devotees as audiences become increasingly fragmented and programmes are marketed directly and with increasing specificity to more select viewer groups. *Babylon 5* was arguably the first television show in the genre to really capitalise on this, precariously putting its potential for continued success and survival on the line by courting niche audiences to a greater extent than any show before or since. By structuring the show as a single continuous five-year story, creator, executive producer, and principal writer J. Michael Straczynski promised viewers of *Babylon 5* a genre show that would be accorded the seriousness normally associated only with its literary counterpart. The boldness of its long-term conception smacked of bravado but for many its hard-won success – in spite of a chain of very public setbacks – turned it into a series with more chutzpah than any other show in the history of cult television.

In the 1960s, *Star Trek* just managed to last three full seasons but no other science fiction show outlasted it on U.S. airwaves until its own sequel, *Star Trek: The Next Generation*, which succeeded in doing so largely by bypassing the networks entirely in favour of being sold directly into syndication, while *The X-Files*, which lasted even longer, appeared on Fox, the then fledgling fourth network.

Although its premise was simple enough to be summed up as 'Casablanca in space', *Babylon 5* (which was initially screened on PTEN, Prime Time Entertainment Network) eschewed the idealistic vision of the future associated with *Star Trek* in favour of a more plausible and urbane vision of the rise and fall of empires in earth's future. The main protagonists were an often dishevelled collection of characters battling addictions to drink and drugs while having to deal with often mundane issues arising from the show's setting, the eponymous Earth space station which acted as a meeting point for both commerce and diplomacy between dozens of races. With a high concept and flawed characters driven by recognisable weaknesses and desires that might more normally be associated with a contemporary drama, it was nonetheless marketed as a show completely out of the norm for SF television. It sought to deliver on this in a number of ways, most notably by structuring the story as a single huge narrative unfolding across 110 hour-long episodes subdivided into five seasons, each set in a calendar year between 2258 and 2262. This meant that entire seasons could go by between plot points being raised and their eventual resolution. Instances such as lead character Jeffrey Sinclair's 24-hour memory gap and the mystery of what was actually inside Ambassador Kosh's atmospherically controlled encounter suit (which completely hid his actual appearance) were flagged in the pilot episode and would be explained only in the second season. Perhaps most famously, the first season episode 'Babylon Squared' (1:20) was the first part of a story that was concluded only two seasons later in 'War Without End' (3:16 & 17). Throughout, the show was filled with premonitory dreams and visions tantalising viewers with possible interpretations of potential outcomes for strands that were to be resolved only several years later. This strategy is, of course, incredibly risky from a production standpoint, especially given the notorious failure of SF shows to last beyond a single season, but was largely justified by presenting the show as a long 'novel for television' in which all important answers would eventually be revealed.

The show's literary credentials were flagged in a variety of ways for the sake of alert and well-read viewers, from the presence of renowned writer and television critic Harlan Ellison as its 'conceptual consultant' to building in several references to such cult texts as Tolkien's *Lord of the Rings*, and even by naming the lead telepath in the series after Alfred Bester, author of *The Demolished Man*, the celebrated 1950s SF novel about ESP. There are also many references to the cult TV show *The Prisoner*, including its catch-phrase 'Be seeing you' and the distinctive thumb and forefinger salute that goes with it.

The insistence on a predetermined five-year arc made the show unusually vulnerable to production difficulties, but when these did occur, it may have in many ways added to its cult status by enabling additional readings from fans and allowing them to speculate on the original intentions against those that are eventually realised on screen. The original star of the show, Michael O'Hare, had to be replaced at the insistence of the studio; so what should have been the final part of the story of season five was brought forward to season three and a new finale, one closer to *Lord of the Rings*, was created in 'Sleeping in Light' (5:22), though this was, in fact, filmed at the end of the preceding season for fear of premature cancellation following the collapse of PTEN.

Keeping fans close was absolutely crucial, even though several stand-alone episodes were also made during the first two seasons to attract more casual viewers. Straczynski made a point of communicating with viewers online via GEnie, CompuServe and USENET groups, fostering a strong sense of community with the show's fans. The show was made on a very low budget, much lower than any of the *Star Trek* spin-offs, for instance, but its underdog status seemed appropriate to fans of a genre usually written off as a minority interest anyway. This sense of allegiance to a marginalised perspective was also part of the narrative as the protagonists would eventually lead a separatist movement against earth's government, aligning themselves with underprivileged minorities and the universe's disenfranchised.

Having made the fans aware of much of the behind-the-scenes strife, in some episodes Straczynski not only provided a framework to develop fan assessments but also paralleled the process of viewer interaction and folded it directly into the narrative by having the five-year narrative set in the much wider context of the *Babylon 5* universe. 'The Deconstruction of Falling Stars' (4:22) analysed the show's own mythos by catapulting the narrative into the future in stages, eventually reaching a million years hence to assess the heritage of the show's characters. Since the show's conclusion, Straczynski has written several spin-offs that fall within the interstices of the show, further opening up the sense of an immersive universe that could be shared by viewers. The role played by Straczynski (known as JMS to friends and fans) in providing viewers with a sense of an 'authored' text is in this case unusually strong as he wrote the vast majority of the episodes by himself – out of 110 episodes, he personally wrote 90, including the entirety of the third, fourth, and fifth seasons (except for a special episode by cult novelist Neil Gaiman).

The show's historical importance and influence has been enormous, even though no one else has yet attempted anything on so grand a scale. For instance, Ronald Moore's re-imagining of *Battlestar Galactica*, with its low-tech environment, mystical resonance, and 'sleeper' characters who are working for the enemy without knowing it, seems to owe a lot more to *Babylon 5* than to its ostensible basis in the original 1970s series. Straczynski's bold, unified vision for a science fiction show aligned to large-scale fantasy and cult literary works, although sometimes battered and bruised, completed its predetermined run – thanks in large part to an unprecedented level of fan interaction. The process of fan engagement continues to be extended and expanded by the publication of new works by Straczynski, including spin-offs, sequels and the long-mooted and much debated feature film version, *The Memory of Shadows*.

5 Playing Hard to 'Get' – How to Write Cult TV

Jane Espenson

Defining terms can be difficult. Or, sometimes, shockingly easy. I'd have to say that cult TV shows are the ones that attract a cult. I take that to mean an involved viewership. Not necessarily large or small, but involved. So the question of how to write cult TV reduces to a previously unsolved question: how do you make an audience feel involved?

Here's my answer, in its simplest form: Don't stuff a cookie in their mouth. Make them walk across the room for it. Make them look under the rug for it. They might even have to lift a floorboard. When they do that, they're a cult.

In other words, if you force viewers to *participate* in order to mine the most enjoyment from a show, then they will feel invested, and if they enjoy what their effort exposes, they will become the cult you're looking for. If a show takes a little more attention, a little more work, or thought, then they know that not everyone is going to 'get' it. And they'll feel proud that they're among a select few. That exclusive club – that's the 'cult' in cult TV.

Notice that this feeling of exclusivity can exist even if, in truth, the club isn't that small. I've had a number of people tell me without irony that they've 'discovered' *30 Rock*. Many of them, generally non-regular television viewers, are not aware that their hip discovery has mass appeal. It is, in fact, mass appeal disguised as cult appeal, which is probably the best thing any show can ever have.

There are some specific things that we as writers can do to force a television audience to engage and work hard to 'get' a show. What I'm about to list is a cluster of properties. You don't need all of them to be cult TV, but they help.

Have Complex Arcs

Story-telling that doesn't reset to status quo after every episode rewards faithful viewers. Make them watch every episode and they'll feel invested. Also, obviously, juggling long and complex stories rewards attention and intellect. *Battlestar Galactica* and *Lost* have long complex arcs. It's often pointed out that this feature discourages new viewership. Jumping in mid-stream takes a lot of effort. But this helps add to the special 'we get it' feeling of the original cult members. They got on the train before the doors closed. Besides, DVDs and downloads – more and more integrated into the average viewer's experience – help latecomers catch up to the train if they're willing to put in the effort.

Under-explain

In addition to rewarding faithful viewers, you can reward careful viewers. Under-explaining what's going on forces the audiences to pay close attention. I recently watched the pilot episode of *The Wire* and I was struck by the fact that no character helps out the audience *even by calling other characters by their names or titles.* The audience has to pick up who they are and how they fit into the overall scheme, simply through intelligent analysis of what they're seeing.

In an episode of *Battlestar Galactica* that we're preparing as I write this, Chief Tyrol spends much of the episode making his way through the ship under difficult conditions without the audience knowing what his ultimate goal is. We're trusting that the suspense of their journey is going to be heightened by the fact that the audience has had things under-explained, rather than over-explained.

The effect of *over*-explaining is exactly as one would predict. I worked for a while on a show called *Tru Calling* about a young morgue worker who was pulled back one day in time to help prevent a death. The show never attained cult status, despite having ingredients that suggested it might. I'm convinced in hindsight that part of the problem was clarity. We made a great effort on that show to be extremely clear, using flashbacks and additional dialogue to remove ambiguity. I might be wrong, but I now think that we took away an opportunity for the audience to feel proud of getting the show by making it impossible *not* to get. I fault no one involved with the show. It's hard to resist handing over that cookie. Withhold the cookie!

Make Them Look

As part of under-explaining, you can also make important information purely visual so that only people who are actively watching will catch it. A camera that pans to capture something that the characters in the scene don't themselves notice can be extremely effective and, obviously, rewards the person who's facing their television.

Examples of this are numerous; one of the most memorable ones for me is the moment at the end of *Battlestar Galactica*'s season three ('Crossroads

Part Two', 3:20) in which, after the body of the episode is complete, the camera plunges through the universe in a dizzying special effects shot to reveal a familiar-looking planet, clearly our Earth. Taken as part of a story in which the very existence of Earth has been an open question, this shot is vital, electrifying, and totally uncommented-upon. I love it.

I myself have become so used to the radio-with-pictures property of most of television that I sometimes have to remind myself to look at the screen (and not at, say, computer solitaire) during shows that are going to require this of me. Instead of assuming that the audience is distracted, a cult show demands that they stop being distracted and face front.

Give It a Documentary Feel

The pilot of *The Wire*, with its refusal to drop names, feels realer for it, since the helpful hand of the writer is noticeably absent. It feels strikingly like a documentary. In fact, a number of cult shows, including *The Wire*, *Firefly*, and *Battlestar Galactica*, are (or were) shot in an overtly documentary-style manner.

By this point, something should be becoming obvious. A world that doesn't reset to zero, that requires inference and visual information because nothing is being adequately explained, that is captured as if it's flying by at its own pace with no accommodation for cameras – that sounds like the actual, real, world. This is the real secret heart of cult TV. It works like life. A lot is made of the fact that many cult TV shows are set in other worlds, but the truth is that cult TV is usually the kind of television that most resembles reality, at least in all the important ways. You'll see that this continues to hold true as our list unfolds.

Mix Dark and Light

Again, this is part of making a show feel real. When a show is uniformly comedic or totally tragic, it lacks the texture of real life. In real life, laughter is often how we combat dark situations, and sadness often tempers joy. The first episode of *Battlestar Galactica* that I wrote contained a moment in which Tigh and Adama confront a serious food shortage on the ship. The moment was scripted this way:

ADAMA
Damn it. Are people still eating paper?

                              TIGH
            No. (deadpan)
            Of course, that's on account of the paper shortage.

It takes a moment to sink in. Then Adama starts to laugh, light-
headedly. Tigh joins in.

Wiping their eyes:

                             ADAMA
            Hys – hysteria. Not a good sign.

                              TIGH
            No sir.

                                          'The Passage' (3:10)

I think the moment works well on film. The audience is challenged to
acknowledge the humour and the sadness at the same time.

The cold open of the pilot for *The Wire* contains another darkly comedic
moment. A detective is interviewing a boy who was a witness to a brutal
killing. The boy explains that the victim, with the unappealing nickname of
'Snot Boogie', routinely stole the money from a poker game. The detective
asks, 'If Snot Boogie always stole the money, why'd you let him play?' The boy
answers, genuinely, 'You got to. This is America, man.' That moment, with its
casual acceptance of both American opportunity and American murder, is
beautifully, darkly, comedic.

I'll continue, because I love these examples. There's a moment I love
in a *Buffy* episode, in which Giles is trying to perform an important ritual.
Unfortunately for him, the ritual, if performed correctly, looks a lot like the Hokey-
Pokey. To me, there's something so obviously true about the fact that only in
the real world would a sober ritual look so ridiculous ('Intervention', 5:18).

The reverse, putting dark into light, is part of what separates a 'cult' comedy
from the others. *South Park*, with its Kenny-killings and other deeply dark
elements, is clearly a cult comedy or was so when it still generated the 'exclusive
club' sensation. And *Family Guy*'s homicidal baby and often cruel humour helped
it come back from the dead through surprisingly strong DVD sales, a sure sign
of cult-ness.

A case can be made that the 'discomfort comedies' such as *Curb Your
Enthusiasm, The Office* (especially the UK version), and *Extras* belong to the
cult category. They certainly mix darkness into the light as they challenge the
audience to laugh while wincing.

Make People Talk Like People

It should be obvious that realistic dialogue helps a show feel real. I love this example from an episode of *Firefly*:

SIMON
Are you Alliance?

JUBAL EARLY
Am I a lion?

'Objects in Space' (1:14)

Real people mishear. Characters rarely do. Real people also stammer, overlap, and use specialised vocabularies without defining them.

If *Friday Night Lights* has validity as a cult show (I waver as to whether it does or not), it would be largely because of its improvised-sounding, overlapping, frequently stuttered dialogue.

Battlestar Galactica's scripts use Final Draft's 'Dual Dialogue' feature more than any show I've ever worked for. This is the part of the program that allows you to print dialogue in two columns to be performed simultaneously by two actors speaking over each other. We listen to people speaking over each other all the time in real life, but far more rarely on television.

Characters on *The Wire* and *The Sopranos* and the fighter pilots of *Battlestar Galactica* have specific vocabularies and ways of speaking that aren't transparent to the viewer and which often go unexplained. Again, the audience has to work, has to invest. Has to work to 'get' it.

Make Complex People

Captain Jack Harkness of *Torchwood* is as complex a character as you're likely to find. The same can be said of Buffy and Starbuck and Captain Mal Reynolds. These characters have interesting complexities built in even at the ground-level. When Ron Moore changed Starbuck from a male character to a female character, he was already making a cultifying choice. Given our expectations of a rowdy Viper pilot, Starbuck as a woman is already a contradiction. Even the name 'Buffy' undercuts our expectations of heroism. And those are just the most basic examples.

Moral shadings and unexpected weaknesses, and the way a character evolves over the course of a show, these all help make complicated people. When an audience has to bring contradictions into focus as they try to understand the totality of a complex character, they cannot help but get involved. Characters that defy easy analysis invite investment for the same reason that we are drawn to complex people in real life.

Cult TV shows generally avoid moustache-twirling villains in favour of villains who think they're heroes – villains with noble impulses or at least reluctant villains. I would love to imagine the conversation that *Buffy*'s Spike and *Battlestar*'s Baltar would have about their choices and why they made them. (By the way, my guess is that the encounter would not end well for Baltar.)

Make Everything Specific

Here's an example from what might seem like an unlikely show. I worked on *Gilmore Girls* for a year. Its cult status is debatable, but I think a case can be made. The cult of Gilmore is less visible than SF fandoms tend to be, but it is very intense. *Gilmore Girls* writers were frequently approached by fans who loved the show and talked about how similar their own mother-daughter relationship was to the Lorelei-Rory relationship. The important thing is that they thought they were the only ones; they didn't realise that other women were saying the same thing. The relationship was presented as having such specific properties, such unique rhythms, that each viewer prided herself on her ability to 'get' it. They *felt* like members of an exclusive club. That's cult TV.

The genuine look of small-town Texas is perfectly captured on *Friday Night Lights*, with attention paid to the specifics of sagging porches and screen doors and lawn signs and car dealerships and diners. Watching it, I'm often reminded of my own small town, even though I grew up in a Midwestern college community, far from Texas both geographically and culturally. It isn't that I'm seeing the same exact details from my own memory, but that the specificity and realness of the details is ringing true and calling up parallel – similar, but not identical – images from my own past.

This may just be another way of saying...

Stay True to the Show's Reality

The pilot-chatter on *Battlestar Galactica* is real. The military procedures are as close to real as we can make them and we make efforts to get the tech and science right. We don't always succeed, but we try. When I first arrived on the show, I needed to write a scene in which a Viper (a small fighting spacecraft) malfunctioned. I put in some made-up language about the part that was malfunctioning and the effect it had on the ship. I was quickly told that there was no such part on a Viper. I had to describe the way in which I needed the ship to malfunction, and then I was told what exactly had to go wrong with the engine in order for that to occur – all of this with a fictional piece of machinery. It may seem like a lot of work for something the audience has no way to check, but I've become convinced that it's absolutely worth it. When something has the ring of authenticity, you can tell, in imaginary worlds as well as in small Texas towns.

We didn't do a lot of research on *Buffy*, but we did have our system of truths about vampires and we stuck to it. And, what's more, we took it seriously and thought about the implications. When vampire Spike discovers that his vampire girlfriend Harmony has been keeping a stake under her pillow, he reacts with disbelief. *'You had that in our bed? Do you know how dangerous that is?'* It's a vampire-specific safety concern that feels real because, given the rules, it *would be* real.

Which brings us to idea of how to ...

Create a World

A lot is made of the fact that cult TV shows often fall into the science fiction genre. There is a common hypothesis that members of the cult of SF television are social outcasts in this world, and that they are looking for another world in which they feel more accepted and at home. I'm not sure the degree of outcastedness among science fiction viewers is as high as is sometimes assumed, but I can personally attest to the vast numbers of *Buffy* fans who state that they never would have survived high school without Buffy's example. It's strange to think of the *Buffy* world, which is infested with demons and full of heartbreak and loss, as an escapist fantasy, but I believe it was. Buffy went through hell (and heaven) and emerged beaten but unbroken – or, perhaps, broken but alive. And that was important for the viewers who identified with her.

Certainly *Battlestar, Firefly, Star Trek* in all its forms, and *Buffy* take place in special worlds. Shows such as *The Tudors, The Sopranos, The Wire,* and *Mad Men* take place in specialised subparts of our world (or our past) in which the rules are somewhat different than our ordinary rules. Even *Friday Night Lights* is so regionally specific that I would count it as having a sense of 'other' in its setting.

It's not a necessary ingredient – *My So-Called Life* has an arguable cult status while existing in an ordinary (but very specific) world – but one that occurs frequently.

So why does other-worldliness mesh so well and so often with cult TV? I'd like to think that it has to do with more than fans who are alienated from the real world. After all, I think I've made it clear that it's these shows *resemblance* to the real world that makes them so engaging for their audience.

In looking for the answer, I fall back on thinking about why I like writing these kinds of shows. It's because it's easier to tell a complex story about our own world when you view it translated through another world. We tell war stories on *Battlestar* that would be hard to take – and hard to sell – if they were told literally. We told more stories of pain and loss on *Buffy* than would be plausible if all those things had to happen in a literal way to a literal girl in this world.

The big lie of making up a whole world is what allows us to tell the truth in our stories. And that's important because cult TV writers...

Have a Reason to Tell the Story

Sometimes an episode offers a moral suggestion. Often it just raises a question where none had been obvious before. And, especially in shows set in a special world, it leaves the audience with the work of translating the reason for telling the story to the real world.

Now, this is nothing new. We've grown so used to the 'morality play' form of television, that from the very first scene we can often tell what lesson a show is going to teach us. The lesson arrives pre-chewed. Cult television avoids this by choosing more complicated lessons. The audience is required to do more work, to pay attention and extract the less-obvious conclusion, if a conclusion is reached at all.

Laura Roslin is the President of the Colonies on *Battlestar Galactica*. Audiences have been trained to expect certain things from characters like her – strong leaders with strong beliefs but with human frailties they work hard to overcome. Characters such as this do the right thing. On non-cult shows, one could easily conclude that such characters *always* do the right thing. So when Roslin strives to fix the vote to ensure her own re-election, what are we to think? She genuinely thinks the other candidate is a dangerous alternative – dangerous to the survival of humanity. So is she justified? Here I'm talking about the complexity not of the character, but of the moral expectations of the audience members. Audiences accustomed to stories that present them with clear moral choices are forced to work hard on that one.

When *Battlestar* viewers consider Adama's decision to save his fleet rather than to engage in a fight over the doomed colonies, or when *Buffy* fans observe Willow's slide into dependency on Magicks, or when *Star Trek: The Next Generation*'s audience watches Lt. Data's struggle to be treated as a sentient being, they don't take those events at face value. They turn them around in their minds, challenged to translate them to our world, and decide what they make of these difficult questions. Can fleeing from the field of battle be the braver choice? When is enough too much? How do you measure the worth of a person? If the cult TV show is real enough, then the audience is empowered to cull those questions from the story-telling and walk away thinking. That's how you really get your exclusive club, your cult.

A Thought about *Star Trek*

Original *Star Trek* is an interesting special case. The fact that the *Trek* world continues to thrive today in novels, fanfiction, conventions, and individual imaginations is stunning and significant, especially since it lacks a lot of the qualities laid out above. It didn't have much in the way of arcs. The dialogue and shooting style weren't particularly naturalistic or documentarian. There were some cardboard villains and some easy moral choices here and there. But in the category of complex characters (Spock remains, to pick a random word, fascinating) and especially in creating a world and in having reasons to tell their stories, *Trek* has everyone beat by a mile.

The *Trek* world contains not just real-seeming things such as dilithium crystals and Jeffries tubes but also heady ideas, viewed in action. Diversity and self-determination and a belief that mankind will overcome its base nature – these are engaging ideas.

I also think that it's interesting to note that many Trek by-products – the later *Trek* series, the early *Trek* novels by James Blish and other SF novelists, and the fanfic that continues to be written to this day – tend to have more cult-TV-like features than the original show: longer, more complex arcs, more complicated relationships, and more moral complexity. *Star Trek* may not have had the entire cluster of properties that make cult TV, but it had the most important ones and it seems to be accruing the others in its afterlife.

To Conclude

The system of television ratings traditionally rewarded shows that were watched, caring little about shows that were loved. Love was nice, but it didn't put delicious ad dollars on the table. Now, however, there's some evidence that things have changed. If you want audience members who don't just turn on the television faucet, but who actually buy DVDs, tune in for special events, and find their way to the network's web sites for commentaries, video blogs, and downloads, then you want an involved audience – an audience that will go out of its way for that cookie.

You want a show that feels real, that challenges its audience to watch carefully, pay attention, listen hard, take the lessons, love the world. You want that engaged, challenged audience. You want a cult. Love wins.

6 *The Twilight Zone* (CBS, 1959–1964)

Stan Beeler

It might be possible to write an article about *The Twilight Zone* without using the term seminal, but it would be unfair to present the series as anything less. The influence of Rod Serling's series which ran from 1959 to 1964 is undeniable. In the roughly 50 years since the first episode aired on the Columbia Broadcasting System, *The Twilight Zone* has provided inspiration for innumerable television series and films. Like many cult favourites, *The Twilight Zone* was slow to develop an audience, although it was an almost immediate critical success, winning Director's Guild, Producer's Guild Awards as well as an Emmy and a Hugo [science-fiction award] in its first season. Serling was one of the very first of the developer/writer/producer/auteur figures who are so important to the history of cult television. His dominant influence on the series may be gauged by the fact that he wrote 92 of the 156 episodes that were aired during the five seasons of the series. One cannot imagine *The Twilight Zone* without Rod Serling.

Rodman Edward Serling was born in Syracuse, New York, in 1924 and shortly afterward his family moved to Binghampton, New York, where he was raised. He maintained strong ties to the area for his entire life and many of his *Twilight Zone* scripts – including the episodes 'A Stop at Willoughby' (1:30) and 'Once Upon a Time' (3:13) – evoke the small-town environment of upstate New York. Serling's company Cayuga Productions which was responsible for *The Twilight Zone* series, was named after his family's summer home on Cayuga Lake, also in up-state New York. At the age of 18, Serling enlisted in the military immediately after graduating from high-school; his time as a soldier was extremely significant in his subsequent career as a creative writer. His experience as a combat paratrooper in the Philippines during World War II was directly reflected in 'The Purple Testament' (1:19) and 'A Quality of Mercy' (3:15) and provided background material for a host of other episodes concerning war and the military. Although he was not a large man (five feet four inches in height), Serling became involved in boxing while in the military and mined the knowledge of the sport for plots and background for some of his most successful scripts – 'The Big Tall Wish' (1:27) and 'Steel' (5:2) are two examples from *The Twilight Zone*. After World War II, his veteran's benefits allowed him to complete his education with a Bachelor of Arts at Antioch

College in Ohio where he worked for the college radio station and honed his skills as a dramatic writer. After graduation he worked as a staff writer for a radio station in Cincinnati for about a year and a half before he gave it up to freelance as a scriptwriter for the new medium of television. In 1955, his script *Patterns*, which was broadcast on the Kraft Television Theater anthology show, had immense critical success and he received a flood of offers to write for both television and film. Within two years he was one of the most popular television writers in the country.

As his career developed, his inclination for social activism and desire for artistic integrity came in direct conflict with the network and sponsors' desire to maintain strict control over the material they broadcast. Serling clearly understood the traditional exemption from censorship enjoyed by fantasy; so when given the opportunity to develop his own series, he chose to work in that genre. He was, however, uncomfortable with the general opinion that writing fantasy was incompatible with serious art. In a famous interview with Mike Wallace which was broadcast in 1959, Serling vigorously defended his choice of genre for his new series, indicating that the sponsors and the network would have no opportunity to 'chop an axe.' He felt that writing fantasy would allow him to produce 'meaningful and insightful' scripts while avoiding the headaches of censorship. In the same interview he also argued that commercial success does not preclude artistic merit. This interview reveals the core of *The Twilight Zone*'s importance to the development of cult television; the series provided socially relevant, well-written plots masked from the censor's hand through the use of metaphor. *The Twilight Zone* is one of the very first – and perhaps one of the best – examples of cult television although it exhibits some significant differences from later examples of the phenomenon. For example, unlike most later cult shows, *The Twilight Zone* does not develop a consistent alternate reality or even have a cast of continuing characters. It is an anthology series consisting of – for the most part – half-hour episodes connected only by genre, the strong thematic harmony of Serling's creative control and his short on-screen introductions and closing statements. These introductions were characterised by Serling's intense on-screen presence and are a highly recognisable (and easily parodied) watermark of the series. Its cult audience, which has been strong for half a century, has never accepted the series as mindless entertainment. One of the reasons that *The Twilight Zone* became such an important success was that its 'unrealistic genre' allowed Serling to deal with questions of social justice and ethics that would otherwise not have been acceptable for broadcast. For example, the question of racial prejudice, which had become so important to the American public in the early 1960s is the focus of the episode entitled 'The Monsters Are Due on Maple Street' (1:22). Serling was born into a Jewish family and although he later joined the Unitarian Universalist Church, he had firsthand knowledge of what it meant to be different in the United States at this time.

To a modern audience the somewhat formulaic structure of *The Twilight Zone* episodes may appear trite. The series employed a plot format popularised by science fiction short stories in the 1950s and the 1960s; the first part of the episode consists of an elaborate build-up, constructing a situation which appears to run in a predictable direction, but the last few minutes provide a plot-twist that undermines the narrative flow. This formula worked perfectly for half-hour-long episodes. The audience invested a short amount of time following a narrative line that was sure to be reversed; their pleasure in the episode was not immersion in a highly developed alternate reality, so the lack of narrative continuity between episodes did not matter. Each week, Serling presented his audience with a brief puzzle and an interesting climax based on an unexpected turn of events.

Despite its formulaic structure, *The Twilight Zone* established the cult television tradition of experimental narrative and cinematographic devices. In 'The Invaders' (2:15), which was written by horror and SF writer Richard Matheson, veteran film and television actor Agnes Moorehead manages to enthral the audience with nothing but her physical presence as the episode included no dialogue. Serling once directly broadcast a French version of the Ambrose Bierce short-story 'An Occurrence at Owl Creek Bridge' (5:22),[1] and 'Five Character's in Search of an Exit' (3:14) is a pastiche of Pirendello's *Six Characters in Search of an Author* and Jean-Paul Sartre's 'No Exit.' 'Eye of the Beholder' (2:6) is shot almost entirely from the point of view of a hospital patient. Except for a few moments in the final plot twist, the audience never sees anyone's face. Serling's intensely loyal audience allowed him room for experimentation that more conventional television could not offer.

Nevertheless, innovative television has inherent drawbacks. Because he opted for quality, Serling had the perennial questions of production costs and audience share to deal with. Often, when the network intervened, changes did not have the desired effect. At one point, CBS suggested that shooting the series on film was an unnecessary expense; however, when 'The Lateness of the Hour' (2:8), 'The Night of the Meek' (2:11), 'The Whole Truth' (2:14), 'Twenty Two' (2:17), 'Static' (2:20), and 'The Long Distance Call' (2:22) were done on video as an experiment in cost cutting, there were problems. These episodes are well written and acted but are egregious because of the reduction in visual quality. Moreover, their cinematography, editing, and the exclusive use of sound-stage settings reflect the restrictions imposed by the unwieldy technology of early video cameras. In season four, CBS decided that the show might garner a greater audience if it moved to a one-hour format. This was also not as successful as hoped and the general consensus was that the half-hour format was far superior, so, in its fifth and final season, *The Twilight Zone* returned to its original format.

By the fifth season, although his artistic judgment was vindicated in most cases, Serling had decided to move on and *The Twilight Zone* was cancelled by mutual agreement. After *The Twilight Zone,* Sirling worked on but did not control *The Night Gallery.* He also wrote a number of screenplays, including *The Planet of the Apes* (1968). Although *The Twilight Zone* did not last as long as other examples of the genre, in the five years of its existence – and in the countless number of reruns in syndication since its cancellation – this series exemplified the lasting influence of great cult television.

Notes

1. Directed by Robert Enrico *La Rivière du hibou* appeared as a short film in 1962.

Part 2

Reading Cult TV:
Texts and Contexts

7   The Avengers/The New Avengers (ITV, 1961–1969)/(ITV, 1976–1977)

Paul Sutton

A n 'offbeat, tongue-in-cheek, British, "pop spy" fantasy TV series' (Murray, 1998: 45), *The Avengers* has been variously described as 'one of British TV's greatest successes' (Clark, 2008: 1), 'the highest pinnacle of spy/secret agent television' (Richardson, 1990: 7), 'constantly kinky' (Macnee, 1997: 69), and 'part of "Swinging London", along with the King's Road, Carnaby Street, Twiggy, George Best, Mary Quant and other such icons' (Macnee, 1997: 50).

As one of the longest running and most popular of the 1960s secret agent series, *The Avengers* has unsurprisingly remained popular with cult TV audiences ever since. Famous for its representation of a certain kind of Englishness and for its juxtaposition of the modern and the traditional, 'the normal with the abnormal', the series 'created its own fantasy world in which the incredible and the unusual were treated as if they were commonplace' (Chapman, 2002b: 89); however, *The Avengers* had its origins in a far more conventional series. Commissioned by Sydney Newman at ABC (a television offshoot of ABPC, Associated British Pictures Corporation), the series was originally to replace the relatively unsuccessful *Police Surgeon*, while retaining the popular actor Ian Hendry who played Dr Geoffrey Brent, the protagonist. Newman was keen to exploit the star potential of Hendry and recalls that *The Avengers* 'would be a fun series that would get away from the realism of *Police Surgeon* [...]. I felt that I could capitalize on the current, literary popularity of the John Le Carré/Ian Fleming genre and send it up' (Macnee, 1997: 15). The surgeon became a GP, with Brent replaced by Dr David Keel. In the first episode, 'Hot Snow' (1:1), drug dealers murder Keel's wife – the title of the series derives from Keel's attempt to avenge this crime – and his investigations lead him to an encounter with the mysterious John Steed (Patrick Macnee). After Keel and Steed discover the murderer in episode two, Steed recruits Keel and they begin a partnership that drew on much of the visual iconography of film noir and the Hollywood private eye films of the 1940s, with both 'wearing raincoats and smoking cigarettes' (Macnee, 1997: 17). The 26 episodes of this first series were broadcast in 1961 with the first third transmitted live and the remaining two-thirds recorded on video. Very little remains of this first series with the first 20 minutes of 'Hot Snow' available and only two fully intact episodes: 'Girl on the Trapeze' (1:6, transmitted 11 February 1961) and 'The Frighteners' (1:15, transmitted 27 May 1961). As the first series progressed, the character of Steed was reinvented. As Macnee explains, the revamped Steed was modelled on his own 'dandy' father (Macnee 1997: 22) and on an amalgamation of Sir Percy Blakeney (the Scarlet Pimpernel) and Bussy Carr, his commanding officer in the Navy (23). The umbrella, the famous prop, completed the image of the elegant English gentleman and served to distance the character from its earlier private detective incarnation. As one critic has noted, Steed 'represented a type of masculinity that had no need for aggressive displays of machismo, men of charm and good manners who nevertheless possessed nerves of steel: the iron fist concealed beneath the velvet glove' (Chapman, 2002b: 62).

In October 1961, an Equity strike over actors' pay meant that the series was out of production. By the time it returned in May 1962, Ian Hendry had left to pursue a film career. Initially he was replaced by Jon Rollason (playing another doctor character, Dr Martin King), partly, it has been suggested, to make effective use of the remaining Hendry/Keel scripts (Chapman, 2002b: 62). After three episodes, the decision was taken to replace Rollason with a woman and so began the format that remained throughout the rest of *The Avengers*. Steed was partnered first by Dr Cathy Gale (Honor Blackman, 1962–1964), then by Mrs Emma Peel (Diana Rigg, 1965–1967), and finally by Tara King (Linda Thorson, 1968–1969). Commentators have suggested that these women were amongst television's first 'feminist female lead(s)' (Andrae, 1996: 115). '*The Avengers*', it is argued, 'refunctioned the patriarchal discourse of the spy genre, transforming woman from an object of male desire into a subject who possessed "masculine" power and independence. For the first time on television, a woman fought back rather than being merely a passive victim' (Andrae, 1996: 116). In the context of Hollywood film and cult television since the 1990s, the extent to which strong female characters may be seen as feminist, exemplified by shows such as *Buffy the Vampire Slayer* and *Alias*, has been the subject of fierce debate; however, there is no doubt that in the mid-1960s Gale and Peel offered viewers heroines who were markedly different from most of the women represented on screen at the time. While Steed was the 'velvet glove', his female partners were the 'iron fists', experts in Judo or Karate, ably dispatching their enemies. Thus in a reversal of the traditional roles of the period, Steed, 'so as not to rumple his clothes [… ,] used his wits to dispose of villains' while 'Mrs Peel carried the gun and did most of the fighting' (Murray, 1998: 46).

It is with the introduction of Gale/Blackman that the series' concern with fashion and style becomes more overt. Early on in the second series, Blackman's leather costumes provided the series with the kinkiness for which it became renowned. Although introduced for practical reasons after Blackman's trousers split during the filming of a fight scene, the leather introduced 'subcultural sexual codes' that were not lost on contemporary viewers' (Chapman, 2002b: 66).

Emma Peel, derived from man or M-appeal, adopted black leather bodysuits but became as well known for her catsuits (known as 'Emmapeelers') and her mini-skirts. As the director of numerous episodes from the Emma Peel era, Roy Baker recalls that the series was among the first in the world to feature mini-skirts and was instrumental in promoting this fashion statement (2000: 122).

As 'extensions of their personalities' (Murray, 1998: 47) the vehicles driven by Steed and Emma are important elements in the series' appeal, both for the audience in the 1960s and for the contemporary 'cult' audience of early twenty-first century. Just as the clothes worn by John Steed, Cathy Gale, Emma Peel, and Tara King are central to the look of *The Avengers*, so too are the vehicles they ride. Steed's vintage 'Speed Six' Bentley, Vauxhall 30–98, and Rolls Royce 'Silver Ghost', all icons of Britain's motoring history, evoke tradition, bespoke craftmanship, and contrast with the sporty and modern but equally iconic Lotus Elans and Europas of Emma and Tara – cars that were signifiers of technological originality and innovative design of the 1960s but which today signify the decade itself.

A number of the key themes that endured throughout the series emerged during the Cathy Gale era, the most notable of which include the conflict between modernity and tradition, visible not only in the contrast between Steed's suits and Cathy and Emma's catsuits, as well as in the vintage Bentley and the modern Lotus, but often also in the inability of reactionary figures to deal with the contemporary world. Contemporary anxieties surrounding scientific advancement both in relation to its perceived dangers and in terms of its political and social necessity are also central to many of the plots of the series, particularly as the science-fiction dimension of the show becomes more visible during the Emma Peel period. The generic possibilities of the series open up significantly as it moves beyond the Blackman/Macnee era to include not only science-fiction but horror and increasingly fantasy as well, although this willingness to play with genre is evident during the earlier period too, especially in an episode such as 'Build a Better Mousetrap' (3:11, 15 February 1964), in which a plot involving apparent witchcraft and the pitting of two eccentric elderly sisters against a gang of 'bikers' turns into a rather more traditional cold war spy story. The cult appeal of *The Avengers* is evident in the final moments of the episode when the role of the sisters as guardians of a revolutionary 'science-fiction' device, which they appear to have been perfecting, is comically juxtaposed with their actual failure to invent a 'better mousetrap'. The show plays continually with generic expectation and continually undermines the seriousness of its plots while nonetheless remaining entirely plausible in its own terms.

Between March 1964 and October 1965, there was a significant 18-month break that marked the end of the third series and the beginning of the fourth. During this period, the decision was taken to shoot on film rather than on video

63

in order to facilitate the sale of the show to the American television networks – a decision that resulted in shifts in the visual style of the series and, by series five, in the adoption of colour (although these episodes were first seen in the United Kingdom in black and white). The larger budgets that resulted also allowed for a greater degree of location shooting and 'more elaborately staged action and chase sequences' (Chapman, 2002b: 75). Julian Wintle, a successful film producer, was employed to oversee the new series, and film directors such as Roy Ward Baker, Sidney Hayers, and Robert Day were brought in to direct. Albert Fennell became executive producer and Brian Clemens, who had written many of the episodes in the previous series, had his role expanded to become associate producer and script editor. Equally important was the decision of Honor Blackman to leave *The Avengers* to play Pussy Galore in *Goldfinger* (Guy Hamilton, UK, 1964). Elizabeth Shepherd was originally cast as Emma Peel but was swiftly replaced by Diana Rigg. For many fans of *The Avengers* it is Rigg's two years as Emma Peel that represent the 'classic' period of the series. The relationship between Steed and Mrs Peel is built around 'a will they/have they?' scenario and thrives on innuendo-laden verbal sparring. During this period, the series begins to foreground its own theatricality, organising episodes around the concealment of plots or plotters behind seemingly innocent facades as in 'Something Nasty in the Nursery' (5:14, 21 April 1967), for example, which features a nanny-training school as a front for a spy ring or 'Murdersville' (6:6, 10 November 1967), where an idyllic, picture postcard English village has become a site for prearranged murder.

For the seventh series, Linda Thorson was cast as Tara King to replace Diana Rigg who had left to play Tracy di Vicenzo in the Bond film *On Her Majesty's Secret Service* (Peter R. Hunt, UK, 1969). While the Macnee-Rigg episodes had been hugely successful in the United States, the Steed-King pairing was less well received, despite its popularity in the United Kingdom. Broadcast in America against the very popular *Rowan and Martin's Laugh-In*, the series saw its ratings inevitably fall and a decision was taken by the U.S. network not to purchase further episodes leading to ABC's cancellation of the series in February 1969.

A resurrection of sorts occurred with the creation of *The New Avengers* in 1976. Produced with French finance from IDTV Productions by Clemens and Fenell, *The New Avengers* updated the original series to the 1970s and featured Steed, still played by Macnee, as a kind of father figure or mentor to the much younger Gambit (Gareth Hunt) and Purdey (Joanna Lumley). The triangular structure introduced an almost Oedipal dimension to the relationship between the protagonists, with Steed and Gambit competing for the affections of Purdey. The witty innuendo of *The Avengers* becomes less effective in this somewhat diluted scenario. Although *The New Avengers* continued to invest in fantasy, it was much more realist in tone and can be seen in many ways as a precursor to the gritty and realistic *The Professionals* that Clemens and Fenell went on to write and produce.

The New Avengers was not a success in the American market and after IDTV Productions discontinued its financial backing of the series, it began to flounder. Despite attempts to rescue the series by moving first to France and then to Canada, it was cancelled at the end of the second season.

The final chapter in *The Avengers* story to date was the production of a Hollywood film, *The Avengers* (Jeremiah Chechik, USA, 1998). Starring Ralph Fiennes as Steed and a miscast Uma Thurman as Emma Peel, the film was set in England and featured well-known British actors in many of the supporting roles. Although the film attempted to retain the feel of the original series, it had a confused and convoluted plot, and despite the inclusion of 'in-jokes' for fans of *The Avengers*, it failed to live up to expectations. As the critic Kim Newman noted, 'the film did not work [...] "because *The Avengers* series is so ineffably itself[;] it doesn't offer the cracks for a revisionary reading"' (Newman cited in Chapman, 2002b: 99). And, of course, the great cult appeal of *The Avengers* is precisely that in its creation of its own generically rich, perversely comic, and thoroughly sixties universe, it is 'so ineffably itself'...

8 Mainstream Cult

Matt Hills

Defining once and for all what is meant by 'cult' status is an extremely tricky if not impossible task (see Hills 2002). However, something that many uses of the term 'cult' tend to share is a sense of what cult is *not*. It is not hugely popular, not culturally omnipresent, not common-place and common knowledge. There is something 'special', something at least a little bit 'underground' or even transgressive about cult media, cult TV included. What this frequently amounts to is a sense that 'cult' television isn't for everybody; only suitably intelligent, discerning audiences 'get it'. Or to put this another way, there's a common notion that 'cult' is anti-mainstream, existing outside the supposed parameters of mainstream culture and entertainment. Mark Jancovich and Nathan Hunt have examined this idea, specifically in relation to cult television:

> There is no single quality that characterizes a cult text; rather, cult texts are defined through a process in which shows are positioned in opposition to the mainstream, a classification that is no more coherent as an object than the cult and is also a product of the same process of distinction that creates the opposed couplet mainstream/cult. (2004:27)

Jancovich and Hunt thus suggest that cult television fandom is a subcultural activity concerned with its 'authentic' exclusivity, therefore constantly policing 'boundaries ... through opposition to the media'(2004: 29). This means that, insofar as 'cult' status is relational, TV shows might gain or lose cult status over time depending on the wider audiences they are reaching. Jancovich and Hunt (2004: 28) offer the example of *The X-Files*, which during the course of its first run in the United Kingdom was shifted from 'minority' channel BBC2 to the rather more 'mass' appeal BBC1 and hence potentially became less 'cultish' for fans concerned with protecting and conserving the exclusivity of their tastes (see Simon Brown on *The X-Files* in this volume). But shows can move in the opposite direction as well, having 'mass' appeal early in their cultural careers before eventually becoming obscure, cult programmes repeated on niche cable channels and remembered and celebrated only by the select few (e.g., *Blake's 7*).

This subcultural mainstream/cult binary is common in relation to cult film as well as television (for further discussion, see Hills 2003b and 2006a).

Joanne Hollows has suggested that the competencies, practices, and dispositions linked to 'cult' have tended to be highly gendered, with a 'masculinity of cult' being (sub)culturally constructed against a 'mainstream ... persistently gendered as feminine' (2003: 37). Where cult TV is 'authentic', demanding 'active' viewership, the mainstream is conceptualised as offering easy, passive pleasures. Hollows' argument is not at all that cult TV shows always lack female fans, nor that all cult TV is definitively detached from connotations of femininity. However, the strength of her argument appears to lie in its ability to accurately capture gendered codes underlying the frequently nominated 'others' of cult TV, for example, soap operas, reality TV, and light-entertainment/celebrity-based formats. TV shows such as *The X-Factor* or *Big Brother* (UK version) may have many highly vocal and dedicated fans, but they are not usually thought of as programmes possessing 'cult' status. These sorts of programmes are instead typically cited as instances of the 'mainstream', and they do tend to be implicitly gendered and feminised; they are thought of as highly commercial and as culturally omnipresent in tabloid coverage.

On this account, there are certain cultural sites and places where cult TV simply does not belong: *Heat* magazine, for instance. Hollows remarks on the fact that even chains of stores selling cult TV merchandise 'take care to define themselves against more "mainstream" shopping spaces' by embracing and celebrating their untidy dinginess and by offering an anti-'glossy' aesthetic for 'a niche audience who wouldn't be seen dead in W. H. Smiths' (2003: 48). Rather than being allegedly feminised consumers, cult TV fans instead position themselves as culturally masculinised collectors or connoisseurs. As Hollows concludes, the ' "radicalism" of cult is only sustained by processes of "othering" and it is always important to remain aware of who, and what, is being "othered" ' (2003:49).

Although these arguments over cult 'othering' have much that is useful to say about the distinctions of cult TV fans, it should also be remembered that mechanisms of cultural othering are, precisely, relational; all that matters is that 'cult' can be defined against something that it is not. Exactly what fulfils this role can shift and change over time, with the underlying structure of meaning staying pretty much the same. The basic opposition underpinning these cult distinctions is, arguably, that of authentic 'culture' versus inauthentic 'commerce'. By distancing themselves from the generally feminised mainstream, cult TV fans can claim an 'anti-commercial' status as the appreciators of televisual art rather than 'mere' entertainment, and as discriminating 'fans' rather than as undiscriminating 'consumers'.

And yet these processes can also play out in a variety of ways; as long as 'cult' status still retains a range of totemic 'Others', it may, after all, be possible for 'cult' and 'mainstream' labels to (uneasily) co-exist or even merge in specific ways (just as 'cult' and 'quality' TV discourses can co-exist in specific settings: see Johnson 2005a and 2005b; Pearson in this volume). To give a few examples, cult TV fans, as part of their exercising of expertise and fan knowledge, may circulate information online about the best deals on DVD purchases (a type of 'active' media consumption). In this context, buying a specific DVD title in W H Smith may make perfect sense to a cult TV fan, who, far from not being 'seen dead' in that high-street retailer, may venture through its doors precisely in line with communally shared and distinctive fan knowledge. This action would still, of course, possess an imagined Other: the consumer shopping for TV DVDs supposedly without thought and without weighing up all the deals on offer. Equally, fans may choose to purchase DVDs and merchandise from specific 'mainstream' retailers (either online or on the high street) because they offer 'exclusive' or 'limited edition' versions of products. Clearly there is once again a constructed Other within this process – the shopper who, again supposedly without thought and discrimination, buys the 'standard' edition rather than one with different packaging or 'collectors' content. In this scenario, the subcultural languages and viewpoints of cult TV fans are evidently being adopted and appropriated by 'mainstream' consumer culture, in order for attenuated subcultural 'authenticity' to be sold back to a niche market of fans. Cult and mainstream are hence not always clearly or singularly opposed in these sorts of processes, and they may interpenetrate even as attempts are made to recuperate some aspect of distinction between the two. The notion of cult TV appreciation as a resolutely grass-roots and non-commercial audience activity set against industry machinations (see Jenkins 1992a) makes little sense in the contemporary TV marketplace, where cult fans have become one niche market amongst others to be surveyed, understood, and catered for.

At the same time, specific practices of fan activity and distinction – against which 'mainstream consumption' has historically been set – have themselves begun to move outside the texts and audiences of cult TV. Janet H. Murray argues that this possibility has been produced, in part, by the rise of digital media:

> In the past this kind of attention [to continuity and textual detail] was limited to series with cult followings like... *The X-Files*. But as the Internet becomes a standard adjunct of broadcast television, all program writers and producers will be aware of a more sophisticated audience, one that can keep track of the story in greater detail and over longer periods of time. (1997:8)

Murray's argument has been shared by others (Pullen 2000; Jenkins 2002), and it represents one way in which concepts of 'cult' and 'mainstream' have started to break down and coalesce into new patterns of cultural meaning. Fan activities such as online posting and speculation, fiction-writing based on the originating TV show's characters, and textual interpretations revolving around specific characters and relationships, have all now begun to revolve around what might otherwise be thought of as 'mainstream' TV shows. To take just one example, the programme *Dawson's Creek* garnered online fans whose activities resembled, in almost every way, those of cult TV fans. And yet, *Dawson's Creek*, with its soap-like storylines and high-gloss images of 'beautiful people', has rarely if ever been described as a 'cult' show (see Hills 2004a). This may partly have to do with the status of *Dawson's Creek* as realist TV rather than as telefantasy, though scholars have argued that elements of the fantastic do not necessarily make for cult television (Johnson 2005a), and some realist, non-telefantasy shows have inspired cult followings, for example, *The Bill* (ITV, 1984–). And although the exnomination of *Dawson's Creek* as 'cult' may be, in part, also due to the continuing role of gendered codes – it being culturally positioned as a 'feminised' text – the binary opposition between cult and mainstream can nevertheless be said to weaken or fracture here. Given the range of online fan activities which came to surround the show, a case can certainly be made for analytically describing it as 'mainstream cult' television. Arguably, practices of cult TV fandom underwent mainstreaming here as a result of the ease with which fans were able to find each other online, and the ways in which they self-consciously appropriated activities that were known to previously characterise cult TV fandom.

Other shows such as *Buffy the Vampire Slayer* could also be described as 'mainstream cults'; there is little sense in which *Buffy,* an international TV hit, can be thought of as anti-commercial or anti-mainstream, and it combines the horror-sf-fantasy themes and subject matter of much cult TV (or 'telefantasy', as this subgenre is sometimes dubbed) with high-gloss production, strong female characters, and a cast of 'beautiful people'. *Buffy* has also appealed strongly across gender lines, being less clearly gendered than much previous cult television, and is much less evidently positioned against 'the mainstream'. However, fans valuing this show have still embraced it as an instance of 'TV Art', treating it as significantly authored ('Joss Whedon's *Buffy the Vampire Slayer*') and hence positioning it against an imagined Other of 'ordinary' or 'ephemeral'/derivative TV drama. Shows such as *Buffy* may not easily or cleanly fit into oppositions such as cult versus mainstream, but by drawing on the binary of authored versus manufactured TV, the culture versus commerce binary underpinning the cult versus mainstream distinctions can instead find a variant outlet.

Henry Jenkins, leading scholar of media fandom, has argued that 'as fandom diversifies' around a wider range of TV shows than ever before, 'it moves from cult status towards the cultural mainstream' (2002:161). But Jenkins does not see 'cult' and 'mainstream' labels as collapsing together in quite the way that Janet H. Murray suggests. For Jenkins, there are differences that continue to characterise cult fandom, even in the context of its ongoing and new-media-driven 'mainstreaming'. This is apparent in Jenkins's study of *Convergence Culture*, where he writes about fans of the science-fiction blockbuster franchise *The Matrix*:

> For the casual consumer, *The Matrix* [*Revolutions*] asked too much. For the hard-core fan, it provided too little. Could any [final] film have matched the fan community's escalating expectations and expanding interpretations and still have remained accessible to a mass audience? There has to be a breaking point beyond which franchises cannot be stretched, subplots can't be added, secondary characters can't be identified, and references can't be fully realized. (2006:126–127)

Although Jenkins notes that this 'breaking point' hasn't been found yet (2006:127), his argument hinges on separating out two very different audiences. And though he doesn't use the terms, the 'casual consumer' can be placed as a figure of 'mainstream' consumption, whereas the 'hardcore fan' seems to stand in for 'cult' fandom. The relational differences and distinctions of mainstream versus cult thus seem to be regenerated here. By contrast, one could alternatively analyse the success of *The Matrix* franchise as a 'cult blockbuster' – a filmic analogue of the TV 'mainstream cult' which similarly hybridises aspects of 'mainstream' exhibition/distribution (or in TV terms, cultural reach and popularity) with the textual layerings, details, and diegetic world-makings of 'cult' media. Different audiences may go on interpreting the 'cult blockbuster' or the 'mainstream cult' in differential ways, but these texts nevertheless appear to unite elements that have previously been linked to cult versus mainstream oppositions.

Indeed, a number of current TV successes could be candidates for 'cult' status, *Heroes*, for example (NBC, 2006–); but is this 'cult' or 'mainstream' television? Like many cult shows, it can be linked to definitions of telefantasy (Johnson 2005a), but its superheroic representations are neither self-evidently niche nor culturally masculinised. In terms of its multinational and mythic tones, it appears designed to 'travel' between and across international audiences, even while simultaneously retaining a strongly U.S.-centric flavour. *Heroes* builds a detailed hyperdiegetic world about which the cult audience can amass textual knowledge, but it also offers a very strong 'hermeneutic code' (or narrative drive) and an ensemble cast which are more often characteristics of soap opera. It is also a high-gloss production which resonates with the concerns of 'teen TV', for example, through the familial storyline of cheerleader Claire Bennet (Hayden Panettiere).

Lost (ABC, 2004–) is another prime candidate for contemporary 'mainstream cult' status. Unusual in its flashback structure, the show deploys a narrative device which enables fans to embrace it as televisual art or 'quality' TV (something which its philosophical subtexts and appropriations seem to almost hysterically bid for). It is filled with clues, details, and narrative layers which can incite and support the types of fan activity linked to 'cult' status (Jenkins 2006), and it seems to demand highly focused, attentive viewing. Perhaps slightly closer to the conventional constructions of 'cult' status than *Heroes*, it nevertheless also involves an ensemble cast and a strong narrative drive at the level of individual episodes, each aiming to hold audience attention through the juxtaposing of 'present' and 'flashback' storylines, even if the specific viewer is not immersed in tracking the bigger, story-arc questions posed. *Lost* may be 'cultish' but it is arguably designed to operate on different levels for audiences who desire to consume it more-or-less intently or to work with it more-or-less casually.

A show such as *Medium* may, instead, strike the viewer as much more unequivocally 'mainstream' despite its telefantasy themes. There is little or no convoluted story-arc to speculate over, and the show is tightly formatted, almost always opening with the dreams of the lead character Alison du Bois (Patricia Arquette). Episodes are predominantly stand-alone and the show has a somewhat 'feminised' profile, centring on Alison and her family life. And yet, within these seemingly 'mainstream' parameters, the programme frequently adopts a highly ludic and excessive tone, with episodes involving clues from a repeated iPod track 'I will survive' ('The Song Remains the Same', 2:2), opening with a sequence where all the main actors temporarily voice themselves as plastic dolls ('Very Merry Maggie', 3:10), or even fusing animation with live-action drama ('Four Dreams', 3:1–2). If *Lost* is multi-coded cult TV leaning towards the mainstream, *Medium* is perhaps mainstream TV toying with cult status, just as much at ease with modelling an episode on Brian de Palma's *Carrie* (complete with narratively motivated use of split-screen: 'Mother's Little Helper', 3:7) as recounting the details of Alison's home life and marriage to an understanding, caring family man. Not coincidentally, *Medium* also shares a number of production staff with shows which have had clearer 'cult' pedigrees, such as Rene Echevarria (the *Star Trek* franchise) and Javier Grillo-Marxuach (*Lost*).

Exploring further into TV genres of horror and sci-fi, we see how the short-lived series *Invasion* (ABC, 2005) began from a classic SF-horror premise: an invasion of body-snatching aliens or 'pod people'. Created by Shaun Cassidy who had previously been behind the cult show *American Gothic* (CBS, 1995–1996), it seemed absolutely designed to catch the attention of cult TV fans – yet at the same time it filtered its SF narrative elements through a heavily soap-operatic focus on what it meant for one female character and mother, Mariel, to be 'changed'. Being 'alien' is not equated with being 'evil' here, nor does 'alien-ness' mean a complete loss of identity and (connotative) humanity.

Like the Cylons of the re-imagined *Battlestar Galactica*, these are science-fictional aliens who are ambivalently and ambiguously represented and not being entirely othered. 'Masculine' and 'feminine' narrative conventions are once more conflated and interwoven in creative ways in these cases.

In hybridised TV shows such as *Battlestar Galactica*, *Heroes*, *Invasion*, *Lost*, and *Medium* – which can perhaps be subgenerically described as a new wave of 'telefantasy-art' television – I would argue that elements of 'cult' and 'mainstream' TV are increasingly being re-articulated. And though the two categories may not wholly fuse together or may not cease to carry distinct meanings, the notion of 'mainstream cult' TV shows, designed to reach a wide range of audiences and intended to be read fannishly as well as less closely, offers a useful purchase on the post-*Buffy*, post-*X-Files* rise in 'artistic' and ambivalent/ambiguous telefantasy. As I have argued here, it also proffers a way of thinking about the new-media-driven rise in fan activities surrounding shows that would not conventionally have been thought of as 'cult'. These developments all suggest that thinking of the 'mainstreaming of cult' as a kind of 'selling-out' would be an unhelpful, if not outmoded, approach. Instead, a range of popular contemporary TV shows seem to be engaged in deconstructing the cult versus mainstream binary, presenting commercially driven TV drama which self-consciously draws on discourses of authorship, sophistication, and quirkiness which have been more traditionally linked to cult TV in its telefantasy mode.

Recommended Reading

Hills, Matt (2004). '*Dawson's Creek*: "Quality Teen TV" and "Mainstream Cult?"' in Glyn Davis and Kay Dickinson (eds) *Teen TV*. BFI Publishing, London: 54–67.

Jancovich, Mark and Hunt, Nathan (2004). 'The Mainstream, Distinction, and Cult TV' in Sara Gwenllian-Jones and Roberta E. Pearson (eds) *Cult Television*. University of Minnesota Press, Minneapolis: 27–44.

Grey's Anatomy

(ABC, 2005–)

Hillary Robson

In the days leading up to the fifth season premiere of *Grey's Anatomy*, Internet message boards were all a-twitter with speculation as to what, exactly, will be the focus of the season. With Season's four catchphrase 'Everything Changes', the doctors of Seattle Grace witnessed changes in their love lives (marriages, divorces, affairs, oh my), the introduction of a gay storyline, and the final answer to the will-they-won't-they love affair plot between super-couple Derek and Meredith (they will). For season five, viewers were titillated with a new and equally promising premise, framed in a question – 'What will you live for?'

For millions, *Grey's Anatomy* is what so many are living for. With an average viewership in the United States of 18 million for original airings, *Grey's* is nothing short of a megahit. While it might be a bit emotionally volatile and soapy at times, it doesn't stop the hoards of men, women, and tweens across America tuning in with a fierce regularity. And *Grey's* viewers are loyal: despite gay bashing,[1] writer's strikes, and the occasional sloppy plotlines, viewer's don't stray from this Thursday night drama.

Grey's defies the typical understanding of cult based on its viewership alone – with 18–21 million tuning in, it is far from the almost-cancelled, teetering-on oblivion cult series that was once the norm. *Grey's*, in itself, represents the new cult audience: consumptive to its core, fans of the series are devout. They spend the Friday mornings after the series talking about what happened the previous night, nitpicking the storyline, the characters – speaking of characters as though they are *real*, live, *human beings* of flesh and blood, imaginary people come to life in a ridiculous hospital world that any doctor will tell you is fully make believe, but that never stops them from tuning in.

While conducting research on the series, I had a sit-down meeting with a psychologist who wanted to discuss the role of the therapist in *Grey's Anatomy* with me. She heard from a friend at the university I teach at that I was writing about the series and had asked to share her thoughts. She is a full-licensed, clinical therapist and sees patients with a variety of problems, from eating disorders to abandonment issues. As we sat together, she told me about how much she loved *Grey's*... despite its poor representation of the medical practice as a whole, disregard for patient-doctor confidentiality, and a blatantly awful representation of modern psychotherapy. In a nutshell, she told me that Grey's was flawed when it came to realistic portrayal of the medical world, of doctors saving lives or of therapists helping patients, but that she never missed an episode. Why? Because the show had a way of making her cry – every episode – and she couldn't imagine spending her Thursday night any other way.

Audience devotion isn't limited to regular viewing. There's an official magazine (Grey's Anatomy Magazine). In it, fans can catch up with patients (quelling the eternal questions of whatever happened to so-and-so); a paper tear out and keep chart of quintessential show moments, and glossy colour poster featuring the 'star-of-the-month'. At just under US$10, you can own a piece of Grey's Anatomy. That's not all: you can also buy the fictionalised diary of a Grey's nurse, or read the musings of Joe the barkeep in Notes from the Nurses Station, play the official board game, or get a wall calendar (Van Dusen, 2006). When a show has that much 'official' merchandise, it points to the fact that it has got a successful cult following, as networks don't often waste time in the production of official, licensed merchandise unless there's a market for it. And for Grey's, there certainly is.

What makes Grey's a cult show has everything to do with the fact that it reflects a cult fandom. An excellent example of this is reflected in the series' marketing power of music. During its second season, a little-known band called The Fray had their song 'How to Save a Life' featured on a promo advertisement for the show. In a week, the song and album had catapulted to the top ten in the pop charts. This unique branding phenomenon – with Grey's serving as the platform for the introduction of new media, particularly music – is in the same vein as the marketing technique employed by Lost's use of imbedded literary texts. Subsequent series have tried to mimic the show's use of music as a marketing and branding tool (Life, Gossip Girl) without a similar success.

Grey's Anatomy defies the typical construction of cult in its genre, format, and mainstream success. It rebels against the conventions that apply for classic cult series, bringing to the forefront a prime example of the present-day cult audience. In droves, the modern cult craves more of their favourite drug – a prescriptive night-time drama with somewhat extraordinary plot lines, a cast of barely believable characters who struggle to define what they live for, what they love for, and, as adults in today's crazy world, what it means to be human. And perhaps that's the appeal, after all, for the millions that tune in each and every week, the fact that we're all on that same journey of self-discovery.

Notes

1. In 2006, actor Isiah Washington allegedly called homosexual co-star T.R. Knight a 'faggot' – a fact that was leaked to the press, then revisited in the 2007 Golden Globes, where Washington repeated the slur in public (AP). The actor's character made his exit at the close of the 2006–2007 series.

9 Transgressive TV

Jes Battis

On 23 January 1926, Scottish engineer John Baird transmitted the first public image of living human faces to an astounded audience in his laboratory. The scanning-disk TV had only 30 lines of resolution – just enough to reproduce a face – but the appearance of that face, we must imagine, was an incredibly uncanny event for the 40 members of the Royal Institution gathered in Baird's cramped laboratory. Like the six-armed alien Pilot who flies the living spaceship Moya in Brian Henson's *Farscape*, or the first CGI creatures to emerge in the 1980s, this 'human' face was actually a moment of human crisis, a wildly transgressive event in the history of visual culture. Colour broadcasting was so transgressive that it didn't emerge in the United States until 1950, due to all sorts of scandalous conflicts and competing patents within the Federal Communication Commission (FCC). So, it is actually difficult to pinpoint a moment in the history of broadcasting during which TV itself *hasn't* been transgressive.

In my History of Television Culture class, I begin with *I Love Lucy* – the first program to feature an interracial couple, a pregnancy, and a disaffected housewife who protests in the pilot episode ('Unaired Pilot') that she doesn't want to be 'just a wife.' Shortly after *Lucy*, *The Honeymooners* was so entangled with the viewing culture that produced it that the show's very first episode dealt with whether or not Ralph and Alice Kramden should buy a television set. In the United Kingdom, *Doctor Who* inaugurated a national obsession with fantasy and science fiction during a period of awkward political transition, when Prime Minister Harold Wilson was attempting to renegotiate Britain's tenure within the European Community (EC) from 1967–1970. Transgressive moments in television often occur during conservative and/or oppressive stretches of government policy-making, such as when shows like *Miami Vice* began to focus seriously on the transnational drug trade during the Reagan 80s, or when *The Jeffersons* premiered to high ratings only a year after the resignation of Richard Nixon due to the 1972 Watergate scandal (which focused intensely on debates around transmission, recording, and surveillance within an increasingly televisual American culture). *The Jeffersons* was the first program to feature an all-black cast trying to balance middle-class foibles with working-class histories. When I showed the pilot episode ('A Friend in Need') to my Film and Media students, they were startled by

George's use of the word 'nigger' and his critical discussion of hate-speech within what was supposed to be a 'funny' program.

The notion of 'transgressive television' has an inextricable association with 'cult television', where spaces of camp and resistance tend to overlap within a playful terrain of desire, devotion, and intertext. Fans are known to be 'cult' once they truly admit to loving a program, just as the program itself gains 'cult status' only once it has either (1) been cancelled, forgotten, and then resurrected by fan intensity or (2) debuted riskily as something that *must* or *ought* to be cancelled within a competitive broadcasting market, only to be surprisingly taken up, authenticated, and loved by an unexpected community of fans and critics. *Twin Peaks* is often cited as the definitive example of the strange, uncanny, non-fitting (and hence non-replicable) show that was embraced and celebrated by a global fan community. The precedent for this kind of reception is *Star Trek*, which was cancelled due to poor ratings, only to be recuperated and adapted by legions of desiring fans who continually restaged Gene Roddenberry's universe through both hetero- and slash-fanfiction. Constance Penley discusses this tradition at length in *Nasa/Trek* (1997).

Often, 'transgression' on television becomes coded specifically as the (unexpected) representation of racial and sexual minorities on screen, which Judith Butler locates as the battle between the 'universal' audience and the 'foreclosed' particular subject who 'makes a claim' for universality – Butler doesn't talk about television, but her linguistic arguments can be applied to televisual culture with productive and surprising results (Butler, 2000: 746). While *The Jeffersons* remains the first African-America family drama on TV, *I Spy* was the first show to feature an African-American performer (Bill Cosby) in a principle role, and audiences would have to wait until the advent of *Good Times* to see a black family living in the Chicago projects rather than in a palatial East-Side New York apartment. *Soap* – itself a parody – was the first show to feature a gay character, and *Thirtysomething* was the first to show two men in bed together; although, Joss Whedon comments that the sight of 'two men sitting ramrod-straight, far away from each other' was 'the most antiseptic thing I've ever seen in my entire life' (2001).

Ellen, of course, was the first primetime show to feature a lesbian main character and was subsequently cancelled when the network decided that scenes of reckless lesbian hand-holding and cuddling were 'too gay' for a 'universal' sitcom. *Will and Grace* has received almost no criticism from straight audiences – and almost nothing *but* criticism from LGBT audiences – but, despite its equally 'antiseptic' portrayal of a sexless, white, middle-class gay man, it remains the first primetime show to feature a kiss between two men (and an interracial kiss at that). Queer sexuality had already exploded in the form of *Queer as Folk* on Channel 4 in the United Kingdom and its 2000

American adaptation, actually filmed in Toronto. For the most part, however, this sexuality has been confined to beautiful, white, able-bodied men with disposable cash and absolutely no viral loads to speak of. The first show to break both the queer and class barriers on HBO, of which I want to offer a short case-study, is *The Wire*, which appeared a few short months after September 11. I want to argue that, where many network shows fail to deal engagingly with 'foreclosed' subjects, *The Wire* succeeds, primarily through its focus on urban poverty and its ability to tell a story largely uncensored on the cable network HBO (see Cathy Johnson on HBO and *The Sopranos* in this volume).

Tony Kushner, a fan of the show, calls it 'substantial, complex, honest ... [a]nd unprecedented' (cited in Alvarez, 2004:). Created by David Simon – whose previous credits include Emmy-winners *Homicide: Life on the Street* and *The Corner* – *The Wire* focuses on a sprawling drug and wiretap investigation in the city of Baltimore. The affective connections and affiliations shared by all of the characters, most of whom are black and working-class, represent a web of Shakespearean proportions, with screen-time equally divided between cops and drug-dealers. Focusing initially on Irish cop Jimmy McNulty as he stumbles upon a transnational drug ring, the narrative widens to encompass warring drug families, dock-workers, union-busters, attorneys, and IV drug-users. The audience is led to engage, at first perhaps uncomfortably, with the heroin-addicted character 'Bubbles' (Andre Royo), who becomes a uniquely ethical figure, caught between resisting the fatal consequences of the drug trade and availing himself of its intense communities, kinship networks, and support systems. The 'villains' in *The Wire* never properly execute a villainous performance, since the Baltimore Police have actually infiltrated the daily lives of a series of overlapping families that are controlled by patriarchs such as Avon Barksdale (Wood Harris), represented by the 'clean' business dealings of Russell 'Stringer' Bell (Idris Elba), and held tightly together by the often dysfunctional presence of Avon's sister, Brianna (M. Hyatt).

The motto of Season One, imprinted on the DVD set, is 'listen carefully', and *The Wire* emerges as a text that relies almost entirely on overheard conversations, eavesdropped moments, and sometimes barely understandable dialogue that jumps between public telephones, swapped SIM cards, and disposable 'burner' cells used prolifically on Baltimore's drug trade. The show's emphasis on impermanence, on *the trace* as all that we know of human interaction, makes it a program almost entirely devoid of the action that commonly moves serial narratives along. An hour might pass within the universe of *The Wire*, but that doesn't mean that a lot will 'happen.' The show stands at a peculiar ontological point, a series of shifting coordinates that can easily confuse even the most devoted of viewers. It is only fitting that actress Sonja Sohn, who plays lesbian cop Shakima ('Kima')

Griggs, began her performance career as a slam-poet (spoken word), and that two other principle characters – McNulty and Bell – are played by British actors who have taken on unrecognisable accents. We are exhorted to 'listen carefully' because most of *The Wire*'s conclusions, if they are that, occur marginally, out of sight, away from the microphone, or through grainy surveillance footage. We are never afforded any sort of privileged, crystalline viewing point, since, like the characters, we remain locked within the vast and labyrinthine machinery of capitalism itself. The show deliberately attempts to radicalise and transgress against its own economic and cultural constraints, as defined by networks, audience shares, and commercialisation.

The Wire features a recurring character – Omar Little – who is black, queer, disfigured (scarred), and transient. He wanders through the drug-choked projects with a double-barrel shotgun, robbing from mid-level dealers and occasionally giving away drugs to addicts while keeping the money for himself (Fig. 9.1). Omar doesn't explicitly position himself against the Barksdale family until Stringer Bell orders the torture and death of his lover, Brandon. 'That boy was beautiful' is the only spoken reason that Omar gives for moving against the Barksdales, and as the seasons progress, Omar's history and motivations remain primarily a mystery. He is certainly the first queer, black, homeless vigilante to appear on a show, and although very little of *The Wire's* narrative energy is devoted to explicit sex-scenes, two of the hottest scenes

Fig. 9.1   Transgressive and Dangerous – Omar Little in The Wire

focus on the show's principle queer characters, 'Kima' and Omar. The Tom Waits song 'Down in the Hole', which plays (through various versions) over the show's credits, in fact, warns us that 'you gotta keep the devil / way down in the hole,' and I would argue that 'the devil' within *The Wire* takes the form of Omar Little, the most cryptic and heavily marginalised character, whose openly queer sexuality and status as a vigilante give him a style of dangerous agency that is constantly mediated by his street-level survivalist existence.

What makes *The Wire*, to me, so emblematic of 'transgressive television' is its equality of narrative focus shared among working-class police, upper-class politicians, survival-level addicts, and sex-workers – all of whom are not allowed to merely remain the silent subalterns of the drug business. Every character in *The Wire* has a voice of some kind and is able to enact unique and creative tactics of resistance against the forces of white-supremacist capital (to borrow a phrase from bell hooks) which seek their disintegration and erasure. Rather than viewing 'addiction' as something that escapes dangerously from the Third World, or describing its drug-lords as invisible 'Colombians' à la *Miami Vice*, *The Wire* displays the drug business as both transnational and local, emerging in the United States at the street level. When Major Howard 'Bunny' Colvin attempts to create a drug 'free-zone', complete with safe injection-sites and HIV-testing, nicknamed 'Hamsterdam' by its inhabitants, the viewer doesn't simply watch a crumbling Babylon of prostitutes, child-dealers ('hoppers'), and rampant disease – instead, they witness the collision of a series of overlapping at-risk communities, an uneasy alliance between police, dealers, addicts, and sex-trade workers (also often addicts), all co-existing for the first time in a monitored space. The climate is undeniably ethnographic, and although police oppose what they perceive as the 'victory' by the dealers, policy-makers, and sociologists on the show are eager to explore the anthropology of the drug business in order to study its durability, even its productive elements.

Many other shows, both cable and primetime, have encoded transgression in unique and startling ways, although the constraints of this article prevent me from covering them adequately. *The X-Files* created an unprecedented amount of audience support and fan-production, so much so that it probably remains the most successful and long-running (nine seasons) 'cult' program in television history. The 1996 episode 'Home' (4:2), which focused intensely on incest and mutation against a gothic setting, was so horrifying in its depiction of an 'alternative family' that it received public protest (i.e., letters written to Fox) and was never re-aired in syndication. Carter's transgression here, far from attempting to showcase some type of marginalised community, was more focused on exposing a set of grotesque sexual relations that – despite their sensationalisation here – might actually exist among abusive families in real life. 'Seeing Red' (6:19), one of the highest-rated episodes of *Buffy* the Vampire Slayer, culminated in the death of Tara McClay (Amber Benson), whose relationship with Willow Rosenberg was probably the most open and visually significant on television at the time, even if its expressions of queer desire were often densely symbolic. This is also the episode where Spike, against character, tries to rape Buffy, which Whedon felt was needed to remind the audience that he was still inherently selfish.

Numerous other cult shows, some surviving for only a year or more, have enacted their own forms of transgressive resistance against the patriarchal codes of network TV. My So-called Life was the first show to focus on the interior emotional life of a teen girl, as well as the first program to feature a principle character – Rickie Vasquez (Wilson Cruz) – who was both queer and mixed-race. Joan of Arcadia, which ran for only two seasons, was possibly the first show to explore an ethically complex relationship between a teen girl, Joan, and a non-specific deity figure, named simply as 'God.' Joan (Amber Tamblyn) would communicate with numerous God-avatars, including a black janitor, a four-year-old girl, and a sexually ambiguous Goth-boy. 'The Election' (2:5) features an unexpected kiss between two teen boys, caught on videotape by a spying Joan (ala The Wire), and Joan's friend Grace (Becky Wahlstrom) is thought to be queer for most of Season One until she falls (oddly) for Joan's little brother. Joan's brother, Kevin (Jason Ritter), is also paralysed from the waist down, but his character retains a visible sex-life (including one instance when he arrives at his girlfriend's apartment, only to discover that the elevator is out of order. Kevin's solution is to have her grab his ankles so that he can walk wheelbarrow-style up three flights of stairs, a testament both to Kevin's manoeuvrability as a disabled person and to his indefatigable eighteen-year-old sex drive). Joan's relationship with 'God' is most fascinating because she never entirely admits to believing or disbelieving in his/her existence.

Numerous other shows have managed to launch creative assaults against conservative representation on TV while still retaining their popularity as prime-time network vehicles. Veronica Mars recast the high-school drama by giving it a noir backdrop, as well as by choosing to focus primarily on a father-daughter relationship, and placed race and class issues at the centre of high-school tensions. And Farscape, an Australian SF import, forced its audiences to care about puppets and CGI-manipulated aliens in new and fascinating ways, disrupting many conventional SF tropes along the way as it chose to focus on dialogue and character-growth rather than breathless plot-arcs. Oddly enough, interspecies romance, a major theme within the show, had already been explored within Disney's animated series Gargoyles, which actually has a banned episode – 'Deadly Force' (1:8) – that has since been reissued on the DVD set. In the episode, a primary character is accidentally shot by one of the gargoyles, and we see her bleeding on the kitchen floor.[1]

Disney pulled the episode due to concerns around gun violence but had no problem adding it to the Season One DVD collection.

Shows such as *Dexter* continue to push boundaries on television, to the extent that a promotional poster for *Dexter* – visible in most New York subway terminals as I write this – proudly displays actor Michael C. Hall covered in blood-spatter, with the tagline 'America's favorite serial killer is back.' I am a fan of the show, but the billboards make me shudder at the thought that a Hollywood serial killer might become a lovable anti-hero. Still, I trust Michael Cuesta to ride the line between transgressive play and exploitative spectacle without crossing it. If Showtime teaches us anything, it is that transgression can be carefully managed and streamlined to appeal to a number of dominant groups. As Foucault suggests, it is really the transgression that *hasn't yet happened* that can still surprise us, and those dark and gem-incrusted possibilities are what Hollywood actually fears the most, since they escape every mode of constraint.

'The fuckin' best trailer park in the goddamn world':
Trailer Park Boys, Homegrown Canadian Cult TV
(Showcase Television, 2001–)
Sharon Sutherland and Sarah Swan

Although not world renowned, the Canadian television series the *Trailer Park Boys* has a small but fervent audience. The low-budget mockumentary follows the escapades of two friends, Ricky and Julian, as they are released from prison and re-enter their lives of petty crime in the Sunnyvale Trailer Park, a low-income community located in the maritime province of Nova Scotia. Much of the show is pure hilarity, but the series also has something more serious to say: The *Trailer Park Boys* is a sly cultural commentary on the cyclical nature of poverty and crime. Through the lens of the mock documentary camera team, we see Ricky and Julian deal in rapid succession with all of the common predictors of criminal recidivism: poverty, drug and alcohol addictions, family disruption, unemployment, and the alienating effects of incarceration. Although arguably a highly successful Canadian program by any measure of viewership,[2] the series is primarily identified – even within Canada – as a cult hit. In this case study, we explore how many of the quintessential qualities of cult television combine with culturally specific Canadiana within the show to create a uniquely Canadian cult series.

Like many of the cult television series profiled in this collection, *Trailer Park Boys* is a genre series – in this case, a mockumentary. This choice itself reflects its Canadian heritage; the show was originally designed as a mockumentary because of sharp budgetary constraints. As executive producer Mike Volpe has commented, 'You have to look for interesting ways of telling stories that you can do for a low budget' (cited in Brown, 2004: 3). Unlike the many cult science fiction series, there are no special effects in *Trailer Park Boys*. The series is designed to look like the uncut and often clumsy work of handheld cameras as filmmakers follow characters around to document their re-entry into society.

Trailer Park Boys also resonates with many of the themes of transgressive television that permeate cult television series (see Battis in this volume). The show engages in the unexpected representation of characters not normally seen as protagonists on television – they are impoverished, addicted, low functioning, and career criminals. In some ways, it can be likened to *The Wire*, the HBO series which Battis discusses in depth. *Trailer Park Boys* is similarly focused on poverty (though suburban rather than urban), its characters speak in a similarly profane way that would normally be censored on television, and both shows oddly share a 'uniquely ethical figure' named Bubbles.

The challenging and subversive subject matter alone is enough to prevent *Trailer Park Boys* from becoming a mainstream hit, but the sheer volume of profanity may be more disturbing to some viewers. For example, one episode alone contained 86 curses, or approximately four swear words per minute (Durbin, 2003: 2). The degree of coarseness is so extreme that a complaint regarding the Season One finale, 'Who the Hell Invited These Idiots to My Wedding' (1:6), resulted in a hearing before the Canadian Broadcast Standards Council to determine whether allowing a child actress to participate in the filming of some of the scenes in that episode constituted child abuse (CBSC Decision 02/02–0909, 2004).

Of course, excluding certain viewers is part of what forms the cult appeal of the show – viewers are 'hip' because they not only feel comfortable with the vulgarity but likely also enjoy the creativity of the characters' coarseness. Trailer park supervisor Mr. Lahey, for instance, is prolific in the creation of colourful compound nouns beginning with 'shit.' His unforgettable tirade about Ricky in the episode 'Propane, Propane' (4:7) illustrates his panache:

> You know he grew up as a little shitspark from the old shitflint and then he turned into a shitbonfire and driven by the winds of his monumental ignorance he turned into a raging shitfirestorm. If I get to be married to Barb I'll have total control of Sunnyvale and then I can unleash the shitnami tidal wave that will engulf Ricky and extinguish his shitflames forever. And with any luck he'll drown in the undershit of that wave. Shitwaves.

Television shows may also earn the moniker 'cult' through intense participation of fans in any number of fan activities. Julian, Ricky, and Bubbles have created such a strong audience response that the actors frequently tour with bands in Canada as an in-character opening act and participate in interviews almost exclusively in character. Moreover, the boys have a fan following which frequently conflates actor with character. In one surreal instance, the actors who play Julian and Ricky (Jean Paul Tremblay and Robb Wells) were in a courthouse waiting to testify at a friends' trial on the day after an episode in which the characters carry out a robbery and are caught had aired. The prosecutor approached the actors to say, 'Oh, I know why you're here' (Durbin, 2003: 3).

As Angelini and Booy note in this volume, 'part of the cult experience is to be in on the jokes' at self-referential moments. For *Trailer Park Boys*, there is a sense in which being in on the joke may equate to being Canadian. Although critics claim that the characters 'embody universal qualities' and that the show could just as easily be set elsewhere (Brown:1–2), aspects of its cult appeal – its 'in-jokes' – are specifically Canadian. For example, in the feature release *Trailer Park Boys: The Movie* (Mike Clattenburg, Can, 2006), we see Ricky's dedication to the beloved Canadian sport of road hockey. When a prison guard releases Ricky from prison 26 days early in order to prevent him from goaltending in a game between the prisoners and the guards, Ricky first begs to stay in prison and then capitalises on an opportunity in court to be sent back to prison for a week purely to play in the game. Similarly, when Ricky kidnaps Rush guitarist Alex Lifeson in order to force him to play in the trailer park, the episode's humour requires the audience's knowledge of Rush songs and other Canadian rock figures ('Closer to the Heart', 3:5). Ricky first asks Lifeson to play 'I Like to Rock' which Lifeson tells him is a song by April Wine, another iconic Canadian hard rock band. Ricky replies, 'Well, play that *Diane Sawyer* song! Just fuckin' play somethin'! That's why you're here!' Of course, Ricky means 'Tom Sawyer', one of Rush's best known songs.

Rush did have significant success outside of Canada and it is possible that the references might be caught by other audience members; however, the humour in another episode, 'Workin' Man' (4:8), is not likely to be appreciated outside of Canada. In that episode, Ricky kidnaps East Coast folk singer Rita McNeil and forces her to assist in the harvest of a huge marijuana crop. While they do so, Rita leads her band in singing her hit 'Workin' Man.' To an audience that knows Rita McNeil's reputation as shy, kind, and decidedly not connected with the drug scene, her participation in this type of activity is hilarious.

Although the Canadian audience appreciates the obscure cultural references, these references may also be partly responsible for the show's lack of widespread appeal. Both the form and substance of the series reinforce its cult identity: the mockumentary form and the transgressive subject matter challenge some viewers and alienate others. These features, combined with the characters' colourful vulgarity, are part of what makes the *Trailer Park Boys* a critically acclaimed and much-loved series, but these same features also prevent the show from becoming a mainstream hit.

Masters of Horror

(Showtime, 2005–2007)

Donato Totaro

Horror fans were on cloud nine when the brainchild of writer/director/producer Mick Garris – bringing together some of the biggest names in the genre for a Showtime cable TV horror series – came to fruition in 2005. By and large, fan expectations were met and, at its best, the two-season, 26-film series brought some of the most outrageously intense, violent, sexual, controversial, and *political* horror images to television screens. Garris enlisted some of the leading auteurs of the genre, including older, established directors (John Carpenter, Stuart Gordon, Larry Cohen, Tobe Hooper, Don Coscarelli, Dario Argento, Joe Dante, John Landis, Norio Tsuruta) and promising younger directors (Lucky McKee, Brad Anderson, Rob Schmidt), which ensured a cinematic look and a varied visual style across each episode (widescreen cinematography, sophisticated mise-en-scène, complex narrative structures, and creative sound design).

In listening to the directors discuss their involvement in the series, the creative, (largely) censor-free control over content, theme, and style was a major factor in their participation, along with the opportunity to compete in a form of cinematic one-upmanship with their peers.[3] Consequently, one of the pleasures of the show derives from watching directors with an established signature style revel in the afforded freedoms and challenge themselves in terms of subject, style, tone, and sensibility. The result is a series that continually pushed the envelope of televised horror formally and thematically, which set it apart from any other television horror series and quickly made it a cult item.

This tendency to challenge norms is related to an important cultural context and an overriding influence on the series: the tradition of the classic pulp horror comics of the late 1940s to early 1980s, epitomised by EC Comics (short for Entertaining Comics), with the titles most closely aligned with the *Masters of Horror* being *Tales from the Crypt* (1950–1954), *The Vault of Horror* (1950–1955), and *The Haunt of Fear* (1950–1954, all published by EC Comics) and subsequent horror comics *Creepy* (1964–1983) and *Eerie* (1966–1983, both published by Jim Warren). The levels of violence and intensity of graphic imagery in the EC Comics went far beyond the equivalent cinematic imagery of the time. This sensibility led to a public backlash, legal battles, and the eventual cessation of the EC Comics horror titles.

87

The *Masters of Horror* can be seen as a retroactive fulfilment and amplification of this pulp horror comic spirit of excessiveness, while feeding into the above mentioned directorial sense of one-upmanship and self-directed challenges.

Although only one of the films was directly adapted from a horror comic – Argento's 'Jenifer' (1:4), based on a story from *Creepy* issue #63, July 1974 – much of the series was in the spirit of this golden age of pulp horror, with morality tales, ironic fate, revenge, and gruesome forms of poetic justice (with twist endings) leading the way. For example, in Tom Holland's 'We All Scream For Ice Cream'(2:10) a group of men bound together by a malicious childhood act against an ice cream vendor get their (literal) 'just desserts' in the form of a voodoo ice cream cone which, when eaten by a child, kills the respective father. Both 'Homecoming' (1:6) (Dante) and 'Haeckel's Tale' (1:12) (John McNaughton) draw inspiration from W.W. Jacobs' famed short story 'The Monkey's Paw', in which a man wishes his recently deceased son back to life – with horrifying consequences. This classic cautionary tale, which was adapted as 'Wish You Were Here' in *The Haunt of Fear* #22, November–December 1953, was a major influence on pulp horror comics. In Argento's 'Pelts' (2:6) – a horror film for sadistic animal activists – poetic justice is served when furriers possessed by supernatural pelts die horrible self-inflicted deaths patterned after their working methods (bludgeoning, skinning, sewing, etc.). Other entries which contain the spirit of the EC Comics include Tsuruta's 'Dream Cruise' and Schmidt's 'Right to Die' (1:3) (both featuring the vengeful ghost of a murdered wife), and Hooper's 'Dance of the Dead' (2:9) and William Malone's 'Fair Haired Child' (1:9) (both featuring children serving poetic justice on their parents).

Joe Dante rose to the challenges set forth by the series with two of the most politically brazen films, 'Homecoming' and 'The Screwfly Solution' (2:7). In the former, American soldiers who died in the Iraqi War return to earth as zombies to vote in an upcoming election in an effort to oust the incumbent war-mongering government. In 'The Screwfly Solution', Dante blends a volatile political cocktail of terrorism, Middle East tension, religious fundamentalism, and female genocide.

While Dante pushed the envelope thematically, the majority of the films in the series pushed the envelope with regards sexuality and violence, a staple of the pulp horror comics. While it is not a surprise that Argento sets the litmus test for violence in 'Pelts', his candid treatment of carnal, ferocious sex between a feral, she-beast and a hapless detective in 'Jenifer' is a surprise. Contentious sex is also featured in McNaughton's 'Haeckel's Tale', a frank exploration of female sexual desire. A beautiful young woman makes nocturnal trips to a nearby necropolis for torrid sex with the reanimated zombie corpse of her first husband, surrounded by groping zombies. What makes this depiction of necrophilia especially transgressive is the mixture of the luridly grotesque with the explicitly erotic.

The final important pulp horror comic aesthetic to address is graphic violence, often highlighted in a gory set-piece. One of the most representative of such moments is the audacious scene at the end of Carpenter's 'Cigarette Burns' (1:8), where an eccentric film collector commits suicide by threading his own intestines into a projector – an ironic salute to the emotional power of *celluloid*. In an equally representative moment, the most extravagant gore scene in 'Pelts' is reserved for the most vile, greedy, and compulsive character in the film, Jake (Meat Loaf), in what is perhaps the series' grandest moment of poetic justice: Jake stands in front of a vanity mirror and proceeds to skin himself alive, pulling his human torso pelt over his head like a sweater, and then presenting it as a 'work of art' to his shocked lover (the 'murder as art' being an Argento signature) (Fig. 9.2).

Like pulp horror comics, the *Masters of Horror* series is marked by an adult sensibility through the employment of older directors, stories featuring older aged characters, and adult subjects and themes (others include infidelity, euthanasia, abortion, mourning, and alcoholism), which stands as a refreshing contrast to the current tendency in theatrical horror of making films for the youth (13–16 years old) market. In more ways than one, television horror and the tradition of pulp horror have come of age with the *Masters of Horror* series.

Fig. 9.2   Murder as art in 'Pelts', Masters of Horror

Notes

1. Thanks to my student Laura Aguinaga for drawing my attention to this in her excellent essay on *Gargoyles*.
2. The average weekly audience for *Trailer Park Boys* is 300,000 in Canada (Johnson, 2006).
3. Being a premium (pay) cable station, Showtime has a far more liberal hand in terms of content than regular network stations. This is only too evident in the NBC horror series *Fear Itself* (2008), Mick Garris' ill-fated attempt to continue *The Masters of Horror* series. Eight episodes in, *Fear Itself* pales in comparison to *The Masters of Horror* in all respects (from writing to visual style); however, it is painfully obvious in the series' lack of graphic violence, sexuality, and overall viscerality that NBC were handcuffed by its status as a network station. Incidentally, as of this writing Garris has left the show. For completists, there was only one noted instance of censorship in *The Masters of Horror*: in Argento's 'Jenifer' several quick yet explicit insert shots of the central character eating a victim's penis were cut out. On a more significant note, Takashi Miike's episode 'Imprint' (1:13) was banned outright from North American television.

10 Innovative TV

Stacey Abbott

In the introduction to *The Cult Film Reader,* Ernest Mathijs and Xavier Mendik argue that one of the distinguishing characteristics of cult film is that it often contains 'element[s] of innovation, aesthetically or thematically' (2008, 2). By their argument, this innovation usually challenges established 'conventions of filmmaking' (2). This challenge, however, can be a result of the 'badness' of the film's production as opposed to a presumed quality the film gains as a result of conscious endeavour. As Jeffrey Sconce has argued, cult film audiences often celebrate films for 'aggressively attacking the established canon of "quality" cinema' (1995:102). Rhonda V. Wilcox, however, has demonstrated in this volume that cult TV has in recent years more often been distinguished by the *quality* of its productions. Gone are the days of the paper maché planet surfaces in *Star Trek* and the wobbly sets of *Blake's 7.* Instead shows such as *Angel, Alias,* and *Battlestar Galactica* deliver sophisticated cinematography, sumptuous art direction, and spectacular, cutting edge special effects. Although cult TV fans, like their film-based equivalents, may see their favourite shows as an alternative to the 'mainstream', what they perceive as separating cult programmes from the mainstream is often their quality. As Mark Jancovich and Nathan Hunt have argued, cult fandom generally privileges 'form over function' (2004: 28) but cult TV fandom specifically 'focuses on ideas and imagination, rather than on taboo material. This leads to a language based on originality and invention instead of independence, subversion, or resistance', which fall within the purview of the cult film (35). Innovation is, therefore, as fundamental a characteristic of cult television as of cult film, but that innovation is largely achieved through experimentation with the stylistic, narrative, and generic conventions of mainstream television.

As a result, most cult television is highly innovative as it is often the innovation that attracts audiences and inspires their devotion to the show. For fans of *Twin Peaks,* David Lynch's unusual stylistic flourishes, such as the repeated shots of an empty staircase and ceiling fan, the isolated street light, or the dangling phone receiver issuing forth the anguished cries of a mother who has just realised her daughter is dead, are as memorable as the mystical murder investigation (Fig. 10.1). Similarly, it was *The X-Files'* highly expressionistic use of lighting that made the show stand out from other programmes, and the revamped *Battlestar Galactica* caught the audience's attention with the

Fig. 10.1   Haunted staircase in Twin Peaks

visually stunning image that opened the initial mini-series: the Cylon basestar, a colossal spaceship designed in the shape of a star, towering over the human space station as its missiles are silently launched. These programmes are characterised by innovative visual flourishes that separate them from the 'mainstream' fare so often despised by cult audiences.

Innovation, however, can sometimes alienate mainstream audiences, leading to a show's premature cancellation. The very premise of some shows can be so unusual or transgressive that they fall foul of audience and industry expectations. This was the case for the quintessentially cult spy series *The Prisoner* that sought to deconstruct narrative and television conventions and reveal in its final episode how its own narrative framework was a fictional construction (see Angelini on *The Prisoner* in this volume). More recently, the short-lived series *Wonderfalls* offered an unusual premise in which its main character was confronted each week by a different inanimate object, including a wax lion figurine, a brass monkey ornament, and plastic garden flamingos, that would speak to her and send her on a rather cryptic and comic mission of goodwill. The producers had shot 13 episodes, of which only four were broadcast, when it was cancelled. Finding a small but loyal cult audience on DVD, the series was just too odd and perhaps too cynical for mainstream TV. Robin Nelson has argued, however, that the multichannel broadcasting climate of TVIII has 'afforded opportunities through new channels aiming only for relatively small audiences in the first instance to try out challenging production ideas', leading to what he describes as 'edgy TV' (2007b: 76). By targeting loyal and niche audiences with such transgressive programmes as *Queer as Folk*, *Sex and the City*, and *Carnivale*, the broadcast climate is, therefore, facilitating an increasing cult approach to television production (see Simon Brown in this volume for a discussion of *Weeds*, *Dexter*, and *Californication*).

While programmes from *Queer as Folk* to *Californication* couch innovation primarily in terms of transgressive subject matter, cult shows have over the years made particular effort to push formal and narrative boundaries upon an episodic level, often disrupting the series' diegesis in the process. This is particularly the case with cult shows that fall within the telefantasy genres of science fiction, horror, and fantasy. A number of the contributors to this volume have noted that one of the attractions of working within telefantasy and cult TV has often been that it is possible to address serious and controversial issues in a way that might be difficult to discuss through more realist narratives or where the expectations of large mainstream audiences must be satisfied. In this manner, *Angel*, for instance, addressed the rarely discussed topic of female genital mutilation through a fantasy narrative about a race of beings from an alternate dimension that make it a ritualised practise to remove a series of ridges on the back of women's necks that glows red when they are aroused ('She', 1:13). The effect of this castration is the reduction of women to controlled and subservient automatons. The feminist agenda of this episode is clear. The fantasy elements enabled the creators to tell a story that might have been deemed unacceptable for prime-time television. Along the same lines, cult television is an ideal space in which to experiment with stylistic, generic, and narrative conventions and break the rules of mainstream television. Devoted fans of cult TV are more likely to accept and often heartily welcome these kinds of deviations from the 'norm' since this reinforces their reading of their favourite series as exceptional and occasionally even as avant-garde.

There is, of course, a long tradition within mainstream television of interrupting the normal flow of the serial narrative with standalone 'event' episodes that break the generic or narrative formula of the series in question. As Jeffrey Sconce points out, 'the sheer textual volume of television production allows producers occasionally to shepherd personal and/ or throwaway projects, episodes with only tangential or strained relations to the overall series architecture.' The televisual serial structure, therefore, allows for what Sconce describes as a level of 'narrative elasticity' (2003: 184). Within mainstream TV, however, there are restrictions upon the extent of this elasticity, as these episodes are usually still expected to conform to the generic or narrative conventions of the show. For instance, the long-running sit-com-turned-dramedy *MASH* undertook a number of 'special' episodes, most memorably 'The Interview' (4:25), shot like a black and white newsreel in which the various members of the 4077 Mash unit are interviewed about their experiences in Korea, and 'Point of View' (7:11), an episode shot entirely from the direct perspective of a patient who is injured and then arrives at the 4077 for treatment. These episodes not only break with stylistic conventions by filming in black and white and with subjective camera work but also challenge the narrative format of the show by telling the story from points of view other than that of the main cast members, instead offering an external perspective of the team and the work they do. Despite this difference, both operate completely within the narrative context established by the series and reaffirm the show's humanist and anti-war themes. Similarly, the live broadcast of *The West Wing* episode 'The Debate' (7:7) in which the presidential candidates stage their debate was daring in terms of the production and performance requirements for such an endeavour. The episode, however, still conformed to the normal diegesis of the show and reaffirmed those aspects of *The West Wing* that distinguished it, namely intelligent and sophisticated political dialogue passionately and convincingly delivered by the show's cast.

In the case of cult television, however, the point of many 'event episodes' is to undermine, albeit briefly, the conventions of the series and to rupture its narrative diegesis, laying bare the construction of meaning within the text. For instance, certain cult series have chosen to experiment with genre by structuring one episode of a series that is generally associated with a very specific generic heritage along the conventions of another completely distinct genre. This type of generic allusion goes above and beyond the generic hybridity which is an inherent quality of contemporary television. Most shows by their very nature draw upon a range of generic influences. The acclaimed BBC series *Bleak House* simultaneously draws upon the conventions of literary adaptation, heritage drama, and soap opera, while the cult series *Battlestar Galactica* vacillates between science-fiction, family melodrama, and war drama. Lorna Jowett has argued that *Angel* is so intricately hybrid that it is virtually impossible to disentangle the generic allusions that circulate throughout the show (2009). In these cases, the audiences are regularly being asked to read the different generic conventions in relation to each other. This use of genre stands in contrast with episodic generic experiments that deliberately undermine the show's traditional conventions by reworking the series through the lens of a completely different genre and by reinventing the show from the inside. These types of episodes force the audience to reorient their expectations and understanding of the show and as a result are rare in mainstream TV. You would not expect to see a musical episode of *The Wire* nor a science-fiction episode of *ER* in which aliens transport the hospital to the moon (a plot used in the episode 'Smith and Jones' [3:1] of *Doctor Who*). This type of playfulness would be too disruptive to the generic boundaries of such 'realist' series. In cult shows, however, the generic boundaries tend to be more malleable and audience expectations more flexible. As a result, these types of experiments are quite prevalent and usually welcomed by the fans.

For instance, the romantic-comedy detective series *Moonlighting* gained a great deal of critical and fan attention when the creators decided to structure one episode as a classic film noir in 'The Dream Sequence Always Rings Twice' (2:4). Initially met with resistance from the network who thought audiences wouldn't watch a show in black and white, the episode was a huge hit with fans of the series. Introduced by Orson Welles, director of *Citizen Kane* (1941) and *Touch of Evil* (1958), and conceived as a deliberate visual and narrative homage to such noir classics as *Double Indemnity* (Billy Wilder, US, 1944)*, The Postman Always Rings Twice* (Tay Garnett, US, 1946), and *Murder My Sweet* (Edward Dmytryk, US, 1944), the episode pushed the limits of the series' self-reverential and tongue-in-cheek humour. As the show's creator, Glenn Gordon Caron, explained he wanted to 'test the audience and test ourselves without taking the whole thing too seriously' (cited in Daley, 1986). This model of generic playfulness was repeated on the Superman series *Smallville* in the episode 'Noir' (6:20) when Jimmy Olson falls asleep and re-imagines his reality as a hard-boiled detective narrative in which he rather than Clark Kent is the central hero. By rewriting the story through the conventions of noir rather than those of superhero, however, Olson does not save the girl à la Superman but is instead arrested for the murder he is manipulated into committing.

The purposes of these kinds of generic experimentation can be numerous. There is, of course, an element of playfulness on the part of the series' creators, and increasingly that sense of whimsy is welcomed by cult TV fans. In both cases, the conversion of the original series into noir enabled the creators, actors, and audiences to enjoy the cinematic allusion to classic Hollywood cinema while also indulging in an alternate universe narrative in which the villains can be heroes, the heroes villains, and the modern successful women can engage in the femme fatale fantasy. The pleasure is in the break from formula. Furthermore, the episode of *Smallville* was specifically an 'event' episode programmed for sweeps weeks, designed to draw in a large audience with this seemingly novel premise. So while this type of experimentation can be seen as transgressive, it is often sanctioned transgression designed to capitalise upon audience's taste for innovation.

In contrast, some shows use episodic generic experimentation to make a deliberate point, often through parody. The horror series *Supernatural,* a show that often engages in quite whimsical play with generic and narrative form, used its episode 'Ghostfacers' (3:15) to make a pointed comment on the state of contemporary television particularly in the light of the writers' strike of 2007–2008. Constructed out of digital footage supposedly shot by amateur filmmakers, the episode alludes to the recent phenomenon of horror films such as *The Blair Witch Project* (Daniel Myrick and Eduardo Sánchez, US, 1999), *Cloverfield* (Matt Reeves, US, 2008), *Diary of the Dead* (George Romero, US, 2008) and *[Rec]* (Jaume Balagueró and Paco Plaza, Sp, 2007). More significant, however, given its TV origins, the episode pointedly parodies contemporary reality television, in the form of such ghost-hunting shows as *Most Haunted* and *Dead Famous*, as well as the host of amateur video footage of 'real ghosts' available on YouTube (www.youtube.com). Shot entirely as a fictional TV pilot for a reality ghost-hunting show called 'Ghostfacers', the episode lampoons the conventions of reality TV and its ghost-hunting sub-genre, such as the seeming sincerity of the investigators, the regular direct-to-camera confessional address, the voyeuristic capturing of private moments, and the humour of the hapless and buffoonish investigating team as they repeatedly scare themselves. The first episode of *Supernatural,* aired after the writer's strike, consciously mocks the popularity of reality TV, a form of programming that generally undercuts the role of the writer. In its opening, the show's moronic hosts, Ed and Harry, comically claim to be the 'bold new future of reality TV', acknowledging that the networks have been 'hit hard by the writers' strike' but claiming 'who needs writers when you've got guys like us'. The irony of this deliberately self-important statement juxtaposed against their ridiculous behaviour throughout the episode serves as a nod to the fans who often share the writers' frustration with this type of amateur programming. Here innovation offers a commentary on the state of television.[1]

Another form of innovation involves foregrounding of the process of storytelling itself and in so doing calling attention to the construction of meaning within the text. Although numerous series from *The Prisoner* to *Buffy* to *Angel* have experimented with these types of episodes, *The X-Files* significantly set the standard for this form of experimentation. Having established both a cult and mainstream following for the series over its first two years, the creators began in their third season to undermine the show's own rules and narrative conventions. The episode 'Clyde Bruckman's Final Repose' (3:4) introduced a minor tonal variation to the series by framing the episode primarily from the point of view of life insurance/psychic investigator Clyde Bruckman, played in deadpan fashion by Peter Boyle. While the episode is primarily a straightforward serial murder case, Bruckman's perspective on the murders and the lead FBI investigators Fox Mulder and Dana Scully is tinged with irony and sarcasm. This shift in perspective is both humorous and slightly disruptive, although by no means overtly innovative.

Disruption, however, takes on highly innovative form in 'Jose Chung's *From Outer Space*' (3:20), a title that seems to be a deliberate echo of 'Clyde Bruckman'. In this episode, author Jose Chung (Charles Nelson Reilley) interviews Scully about the investigation of a particular alien abduction case which he has decided to make the subject of his next novel. A simple premise it may seem but within the flashback structure the audience is introduced to a wide range of subject positions as the story is constructed à la *Rashomon* (Akira Kurosawa, Jap, 1950), as a series of characters recount their version of what happened. Like *Rashomon,* the episode questions the notion of truth in favour of subjective perspective. As Jose Chung tells Scully, 'Truth is as subjective as reality', laying bare the thesis for the episode. The episode, however, does not stop at raising these questions about truth and reality, nor is it purely a homage to Kurosawa's film. The episode also interweaves within this tale a series of intertextual allusions that call attention to *The X-Files'* place within a broader media and science-fiction landscape. The episode begins with an alien abduction that draws upon the visual imagery associated with abduction mythology, the car stops abruptly, a bright light from the sky engulfs the vehicle, and the aliens appear with large heads, wide eyes, and grey skin. This imagery is subsequently disrupted by the appearance of another alien who is, by contrast, designed in homage to Ray Harryhausen's classic stop-motion animation and appears to be more of a mythical monster from *Jason and the Argonauts* (Don Chaffey, US, 1963) or *Clash of the Titans* (Desmond Davis, UK/US, 1981) than an alien from *Close Encounters of the Third Kind* (Steven Spielberg, US, 1977). Later Mulder interviews a man who distractedly sculpts his mashed potatoes like Richard Dreyfuss does in *Close Encounters,* and in a separate flashback Mulder orders piece after piece of sweet potato pie as he questions the diner owner about the case, echoing Agent Cooper's pie obsession in *Twin Peaks.* Finally Scully's autopsy of a supposed alien corpse is shot on video and composed and edited to deliberately evoke the infamous alien autopsy footage in *Alien Autopsy: (Fact or Fiction?)* that was aired on the Fox network. The entire approach of this episode is to call attention to its own constructedness and to undermine any notion of the 'truth', a highly transgressive action in a series with the tag line 'the truth is out there'. Here the show openly challenged its own premise.

The success of this episode with audiences and critics enabled *The X-Files* to regularly return to this type of experimentation, often including one-off episodes that diverged from the show's established narrative trajectory by playing with stylistic and generic conventions. This playfulness with the televisual form has in recent years been seen as a characteristic of 'postmodern' TV drama, a form of television that 'tends to reject historical authenticity, mixes styles and genres of television using the techniques of bricolage, and even draws attention to its own constructedness like Brechtian theatre in order to frustrate the temptation to derive meaning from an open text' (Page, 2001: 43). The postmodern quality of *The X-Files* was overtly acknowledged by the show's creators with their episode 'The *Postmodern* Prometheus' (5:5) where their homage to Mary Shelley's *Frankenstein* and Universal's adaptation of the novel, which included black and white cinematography, atmospheric electric storms, and angry, torch-carrying villagers, was juxtaposed with the songs of pop Diva Cher, clips from Bogdanavich's *The Mask* (1985), and extracts from *The Jerry Springer Show*. Jim Collins further argues that 'within postmodern culture, identity must be conceived as an intersection of conflicting subject positions' (1992: 337), a perspective reflected in *The X-Files*' use of 'event episodes' to disrupt conventional storytelling by introducing different narrators (as in the episode 'The Unusual Suspects' [5:3] told from the point of view of conspiracy theorist organisation The Lone Gunmen) or various subject positions (as evidenced in 'Bad Blood' [5:12] where Scully and Mulder each tell their own version of their encounter with a vampire). In *The X-Files*, innovation was, therefore, characterised by intertextual referencing, generic manipulation, and the undermining of authoritative subject positions, all of which conforms to or established the parameters of postmodern TV.

The success of *The X-Files*, particularly these highly memorable event episodes, demonstrated the manner in which postmodern TV and cult TV dovetailed as cult audiences increasingly welcomed these transgressive breaks with narrative continuity, paving the way for subsequent cult series to be equally daring (see Abbott on *Buffy the Vampire Slayer* in this volume). The horror series *Supernatural* includes numerous episodes such as 'Tall Tales' (2:15), 'The Usual Suspects' (2:7), and 'Mystery Spot' (3:11) that not only extend the narrative experimentation witnessed in *The X-Files* but also overtly cite *The X-Files* as a cultural reference. *Supernatural*, like *The X-Files* before it, also demonstrates that the telefantasy genre is predisposed to include episodes that bend stylistic rules, blur generic boundaries, and break with narrative conventions because so much can be explained through science, mysticism and the supernatural. For instance, the show can feature a *Groundhog Day* (Harold Ramis, 1993) parody, as in 'Mystery Spot', where ghost-hunter Sam repeats the day of his brother and partner Dean's death over and over again in increasingly cartoonish fashion because the series has already established the presence of a 'trickster' demon who can alter reality ('Tall Tales'). In *Angel*'s Los Angeles, it is possible for demons to appear in the form of puppets, transform the series hero into a puppet ('Smile Time', 5:14), and make a character jump back and forth within the episode's narrative, repeating moments previously witnessed, because she 'has been pulled out of linear progression' through a temporal shift ('Time Bomb', 5:19).

In a similar fashion, it is possible in a science-fiction universe where the notion of time travel is well established, as in the *Star Trek* franchise, to have a story in which characters from *Star Trek: Deep Space 9* (*DS9*) travel back in time and interact with characters from *Star Trek* the original series (*ST: OS*) as was the case in 'Trials and Tribble-ations' (5:6), an episode produced to commemorate the thirtieth anniversary of *Star Trek*. In this episode, a number of *DS9*'s regulars inadvertently travel back in time not only to encounter the original Starship Enterprise but to actually become integrated within one of the most popular episodes of the original series 'The Trouble with Tribbles' (2:13). Significantly, this example highlights how the cult nature of the show and its audience facilitates the playfulness involved in this type of experimentation. It is not simply that the generic form will absorb these types of variations within the diegesis but that part of the pleasure of the episode comes from being pulled out of the diegesis to watch how the show's creators integrate the contemporary cast within the clips from the highly familiar classic episode through very clever digital imaging. The audience watches the episode at two levels, one following the diegetic narrative in which Captain Sisko and his crew attempt to prevent the Klingon villain from changing the past and the other focusing on how the effects of integrating the old and new episodes are achieved (as in the fight sequence on the space station where Worf, Obrien, and Dr. Bashir [DS9] fight alongside Scotty and Checkov [ST: OS] or in the sequence when Captain Kirk from the original series reprimands his crew including Engineer Obrien from *DS9*). Finally, the episode also offers pleasures specifically aimed at its cult audience, as the *DS9* characters hero worship Captain Kirk and First Officer Spock. Dax comments that Spock is much better looking in real life and urges Cisko to admit that he would like to meet Kirk, 'one of the most famous men in Starfleet history!' Cisko finally relents and acknowledges that he would love to meet Kirk and ask him about fighting the Gorn on Cestus Three, a reference to the popular episode 'Arena' (1:20). This episode fosters the perception of a shared passion for the original show on the part of the fans and the creators of the new series and as a result indulges in the series' cult-ness.

While the worlds of telefantasy series usually allow for a degree of narrative disruption, these particular episodes push the parameters of 'narrative elasticity'. They specifically invite audience indulgence in their stylistic, narrative, and generic experimentation, an indulgence that cult TV audiences embrace for part of the pleasures of cult TV is the shared recognition among fans that their show is doing something unique, transgressive, and innovative.

Recommended Reading

Abbott, Stacey (2009) ' "It's a Little Outside the Box": How *Angel* Breaks the Rules', in Abbott (ed.) *Angel*. Detroit: Wayne State University Press, 83–103.

Nelson, Robin (2007) 'Pushing the Envelope: "Edgy" TV Drama, *Queer as Folk, Sex and the City, Carnivale*', in Nelson (ed.) *State of Play: Contemporary 'high-end' TV Drama*. Manchester: Manchester University Press, 76–108.

Buffy the Vampire Slayer
(WB, 1997–2001/UPN 2001–2003)
Stacey Abbott

Although *The X-Files* may have demonstrated how a successful cult TV series could be highly innovative on a narrative and generic level by regularly disrupting the narrative arc with one-off event episodes, Joss Whedon's *Buffy the Vampire Slayer* took this penchant for experimentation even further. Much has been written about the most high profile of these event episodes, specifically 'Hush' (4:10), 'Restless' (4:22), 'The Body' (5:16), and 'Once More with Feeling' (6:7) in which showrunner Whedon stretched his own creative abilities as a writer and a director. 'Hush', a fairy tale featuring demons who steal voices, was Whedon's response to comments that his primary talent lie in dialogue. 'Restless' abandons conventional narrative in favour of a non-linear dreamscape, while 'Once More with Feeling' was the show's highly acclaimed musical episode. Finally, 'The Body' breaks televisual conventions around image composition and sound, specifically Whedon's choice to use only carefully selected diegetic sound, to express the surreal and disconnected experience of a death in the family. Each of these episodes is a testament to Whedon's artistry as a writer and director but they also convey his and the production team's commitment to undermining televisual convention, and to fostering an environment in which experimentation and innovation are not only welcomed but also made a fundamental feature of the series' matrix. The innovations stretch well beyond these acclaimed episodes.

Once the mythology and character relationships were established in season one, *Buffy* increasingly demonstrated stylistic and narrative innovation by deliberately foregrounding the art and construction of storytelling. Repeatedly the series drew upon unusual and disruptive narrational devices such as the split screen in 'Him' (7:6); the shadow puppets that recount the story of the men who created the first slayer in 'Get it Done' (7:15); and the poetic use of voice over in 'Passion' (2:17) and 'Becoming (Part I)' (2:21), delivered primarily by Angel(us) as if he were standing outside of the text, observing and reflecting upon the events as they unfold. 'Conversations with Dead People' (7:7) bookends its four distinct and parallel explorations of death and loneliness with a musical performance in the nightclub The Bronze, while 'Selfless' (7:5) uses diverse stylistic and generic devices to convey the different episodes and identities that have come to define Vengeance Demon Anya's life. These include presenting her original human existence in Sweden like a bad foreign movie, replete with sub-titles, scratches on the print, and jarring editing, and the highly disruptive and disjunctive cut from Anya, in a flashback to the musical episode, singing about her pending marriage, to Anya pinned to the wall with a sword thrust through her chest. These episodes single themselves out as unusual from the standard structure of *Buffy* by disrupting any form of classical narrative diegesis and by overtly inviting the audience to reflect upon the nature of storytelling. The show developed this self-reflective approach, not to empty the meaning from the original text, a criticism often levelled at much postmodern art, but to introduce layers of meaning that require active viewing on the part of the audience. These episodes demand discussion and analysis, acts that the cult TV viewer and scholar are eager to explore.

Furthermore, although *The X-Files* and *Supernatural* often challenge the notion of an authoritative narrative voice through the introduction of differing subjective positions, *Buffy* far more regularly decentres the narration by privileging a range of narrative voices across the series. The show may be named after Buffy, but many characters are given the opportunity to take centre stage. In the episode 'The Zeppo' (3:13), the mythic battle undertaken by the show's primary heroes, Buffy, Angel, Willow, and Giles, is undermined by focusing upon Xander's seemingly peripheral, although equally heroic, actions as he fights zombies and stops a bomb from blowing up the high school; all actions that go unseen by his friends. Similarly, episodes such as 'Superstar' (4:17), 'Real Me' (5:2), and 'Storyteller' (7:16) hand the narration over to even more peripheral characters than Xander, who is, of course, a central member of the Scoobie Gang, and in so doing unsettle the narrative premise for the series. These episodes not only focus upon the actions and perspectives of marginal characters but also provide them with a structuring voice that influences the format of the episode. This is most obvious in 'Storyteller' in which former super villain turned ally Andrew is purporting to be making a documentary about the final battle of Buffy against the seasonal big bad, the First Evil. Much of the episode is shot on video with Andrew directly addressing the camera, interviewing the other characters or describing events from his perspective. Furthermore, these scenes are intercut with comic fantasy sequences in which Andrew recasts himself as the hero of events from the show's past.

In 'Real Me', Buffy's sister Dawn, who was suddenly introduced without explanation in the last minutes of the previous episode ('Buffy vs Dracula', 5:1), provides the narrative voice over for the episode as she explains what it is like being the sister of the Slayer. No explanation for her presence is

101

offered, something that startled fans were eager to receive, and instead the audience is forced to engage with Dawn's point of view as she guides them through her perspective on the Buffyverse. Similarly in 'Superstar', former Sunnydale High classmate Jonathan, a character who has appeared in the background of the show since its first season, concocts a magical spell that not only transforms him into a writer, spy, inventor of the internet, and star of *The Matrix* (Andy and Larry Wachowski, US, 1999) but also rewrites the premise for *Buffy* by placing him at the centre of the narrative, even reconstructing the show's credit sequence to feature Jonathan's heroic actions instead of Buffy's. In each of these cases, the line between text and extratextual narration is blurred and the foundations for the series are briefly challenged. While these episodes may be seen to be occasional disruptions in the overarching story arc, disruptions that are eventually resolved when Buffy reclaims the narrative, they do, however, highlight the constructedness of the cult TV experience in which any fan can write themselves into the centre of their favourite TV show.

The manner in which these characters reconstruct *Buffy* to suit their own personas presages one of the most narratively transgressive episodes for a cult television series that has engendered intensive loyalty on the part of fans: namely, 'Normal Again' (6:17), an episode in which the entire *Buffy* universe is revealed to potentially be the imaginings of Buffy's psychotic mind. In this episode, Buffy, seemingly under the influence of demonic poisoning, leaps back and forth between her Sunnydale existence and her life in a mental institution, where her psychiatrist claims that Buffy is suffering from psychotic delusions in which 'she is the central figure in a fantastic world beyond imagination'. This episode startled fans by undercutting the entire premise of the series and challenging fans' own devotion to this fictional universe, particularly through the ending in which Buffy seemingly chooses to live the delusion by 'returning' to Sunnydale. The final shot of the episode is of a catatonic Buffy crumpled on the floor of her hospital room. This episode demonstrates the commitment of the show's creators to transgressing the boundaries not only of televisual convention but also of their own narrative universe. In this they risked alienating not only television executives and advertisers but also their own loyal viewers. But while the response to 'Normal Again' was mixed, provoking praise alongside outrage, it also engendered respect. Here was a show that was prepared to risk all for the sake of its own creative vision.

The Prisoner
(ITV, 1967–1968)
Sergio Angelini

Patrick McGoohan's *The Prisoner* wanted to use the science-fiction/fantasy form to turn 1960s traditional episodic television drama on its head. Quickly revered by genre enthusiasts as a genuine cult classic, even this niche success is surprising if one considers that *The Prisoner* lasted for only one season and is comprised of a scant 17 episodes. At the time, critics and mainstream audiences were, in fact, outraged by *The Prisoner,* which gives at least some indication of the show's ability to shock and surprise, especially if one considers its pedigree. It followed on directly from McGoohan's hugely popular spy show *Danger Man* (screened in the United States as *Secret Agent*) and was initially perceived as a sequel, in which its focal character John Drake resigns from the British secret service and is kidnapped. However, within only a few minutes of the opening episode 'Arrival', the use of science-fiction/fantasy elements (most notably 'Rover', a large menacing balloon launched from the depths of the sea that patrols the jailed citizens and can smother and kill them) start to restrict the appeal of the show more tellingly than its naturalistic predecessor. Its broader allegorical underpinnings have subsequently given it a critical credibility unlike that of any other show made for ITC, the company set up by Lew Grade specialising in such popular and undemanding fare as *The Saint* and *Thunderbirds,* which financed McGoohan's conception.

McGoohan owned the series' production company, Everyman Films, starred in each episode, and is credited on screen as director of three episodes and writer of two of these, although he also wrote another script as 'Paddy Fitz' and directed two further instalments as 'Joseph Serf'. No other series of its type from this era was ever so completely in the control of a single individual, and this has undoubtedly been crucial in its absorption as a cult text (Fig. 10.2).

To help put the achievement of the series in context, one may look to the show it almost became. The first 39 half-hour episodes of *Danger Man* were screened from 1960 to 1961 and pre-dated the huge success of the James Bond film adaptations; in 1964, the show was renewed as a 60-minute show and reformatted to reflect the emerging spy boom. Drake thus moved from NATO to 'M9', was made more explicitly British, and given an 'M'-like boss. When McGoohan curtailed the fourth season of *Danger Man* to make *The Prisoner,* he

103

Fig. 10.2   Patrick McGoohan – creator and star of The Prisoner

took much of the crew, including script editor George Markstein, producer David Tomblin, and cinematographer Brendan J. Stafford, with him. Others, including producers Sidney Cole and Barry Delmaine and editor/second unit director John Glen, were instead reassigned to the new project 'McGill'. Like *The Prisoner,* it featured a fiercely independent ex-secret agent who leaves his agency under a cloud, only to find his ethics and sense of self constantly tested while still being dogged by his past. They both boasted instantly recognisable theme tunes by Ron Grainer and were initially broadcast within only a few days of each other throughout the 1967–1968 season. If *The Prisoner* sought to undermine the genre, *Man in a Suitcase* (as 'McGill' would become) became the toughest and most physically and emotionally violent of all ITC series, taking the lone-wolf format beloved of ITV adventure series to its limit, but no further. The makers of *The Prisoner* had much more on their mind than extending that format. With its strong anti-authoritarian stance (the village is littered with Orwellian slogans such as 'Questions are a burden to others'), its heavy use of symbolism, and its embracing of narrative incoherence, it infuriated audiences for its stubborn refusal to yield forth sympathetic characters or traditional plots.

Following his kidnapping, the anonymous hero, known only as 'Number Six', is transported to a mysterious village (also unnamed) and subjected to various interrogation techniques by a succession of 'Number Twos' in an effort to discover why he resigned. Duality and mind control are the most persistent themes, seen at their best in 'The Schizoid Man', an ironic look at behaviourism in which the hero is made to think that he is actually impersonating 'Number Six', with the result that he has to fight to retain control of not just his own identity but also the one that has been imposed on him by his captors (his mantra, 'I am not a number I am a free man' is derided each week by the new 'Number Two').

The Prisoner, as it progressed, was a show that was clearly unwilling to provide any sort of narrative closure. Even the exact running order of the episodes (save the opening episode and the two-part conclusion) is unclear, not least due to internal inconsistencies in the episodes in the order in which the network decided to put them out; fans of the show endlessly debate the 'correct' order in which the series should be seen. When it was cancelled, McGoohan decided to show up the espionage premise as a formulaic charade. After a production hiatus, its final four episodes reshaped the narrative as a Western ('Living in Harmony'), a bed-time story presented as a parody in the style of *The Avengers* in 'The Girl Who Was Death' and finished with the long-awaited conclusion that satisfyingly revealed the severe limitations of most episodic television drama but provided only derisory plot 'resolutions' to those viewers requiring them. We found out where the village was (Portmerion, North Wales) but only via an undramatic onscreen title; a hooded Number One is unmasked, only to reveal that he is a grimacing version of Number Six; and the hero finally destroys his prison (via perfunctory stock footage) and escapes, but with the clear indication, however, that he is not actually free at all as his return matches exactly the opening sequence in which he was initially captured. After the final episode was first shown, the switchboard of the UK broadcaster was jammed with furious viewers demanding to know what it all meant, while in America the episode 'Living in Harmony' was pulled and cut from the original network screening. The richness of the text has ensured that this allegory masquerading as an adventure series with SF trappings has been the subject of dozens of books and led to the creation of the one of the first organised cult appreciation societies, 'Six of One'.

Subverting genre conventions from within involves at a basic level a fundamental betrayal of audience expectations, the laying down of a challenge to the accepted norms of television appreciation as a mass media. For devotees of cult television, part of the appeal can come in finding shows such as *The Prisoner* that bring something genuinely new to one's appreciation of genre and the syntax of television, even questioning the orthodoxy of programming itself.

Notes

1. The episode 'Smile Time' of *Angel*, in which the show's hero is turned into a puppet while investigating a case based around a children's TV programme, also uses this unusual and innovative premise to offer a similarly pointed commentary about contemporary television. This commentary was made all the more poignant for the fans as the episode aired only days after the announcement that the series was cancelled. See Abbott 2009 for a closer discussion of this episode.

11 Representation: Exploring Issues of Sex, Gender, and Race in Cult Television

Lorna Jowett

How realistic is it to expect cult television, something many consider a niche market, to impact on perceptions of sex, gender, or race? Yet television fiction, striving to remain relevant and credible to audiences, must negotiate questions of identity that change as understanding of ourselves and our society changes. In turn, television's popular nature makes these negotiations influential. Television drama deals with sex, gender, and race because it tends to centre on character. Often, representations are mobilised in a liberal humanist fashion which embraces diversity and freedom of expression but does not acknowledge the political significance of identity. Despite successive waves of feminism and gay rights activism, sex and gender tend to be depoliticised because they may be dealt with as individual concerns, playing down their social significance. Race, perhaps especially in the United States, is seen to be more political. Naturally, the mainstream, commercial nature of television means that sensitive subjects will always be handled carefully, often leading to a 'least offensive programming' strategy (though what is considered offensive will vary from country to country and from individual to individual). Yet the increasing segmentation of television markets has caused a shift to what some describe as 'narrowcasting', and in an industry that now values products aimed at specific audiences, cult television has come into its own. Cult, through its negotiation of genre, potentially enables representations to be less mainstream. Furthermore, given the overlap between cult and some 'quality' television, its audience may be more willing to embrace challenging representation as part of contemporary television drama.

The genre categories frequently labelled cult (science fiction, horror, action) are historically associated with young, white, male viewers. Why would shows that apparently target such an audience have anything to say about sex, gender, or race? Firstly, whiteness, masculinity, and heterosexuality are no longer the invisible 'norms' of society and representation of them can be equally revealing about the ways we construct identity. Secondly, Sara Gwenllian-Jones and Roberta E. Pearson argue that despite the notion that cult has a limited market, 'unlike many low-budget films aimed at niche audiences of aficionados, cult television is fairly mainstream fare,' so it is hardly surprising if it reaches a wider audience than its perceived target (2004b: xii). Some shows classed as cult have always had large numbers of viewers, *Doctor Who* being one obvious instance. *Doctor Who* is a 'quality' production from the BBC and its scheduling in the United Kingdom during early evening primetime (around 7 pm on a Saturday) indicates its intended status as mainstream family television *and* as science fiction cult fare. A crossover with teen television can also 'mainstream' cult products (such as *Smallville*, or *Buffy the Vampire Slayer*) as well as position them to debate sexuality and gender as teen concerns.

In addition, cult television's genre leanings may offer latitude for innovative representations of gender, sex, and race. The fantastic elements of many cult shows lend themselves to defamiliarising the customs, interactions, and morals that structure social identity. This does not mean that all fantastic television makes use of this potential, of course. Nor does it mean that all cult television is fantastic. 'Genre' has less authority in the blended landscape of contemporary television, yet its conventions still affect representation. The term 'fantasy violence' in ratings (for television, film, and games) demonstrates how audiences and regulators see the fantastic as a mode that does not work in the same way or require the same rules as 'realistic' fiction. The allegorical or symbolic nature of the fantastic enables cult shows to debate sex, gender, or race under cover of stories about aliens, robots, demons, other worlds, or other times. *Star Trek* is a well-known example, being credited with the first interracial kiss on U.S. network television (though in 'Plato's Stepchildren' [3:12], the kiss, between Captain Kirk and Lieutenant Uhura, was 'excused' by the plot as being compelled through alien telekinesis). Creator Gene Roddenberry relates, 'I could make statements about sex, religion, Vietnam, unions, politics and intercontinental missiles ... we were sending messages, and fortunately they all got by the network' (cited in Johnson-Smith, 2005:59).

Perhaps this is one reason why cult television has been criticised for its poor representation of race. Although other, more mainstream genres such as police drama have a history of including characters from a range of racial and ethnic backgrounds (*Hill Street Blues, NYPD Blue*), 'cult' genres have not done the same. But what constitutes positive representation? It is not simply a question of counting up white and non-white characters: the starship Enterprise of *Star Trek* has a multi-cultural bridge crew but still a white male is in charge and the (mainstream, white) ideology of the Federation is valorised over Other cultures. Representation of race in cult television is not always recognisably about existing racial issues; it often concerns attitudes to race (species) and our (human) relations with Others. Immigration, naturalisation, and the tensions within diverse populations can be mediated through the trope of the alien/Other in a safely defamiliarised story. While *Star Trek*'s utopian Federation (at least in most of the franchise's incarnations) is supposedly above prejudice of any kind, other cult shows such as *Babylon 5* or *Farscape* overtly engage with interspecies conflict motivated by race and nationalism. *Babylon 5* is a multi-species critical utopia (a utopia in progress, striving for a better world, rather than having achieved it) set not long after the Earth-Minbari War, with a complex history of other conflicts both between and within its various species, such as the Centauri occupation of Narn, the Shadow War, the past oppression of telepaths, and the current power of the Psi Corps. *Farscape*'s Peacekeepers value racial purity and the basic premise of the show is that the hero Crichton must adjust to living in a multi-species population as the only human (though Sebaceans/Peacekeepers are noticeably similar, aligning their tendency to racial oppression with the human).

Fantastic settings can invite comparison with the viewer's own world. *Doctor Who* episodes from season three feature passing comment on companion Martha's blackness during a visit to New York City in the Depression era ('Daleks in Manhattan' [3:4] and 'Evolution of the Daleks' [3:5]) and to rural Britain immediately before World War I ('Human Nature' [3:8] and 'Family of Blood' [3:9]). Notably her gender is a matter for less comment in these adventures. Having characters note racial identity highlights how our society has moved on from the prejudice of the past (a strategy also employed by *Star Trek*). In the 1920s or the 1930s, Martha's identity as female might be equally remarkable to the inhabitants of societies accustomed to male dominance and particular perceptions of gender as well as race. Yet the Doctor has had female companions since the show's debut in the 1960s, and they are often as active as male counterparts. In the context of viewing the show, then, gender seems less noteworthy than race. Through characters such as Martha, and previously Mickey in seasons one and two, the updated version of the show now works to incorporate blackness as an everyday aspect of British identity, noted only by less enlightened characters.

In contemporary cult television, point of view can be shifted to give various sides of the story. However, if the main characters are almost all white (as well as middle class and heterosexual), then the boundaries of normality are still reinforced, despite narratives interrogating hegemonic values. Similarly, if Otherness is almost always projected onto aliens or vampires and negotiated in allegorical ways, it is at risk of remaining (or being read by the audience as) 'just a story about vampires [or aliens]', one without any social relevance. Roddenberry's comment about getting past the network censors highlights the importance of interpretation for any given scenario, and audiences may choose to ignore apparently progressive messages, rendering their viewing safe escapist entertainment.

No single facet of identity can easily be separated from the whole, and representation of race links with sex via reproduction and discourses of racial purity or hybridity in cult television characters such as Spock (*Star Trek*), Delenn (*Babylon 5*), alien/human hybrids in *The X-Files*, human-model Cylons (organic androids) in *Battlestar Galactica*, or human/demon characters in *Buffy* and *Angel*. These characters often experience culture clash or dual consciousness and have sometimes been read as figures of the 'tragic mulatto' (a term which in American literature denotes a mixed-race character who, because of racial divides, is caught between two cultures while fitting into neither). Interspecies liaisons (like that of Chiana and D'Argo in *Farscape*) can also stand in for interracial relationships. Their presence raises questions about what constitutes humanity in a wider frame than our current society.

While the fantastic offers specific strategies for exploring race, the handling of romance remains heavily influenced by the codes and conventions of television drama, and this inevitably affects representation of sex and gender. Emphasis on serial narrative or the ensemble cast prioritises character development, and it means cult shows can demonstrate emotional realism despite their fantastic elements. Early cult television such as the original *Star Trek* focused on characters and their relationships as a strategy to attract the female viewers considered desirable by advertisers[1] – one deliberate attempt to widen the target audience. The high-profile but short-lived *Twin Peaks* uses style and narrative quirkiness to distinguish itself *as* cult, yet this is adapted in longer-running successors such as *The X-Files* which combines *Twin Peaks'* darkness and idiosyncrasy with strong lead characters and ongoing speculation about their relationship (*The X-Files* aired for nine seasons in comparison with *Twin Peaks* two).

The boundaries of acceptable topics related to sex on television may have relaxed in recent decades but some conventions still hold considerable sway. While representation of homosexuality has generally moved from invisibility to visibility, for instance, a heteronormative perspective tends to dominate. Television drama, including cult, often explores heteronormativity in terms of morality, gender roles, violence, romance, monogamy, and appropriate coupling, and in doing so it can undermine its privileged status. The nature of serial television also contributes here: romance may be appealing, but unresolved sexual tension satisfies the demands of serial narrative better (as in *The X-Files*) and many cult teen shows featuring independent female protagonists problematise traditional romance. The rules of appropriate coupling still generally apply to cult television, yet, when a character is a superhero, a warrior princess, a vampire, or a secret agent, the struggle to find an 'appropriate' partner and maintain a relationship is fraught with difficulty. *Dark Angel* took this to parodic extremes in its second season when protagonists Max and Logan were unable to share physical contact because an engineered virus put Logan at risk if Max even touched him.

Sex may be easier to find than romance, and certain genres in cult lend themselves to negotiating sexuality in less 'vanilla' terms: the gothic elements of *Buffy* and *Angel* allowed a range of BDSM sexual practices to appear on screen, for example. Generally, however, especially in shows featuring younger characters, the boundaries of 'appropriate' sexual behaviour are tested but adhered to: bad partners and bad sex may be entertained by the narrative (and serve to entertain the audience) but are eventually rejected or condemned. Some shows have attempted to challenge standard morality by introducing characters who accept and enjoy or overtly profit from their sexuality (Inara in *Firefly* is a professional Companion, with status roughly equating to a Geisha; Chiana from *Farscape* is exiled from her own strictly regulated society because she chooses freedom in all things, including sexual behaviour). Yet even fans admit that such representations have difficulty rising above stereotype (Chiana's character development is often critiqued along these lines).

Sexual innuendo might slip past the regulators, but open displays of homosexuality on screen attract criticism as well as praise. *Star Trek: Deep Space Nine*'s same-sex kiss between joined Trills Jadzia Dax and Lenara Khan in 'Rejoined' (4:5) is one example, though, as with the original series' interracial kiss, this was carefully 'justified' by the plot. (Joined Trills are a humanoid race who host long-lived symbionts. Jadzia, a regular character, hosts Dax. In this episode she meets Lenara, whose symbiont, Khan, was married to Torias, a male host of Dax, while joined with another body. Despite taboos against such relationships and based on the history of their symbionts, Jadzia and Lenara are strongly attracted to each other and share one kiss before agreeing to part. The 'lesbian' kiss is, therefore, displaced onto a historically 'heterosexual' relationship). On the other hand, viewers may develop subtextual or resistant readings that actively queer characters or relationships, as an abundance of slash fan fiction testifies. More self-conscious shows encourage such readings, witness *Buffy* creator Joss Whedon's often-quoted Bring Your Own Subtext invitation (cited in Saxey, 2001: 208). Glyn Davis states that in *Smallville* 'the friendship between Clark and Lex is ... fairly evidently homoeroticised' and suggests that such representations 'complement the overt representation of queer teens in the teen series' (Davis, 2004: 137). Regular viewers of *Xena: Warrior Princess* may have ridiculed the notion that Xena and Gabrielle's lesbian relationship was subtextual; by the end of the show's six-season run, it had become canonical to many.

Such readings are not, of course, restricted to cult television, though fan activity perhaps makes them more apparent. Television as a medium seems to lend itself to queering or otherwise disrupting the supposed 'male gaze' of cinema. The male in cult shows, as in current mainstream television, is just as

111

likely to be displayed openly as an object for the gaze as the female, whether this is via Clark Kent's too-tight shirts in *Smallville* or Angel's torture scenes in *Buffy*. Science fiction, gothic horror, and superhero narratives also tend to particular dress codes, frequently involving leather or Lycra and sometimes verging on fetish wear (like Scorpius' bodysuit in *Farscape*). Despite understandable reluctance to step too far outside of the usual conventions for representing sex, the overt spectacle of semi-clothed bodies, the outfits worn by attractive stars, the focus on relationship arcs, and the prevalence of self-consciousness or even camp, all mean that via a medium perceived to be mainstream because of its domesticity, cult television brings all kinds of potentially queer or resistant images directly into the home.

Representations of sex inevitably connect with representations of gender. Notions of appropriate coupling and 'good' sex affect representations of both femininity and masculinity. Biological essentialism is sometimes upheld by these fictions but is also challenged, not least by hybridisation of what were once identified as masculine or feminine genres, combining action and professional life with relationships and domesticity. The primacy of the white male hero has been questioned or, at the very least, recent cult shows focused on white male heroes tend to problematise these aspects of identity (see Jowett on *Angel* in this volume). Likewise, the postfeminist terrain of apparent freedom and equality for women has also been mapped, if mostly via white, middle class protagonists. Role reversal is common, with a range of female action heroes and sensitive, nurturing males in evidence. One of the forerunners here is the pairing in *The X-Files*, which presents the female Scully as logical, rational, and scientific and the male Mulder as impulsive, intuitive, and open to 'irrational' explanations. While the value of direct role reversal is questionable, such representation helps develop contemporary cult characters who no longer match up neatly to traditional gender roles or gendered characteristics. Even within the parameters of genre conventions, such characters maintain gender fluidity; indeed the vogue for generic hybridity may even encourage this.

In some senses, then, the representations of sex, gender, and race found in cult television are no different from those in other types of television. However, unconstrained by conventions of realism, the genre elements of cult allow greater scope for addressing these issues in speculative ways. Critically acclaimed cult television shows (such as the re-imagined *Battlestar Galactica* or *Heroes*), perhaps understandably, are often those that strive for aspects of realism in representation. Because these tend currently to revolve around characters and relationships, the focus is on identity constructed as an individual and is often directed to a mainstream audience (hence, perhaps, the primacy of sex or gender rather than race). The political nature of identity is rarely raised, or raised only in a disguised fashion, leaving the viewer either to applaud their own liberal reading of a particular story-arc or character, or to dismiss these as fantasy with no real foundation.

Yet the postmodern cult television text, which tends to be contradictory and unstable in all kinds of ways, is arguably an ideal vehicle for allowing viewers to recognise their own contradictory and unstable sense of who they are, whether this relates to sex, gender, or race. The blurring of boundaries in contemporary cult drama might work against a clear political context, but it also tends to deny traditional linear narrative and to work against a neat resolution. In this sense, the problem of identity is never solved, it remains fluid and contingent.

Recommended Reading

Battis, Jes (2007) *Investigating Farscape*. London and New York: I.B.Tauris.

Bernardi, Daniel Leonard (1998) *Star Trek and History: Race-ing Toward a White Future*. New Brunswick, NJ: Rutgers University Press.

Jowett, Lorna (2005) *Sex and the Slayer: A Gender Studies Primer for the Buffy Fan*. Middletown, CT: Wesleyan University Press.

Angel

(WB, 1999–2004)

Lorna Jowett

Angel's title character became a soulless vampire in 1753. Known as Angelus, he wreaked havoc for decades, until killing a gypsy girl led to a curse that returned his soul and, with it, his guilt for his evil deeds. It also stipulated that if he ever experienced perfect happiness, his soul would be removed again. Angel, as he now calls himself, seeks redemption by fighting evil. His soul is temporarily lost when he feels true happiness during sex with Buffy (in *Buffy the Vampire Slayer*) but is returned by magical means. This ends any hope that he and Buffy can have a normal relationship, however, and he moves to LA. Now the focus of a new spin-off show, Angel sets up an agency dedicated to 'helping the helpless', assisted by assorted regular characters (Wesley Wyndam-Pryce, Cordelia Chase, Charles Gunn, Winifred 'Fred' Burkle, Lorne, Doyle, and Spike).

This backstory alone demonstrates how cult television deals in complex stories about character and, therefore, with issues of identity. *Angel*'s fantasy vampires and demons can 'stand in for social issues', as Brian Wall and Michael Zryd point out (2001: 66). Thus as well as figuring Otherness via gender or sexuality, demons in *Angel* are sometimes deliberately constructed as ethnic groups, or slavery is displaced onto demon-human relations. Other episodes highlight racism and prejudice. 'You wouldn't get it. You're passing. ... You can walk down the street,' says one demon to another whose demon features are not always visible ('Hero', 1:9), as with vampires, who invariably 'pass' in *Buffy* and *Angel*.

Yet *Angel* also negotiates race via its characters such as the dead white European Angel or the street-smart black Gunn. While it may be difficult for white writers to render Gunn consistently convincing, the character does allow for a more 'realistic' commentary on race – that is, one situated in our world, rather than in fantasy. Gunn's overall arc can be read as assimilation, but the recognition that he must lose touch with his old neighbourhood when he starts work with Angel Investigations acknowledges that his world remains separate from that of white professionals.[2] Gunn also challenges traditional constructions of the hero as white, though both Angel and Wesley's whiteness is complicated by their identification as European.

Although the show does have fascinating regular female characters, *Angel* deals predominantly with masculinity: producer David Greenwalt says, '*Buffy* is about how hard it is to be a woman, and *Angel* is about how hard it is to be a man' (cited in Nazzaro, 2002: 158). Regular characters such as Angel, Doyle, Wesley, Gunn, Lorne, Connor, Spike, and Wolfram & Hart lawyer Lindsey McDonald offer a range of masculinities that develop in concert. *Angel* explores and develops male relationships via its mixture of action/horror/superhero/noir, from workplace relationship (Wesley, Gunn, Angel, Lorne) to friendship (Wesley and Gunn, Angel and Doyle), to rivalry (Angel and would-be nemesis Lindsey, Angel and Spike), to father-son conflict (Angel/us and his father, Wesley and his father, Angel and his son Connor). Wesley's gradual transformation from effete bumbling fool to competent demon fighter takes in comedy, action, and melodrama,[3] while Connor, as well as being Angel's troubled son, functions as a contrasting version of the vigilante superhero (just as the Groosalugg, a champion from another dimension, offers another take on the noble hero). Moreover, while Wesley, Gunn, and Lindsey struggle with human constructions of manhood, Angel, Spike, and Lorne face further challenges in constructing a version of masculinity that incorporates their Otherness as demons – as Cordelia says of Angel, they are literally 'not like other men' ('Carpe Noctem', 3:4).

Similarly, the show explores a range of sexualities from conventional workplace romance (Gunn and Fred, Wes and Fred, Angel and Cordelia) to more antagonistic and kinky relationships (Angel/us and Darla, Wesley and Lilah). Given concerns about taste and acceptability, much of the 'bad' sex is displaced onto 'bad' characters, as with Angel/us' history, or onto characters going 'dark', such as Wesley in season four. Even here the level of emotional realism can be high, demonstrating that relationships pose problems to both vampires and regular people alike. Yet the fantastic mode exaggerates situations, and heterosexual romance is dealt with via Angel's hyperbolic relationships with Buffy, Darla, and Cordelia, offering another twist on the impossibility of romantic/sexual fulfilment since the protagonist seems forbidden from consummation of his love. Even this is redeemed in the final season: Angel finally realises that most relationships will never offer perfect happiness, so he may as well enjoy the chances he has.

Angel is overtly sexualised because of the attention paid to his body, a now commonplace focus in other television shows, offering the male as spectacle and attraction for the viewer (Fig. 11.1). Here it also derives from horror and action, which have always focused on the body and its vulnerability. In *Angel*, this fascination with the physical and the un/controlled body is

115

Fig. 11.1   Male body as spectacle in Angel

carried through to sexuality because of the curse. In addition, the show uses vampirism as Otherness to question Angel's heterosexuality. Through all five seasons, runs a stream of assumptions made by minor characters that Angel is gay. His interactions with camp demon entertainer Lorne highlight this, and overt homoerotic elements underpin his sparring with both Lindsey and Spike. Angel spends three seasons of *Buffy* and most of *Angel* pining after unattainable blonde women, but the inclusion of vampire Spike in season five shows that his attraction to blondes may extend beyond heterosexuality, and their interactions veer between buddy movie and 'perfect couple' (Whedon, 2005).

While other 'quality' television dramas address changing masculine roles, few do so extensively within a genre context that draws on action and heroism and that directs attention emphatically to the body. Like other cult television, therefore, *Angel* continually uses genre and the fantastic as a means to expand the possibilities for representing sex, gender, and race.

Cylons/cyborgs in *Battlestar Galactica* (Sci-Fi Channel, 2003–2009)
Bronwen Calvert

When Ronald D. Moore and David Eick re-imagined the 1970s U.S. show *Battlestar Galactica* (ABC 1978–1979) for the twenty-first century, they included a wide variety of themes and issues for exploration. It has been noted that the show has 'no single political subtext. The show has all the subtexts at once' (Rogers 2006). And not just politics: there are storylines following justice, faith, and religious belief; there are strong female characters – including original characters Starbuck (Katee Sackhoff) and Boomer (Grace Park) re-imagined as women – along with narratives that reflect many preoccupations of post-9/11 America. Yet of all the re-imagined elements that have taken their place in the new *Battlestar Galactica* none is more potent than the reworking of Cylon mythology and the theme of embodiment. While, in the original series, the entities referred to as Cylons[4] were clearly artificial, non-human enemies, appearing as metal, mechanised humanoid shapes, in the new version of the series 'the Cylons look like us now'. Completely humanoid versions of the mechanised Cylons take a prominent place in the new narrative, troubling and subverting what it means to be 'human', a prominent theme within science fiction and cyborg theory.

Cyborg embodiment (as both theoretical concept and future possibility) is lauded by theorists such as Hans Moravec (1990), who posits a future in which the human body will become obsolete. Yet a key element of cyborg theory includes recognition of the limits of cyborg embodiment and the impossibility of separating human consciousness from human bodies (see, e.g., Morse, 1998; Hayles, 1999). Donna Haraway (1991) posits another kind of utopian vision in which the existence of the cyborg makes it possible to unite oppositions and erase difference between the organic and the mechanical or technological. In *Battlestar Galactica*, the humanoid Cylons are the latest of several 'models' which range from the raiders (small spaceships) and centurions (humanoid metal warriors) to the 'hybrids' (humanoids who control the Cylon Basestars). All of these fit the science-fiction concept of the cyborg body, which comprises an organic body overlaid with mechanical and/or cybernetic elements, enabling the cyborg to perform feats beyond human capabilities. However, while the mechanic or cybernetic aspects of Cylons are clearly shown in fight scenes, including battles in space, the newest form of Cylon embodiment places emphasis on the organic body. And while the

117

Cylons are presented as an implacable enemy, there is also emphasis on the ability of the new humanoid Cylons to 'pass' as humans, which ties in with the show's preoccupation with the themes of terrorism and racism.

The humanoid Cylons overturn the notion that the human body might be so improved upon that, as Moravec suggests, it can be discarded for a disembodied cybernetic future. These Cylons, so like humans that they can masquerade as humans and, on occasion, believe that they *are* humans, seem to have no wish to transcend embodiment. Paradoxically, the Cylons as presented in *Battlestar* both emphasise and erase difference, but this is a difference that remains located within an embodied self. Multiple copies exist of twelve 'models' of the humanoid Cylons. Like the other types of Cylon, this latest version is able to download consciousness into a new, identical body when an existing body dies. The copying and recopying of identity and embodiment recalls Walter Benjamin's notion of a 'work of art' copied until it loses the 'aura' of the original (although, in the case of the Cylons, no obvious original exists) (1969). Similarly, Jean Baudrillard outlines successive stages of simulation culminating in a stage at which no distinction exists between the artificial and the real ('the real is no longer real' [1988: 174]). This chimes with what occurs in *Battlestar* where Cylons are engaged in a battle of simulation – including multiple replica bodies and manufactured memories – against humans.

Despite the multiplicity of identical bodies, some Cylon models become highly individual characters as the show's narrative progresses. For example, Sharon Valerii known as 'Boomer', the sleeper agent on the Galactica, is distinct from the Sharon Valerii version known as 'Athena' who gives birth to a human/Cylon child. There are also many different versions of the 'Number Six' model including 'Caprica Six' who had a relationship with Gaius Baltar, Shelley Godfrey who tries to expose him as a traitor ('Six Degrees of Separation', 1:7), Gina Inviere who infiltrates the Pegasus (*Razor*), and Natalie the leader of the rebel Cylons ('Six of One', 4:2). The opposition between Cylon and human becomes steadily more blurred as the show progresses. Caprica Six and the resurrected Boomer attempt to disengage the Cylons from battle and to form a truce with humans ('Downloaded', 2:18, 'Lay Down Your Burdens, Part 2', 2:20); Natalie and the rebel Cylons ally with the Galactica against other Cylon models ('The Ties That Bind', 4:3). Athena combines the organic and the cybernetic when she uses her Cylon abilities to aid the Colonial fleet ('Flight of the Phoenix', 2:9, 'Lay Down Your Burdens, Part 1', 2:20), and the blurring of the human/Cylon opposition is evident when her unborn child's foetal blood cures President Laura Roslin's cancer ('Epiphanies', 2:13). Although they can download into a succession of replica bodies, Cylons are said to be unable to breed with each other[5] but can have children with humans, further disrupting the boundary between the organic and the technological ('The Farm', 2:5, 'Final Cut', 2:8, 'Downloaded').

With their distinct identities and memories, the humanoid Cylons become ever more indistinguishable from humans. Their cyborg bodies do not always appear to afford them much additional strength or power; and it is also revealed that Cylons can die as permanently as humans if the 'resurrection ship' containing their replica bodies is out of a certain download range. Thus, as the show continues and both humans and Cylons venture further from their home planetary system and from the resurrection ship, this particular difference is also eroded; with the destruction of the resurrection hub ('Revelations'), that difference is erased altogether. Just as Cylons become progressively more like humans, a parallel narrative strand sees humans losing touch with aspects of their humanity, for instance, morality, democracy, and justice. Evidence of this is seen on the battlestar Pegasus where violence, including rape as torture, becomes commonplace (see 'Pegasus', 2:10; 'Resurrection Ship, Part 1 and 2', 2:11–12). Along with this cult show's attention to political, religious, and philosophical debates and, of course, kick-ass action and spectacle, these conventions of science fiction enable engagement with broader questions about the nature of humanity, thus producing a combination of elements that continues to fascinate its fans.

Notes

1. See Johnson, 2005a: 77.
2. For more on Gunn and racial representation, see Meyer, 2005.
3. See Stacey Abbott on Wesley (Abbott, 2005a: 189–202).
4. The 'Cylons' of the original series were a reptilian race who created these metal beings as servants.
5. Although this is called into question when Caprica Six becomes pregnant with a child, fathered by Tigh ('Revelations', 4:10).

12 Boldly Going: Music and Cult TV

Janet K. Halfyard

Does music work in a distinct manner in cult TV? Labelling something as 'cult TV' tends on one hand to indicate the attitude of the fans, typically displaying extreme levels of loyalty and interest in the minutiae of all aspects of a programme, and on the other to position it as a complementary idea to mainstream. With their often complex and extended narrative arcs, and their frequent use of the monstrous as metaphor for the many and various problems that beset contemporary society, cult TV series require an engagement that is both imaginative (the willingness to engage with alternative realities as credible constructions) and thoughtful (the willingness to understand the process by which characters reach their moral decisions in scenarios that are often both challenging and completely outside the lived experience of the viewer). Cult TV has a tendency to engage with narrative ideas at a metaphorical and mythic level and as such, it is – certainly in narrative and moral terms – the avant-garde of TV. Cult TV is often not reassuring: it does not merely confirm our existing cultural values but challenges them and in doing so both reflects and acts to shape the way those values gradually change over time.

These then are some of the things that set cult TV apart from the mainstream in terms of narrative agendas and audiences, but the musical strategies that it employs also set it apart in some areas. To examine this fully requires an understanding of how music works in TV overall and, although a variety of writers over the last 20 years have set about theorising how music works in film, much less work has been done on a taxonomy of TV music, something I will now briefly attempt.

Looking at the range of televisual production, I can identify six basic categories of music in TV, noting that I have failed to find an example of TV that uses no music at all.

1. Opening title (and end credit) music.
2. Diegetic (source) music
3. Segue or link music
4. Instrumental scoring
5. Pre-existing popular music compilations as scoring
6. Any combination of the above five categories

On the surface, this is not too far removed from film music categories, but there are some important differences. Firstly, there are occasionally films which have no opening title music (or main title, as it is known filmically): they are unusual and invariably positioned as art films, such as *21 grams* (Alejandro González Iñárritu, U.S., 2003). Moreover, the opening of a film is a different kind of moment in a narrative/structural sense from a TV programme: designed to be watched in a cinema, where they are specifically the central and self-contained point of the viewing experience, films may simply drop the viewer straight into the story without a credit sequence at all, leaving all the production information for the end credits.[1] A TV show, on the other hand, positions each episode in a wider broadcast schedule, and so the need to delineate its opening and closing in a structural sense is much more pronounced. There may be programmes for which this is the only type of music normally found in the show, usually factual shows such as current affairs programmes like *Newsnight, Question Time,* and *Panorama* or the children's educational entertainment show *Blue Peter*.[2]

Some films may restrict themselves to opening/end credit music but then have no score: *The Asphalt Jungle* (John Huston, U.S., 1950) is a good example of this, with 'framing' music by Miklós Rósza but then nothing but diegetic music in the rest of the film.[3] Shows which, in addition to adding opening credit music, use diegetic music include factual programming such as pop music shows, variety and talent shows, and also fictional programmes, where it is used in much the same way as in film: someone somewhere in the diegetic world of the show has chosen to play this music, and it will often have some textual significance. Although they may not realise it, the musical choices of fictional characters are rarely arbitrary but are mechanisms through which writers and directors construct meaning either in relation to how a character is positioned or as a commentary on the narrative.

Although music is used to segue between scenes in both film and TV, softening the transition from one scene to the next, film has no true equivalent of the type of segue music found in shows such as *Friends, Will and Grace, The Fresh Prince of Bel Air,* or *Spin City*. What all these have in common is that they are filmed live in front of a studio audience and this effectively precludes the use of any form of underscore, both because of the logistical nightmare of attempting to cue music second by second to the visual action and because to add it afterwards would mean that the studio audience's experience of the show was substantively different from that of the television audience. The result is that a great deal of TV uses very little music compared to film and tends to use it specifically in the transition points between segments, which is as true of news programmes as it is of studio-based fictional ones.

Categories four and five of my taxonomy have precise parallels in film music and so are likely to be found in those TV programmes that most resemble film in terms of their production values: and this includes most of what is commonly referred to as quality television. Here, specially composed instrumental (in whatever idiom) or pre-existing popular music is used to create a non-diegetic underscore that interprets and paces the onscreen action in much the same way as it does in film. The final category simply allows for all the other categories to be used in combination. There is, however, one category of film music notably missing from this list, and that is the use of pre-existing classical music in the non-diegetic underscore, something relatively common in film scoring. In fact, classical music is almost entirely absent from the scoring strategies of television music in general and is most likely to occur in documentary and other factual programming but not in fictional TV. As I have discussed elsewhere, in American film narratives, classical music is generally used in relation to European characters (Halfyard, 2006). TV, perhaps because it is more firmly situated in domestic markets, generally engages less with the idea of Europe and Europeanness.

Turning to how music functions distinctively in cult TV, there is no single common strategy. The most obvious aspect that unites the various series that come under cult TV's aegis is that they tend to use a lot of music and they tend to use it in a way very close to the manner in which it is utilised in film. These are thematically driven, often 'orchestral' scores (even where TV budgetary constraints mean that the sound is produced on synthesisers rather than by a live band or orchestra); for some of them, a source of the thematic material is the series theme tune. However, this is nonetheless an area where cult TV differs from the filmic model it otherwise emulates. Firstly, a great many recent cult TV series do not use the theme tune as a major element of the episode scoring's thematic material: *Twin Peaks*, *Xena: Warrior Princess,* and *Hercules: The Legendary Journeys* do, while *Buffy the Vampire Slayer*, *Angel*, *Alias*, *Dark Angel*, *Supernatural*, *Heroes*, as well as the relaunched *Doctor Who* do not. This is a strategy that would be highly unusual in film scoring, where the main title often acts as an overture that establishes the major themes. Secondly, films are normally standalone narratives. Those that extend their narratives into a series of films (which, interestingly, are most likely to be in the same areas of fantasy that are common to cult TV) rarely go beyond a sequence of three or four films. Such series will frequently reuse the same theme established in the first film but, with some exceptions, the basic theme is reworked – reorchestrated and differently developed – for each subsequent main title cue and film. TV, on the other hand, normally reproduces its theme identically from one episode to the next and from one season to the next, often altering the visual title sequence to reflect narrative and character developments, but rarely altering the theme in any audible way. In this way, the theme tune itself is a fixed point that is central to the creation of a series identity, and this is particularly evident in much cult TV. Perhaps the clearest model for the consolidation of cult TV theme tunes and series identity is the *Star Trek* franchise, which uses common elements in the theme tunes of all the individual series apart from *Enterprise*. The musical identity of the franchise as it reinvented itself in the 1980s is firmly rooted in another musical model, that of Aaron Copland's distinctively 'American' sound, most notably in the brass and percussion fanfare of *Fanfare for the Common Man* (1942) and the early Western pioneer spirit of *Appalachian Spring* (1944).

What is most notable about *Enterprise* in relation to cult TV is its relatively unusual strategy of using a song for its theme tune and, therefore, as a central point of its series identity. Of all the programmes that fit under the very broad umbrella of cult TV, this is the least common strategy when choosing a series theme. In fact, it is a very common strategy in what might be loosely called 'soft cult', programmes which have a clear relationship to cult TV in terms of their premises, plots, and characters but which generally subscribe to more mainstream values, finding neat (sometimes trite) ways of resolving conflicts and only occasionally challenging the assumptions and values of the audience with alternative constructions of reality that jar with mainstream axioms of cultural normalcy. These include programmes such as *Charmed*, *Roswell*, *Smallville,* and *Veronica Mars*, where the central characters are generally firmly located in strong, largely conventional, functional family units and where the process of testing boundaries tends not to result in the central characters being lastingly damaged. That all these series use an existing song as their theme tune is also potentially part of the reassuring nature of the programmes. Songs function quite differently from instrumental themes and can be a very useful and productive scoring strategy, offering the audience a different type of engagement. The words of a song anchor the music in specific, articulated meaning. They work more on the conscious level of the mind than an instrumental theme does, and while these instrumental themes may contain a wealth of associations and cultural musical codes that allow us to hear the music as meaningful in relation to the visual image, we are not necessarily consciously articulating these to ourselves as we listen. A song does precisely that: as such, it can act to collapse the range of possible narrative meanings available to an audience into one specific meaning, the song acting as a commentary to a scene, such as 'Goodbye to You' at the end of *Buffy*'s 'Tabula Rasa' (6:8) or the songs which are used to close every episode of *The Sopranos* and *Queer as Folk*. These examples demonstrate how powerful a song can be in a score; but placing a song as the theme tune potentially over-anchors the meaning of the entire series. Particular types of music have strong cultural links to specific demographic groups, links which are fostered by the music industry as an aspect of how music is positioned within the marketplace. Young people, in particular, are encouraged to develop their sense of identity in relation to particular types of music, to find a space for themselves within an identifiable musical brand. The mechanisms by which music then comes to be placed within TV shows contribute to the overall, market-led synergy: targeting a specific audience for a particular show leads to popular musical choices that further reinforce the attachment between show, music, and audience, something likely to be particularly pronounced when a popular song is closely tied to the overall series identity by placing it in the opening credits.

This may well have caused the problem that *Enterprise* encountered: there was nothing which obviously suggested that Russell Watson and/or Rod Stewart were singers whom fans of *Star Trek* were likely to list among their musics of choice, with the result that the song was simply insufficiently appealing to the *Star Trek* fan base for them to collectively identity with it; instead, many appear to have felt alienated by a music that apparently betrayed the franchise's Copland-esque identity, replacing it with something that intruded too much and too ineffectively into the already well-defined musical space of the franchise and its fans.[4]

It is likely that any song would have failed to be greeted warmly by *Star Trek*'s fans: musically, the post-1980 series were simply too bound up in their apparently timeless (certainly not futuristic) classical orchestral sound world, from the 'cowboys galloping across the prairies of space' theme of *The Next Generation*[5] to the sophisticated cross-rhythms of *Deep Space Nine* and the sheer lyric elegance of *Voyager*, with the result that the pop song came across as too specifically temporally located in contemporary pop music culture. Another space-based cult TV programme did, meanwhile, successfully use a song as its theme, but with significant differences that both account for its success and point to the ways that cult is able to move the boundaries of musical practice in TV.

The series was Joss Whedon's short-lived *Firefly*, which took the same premise of space travellers as the futuristic equivalents of early American pioneers and settlers underlying other space-based narratives such as *Star Trek* but explored it in a much more overt way, at the same time introducing a North/South U.S. Civil War dimension into the cowboy mix. The music is highly original in several ways: the song is not a pop song but a quirky, almost awkward ballad in a bluegrass/country style that in no way presents any clear indicator of the musical genre's current target demographic in the commercial world of music marketing. If it points to anything, it points to the past: the song comes across as archaic, idiosyncratic, and more field-recording than marketable single. It, therefore, positions itself less in relation to the potential audience and more in relation to the narrative, and here lies its difference and its success. The music at the top of a TV show needs to do at least one of two things: inform the audience as to the genre of the show they are about to watch and/or indicate whether this is a show that the individual viewer is likely to want to see. To use a crass example, a middle-class English grandmother turning on her television and hearing a show that opens with the strident techno of *Queer as Folk* is likely to change channels before the programme even begins: the music has

125

told her everything she needs to know both generically and personally. Popular music performs both of these two functions effectively but performs the second function more effectively than orchestral scoring. Orchestral scoring, using the 'default classical' idiom of film, performs the first function very well, informing us about the narrative's genre, but performs the second less well as it does not come with the same kind of culturally loaded 'baggage' that governs how we identify with and respond to music in a film or TV context. Instead it functions on the basis that it will draw all viewers into the same set of interpretations and responses (which Anahid Kassabian, in a suitably *Star Trek*-like theorisation, describes as an *assimilating* identification, compared to the more individualised *affiliating* identifications produced by popular music [2001]).

Firefly's song may be popular music rather than classical scoring but, although its idiom is still generally identifiable as some subset of 'country' (so pointing culturally to the American South and/or to the Wild West), its distance from familiar contemporary popular idioms and genres means that for a large part of the audience it works more like orchestral scoring: the relative obscurity of the musical genre means that it will tend not to produce affiliating identifications among audiences but instead will tend to assimilate us all into a single reading of its meanings. Another important feature here is that it was specially composed for the show by Whedon rather than being an existing song, as is the case with almost all uses of songs as themes in other TV programmes.[6] This provides the song with an additional level of significance that makes it far more likely that the audience will accept it as part of Whedon's overall auteurist vision of *Firefly*'s universe, adding to the cult-ness of the show rather than detracting from it as seems to have been the case with *Enterprise*.[7] The result of the song being specially composed in an old-fashioned, non-mainstream musical genre is that it is able to perform the referential narrative function of classical scoring. However, at the same time, it combines the visual images of the opening credits with the song's lyrics to communicate ideas of loss and defiance alongside juxtapositions of horses and spaceships. With quite remarkable economy, the series' musical and visual opening sequence establishes a detailed and specific sense of how the U.S. past acts as both metaphor and structure within an apparently futuristic narrative.

A more recent development in cult TV main titles is the disappearance of the theme tune, an altogether more radical strategy in relation to any TV programme. An early example of this is the first season of *Alias*, where the title sequence was remarkably brief – less than 30 seconds – and consisted entirely of white words played against a black screen accompanied by thematically very limited techno music, at a point where a normal opening sequence was highly visual and generally lasted around a minute. Later seasons of *Alias* expanded the title sequence considerably, introducing first multiple images of Sydney/Jennifer Garner and later images of the entire ensemble cast, so *Alias*, in this respect, became gradually more conventional. Nonetheless, the idea of effectively omitting the title sequence is something that is becoming quite common in cult TV. *Heroes*, *Supernatural*, *Pushing Daisies,* and *Eli Stone* all have opening titles that entirely omit any credits and simply present the title of the series with a brief instrumental flourish in sequences lasting less than six seconds. This is an overtly filmic gesture, as mentioned above, and marks a significant move away from the centrality of the series' musical theme in establishing the series identity. As a strategy, it replaces this as an overt process with something more open-ended that encourages a sense of ambivalence – and moral ambivalence is a narrative idea that is central to all these series.

Cult TV explores other musical areas generally avoided by the mainstream. Although classical music is still generally rare, it nonetheless uses it much more (and much more interestingly) than other fictional TV, such as the uses of and references to opera in *Star Trek* (both Klingon and Italian), *Buffy,* and *Queer as Folk* (which also makes breathtaking use of the sixteenth-century Latin motet 'Parce mihi Domine' in the final episode of its first season). It plays with ideas of music and dance – such as the *Hercules* episode '... And Fancy Free' (4:8), which alludes throughout to *Strictly Ballroom*, and Emmett's *West Side Story* and Tchaikovsky fantasies in *Queer as Folk* – and experiments with singing in surreal and fascinating ways, such as the demon karaoke bar of *Angel* and the musical episodes of *Xena* ('The Bitter Suite', 3:12) and *Buffy* ('Once More, with Feeling', 6:7). Any one of these areas could (and no doubt eventually will) provide ample material for other discussions of music in cult TV. There are no absolute rules in the way cult TV uses music, but there is a clear and continual process of invention and innovation.

Recommended Reading

Halfyard, Janet K. (2001) 'Love, death, curses and reverses (in F minor): music, gender and identity in *Buffy the Vampire Slayer* and *Angel*', *Slayage: The Online International Journal of Buffy Studies* (1:4). Available at http://www.slayageonline.com.

Kassabian, Anahid (2001) *Hearing Film: Tracking Identifications in Contemporary Hollywood Cinema.* New York and London: Routledge.

Negus, Keith and John Street (2002) 'Introduction to "Music and Television" Special Issue', *Popular Music* (21:3), 245–248.

Notes

1. The result is that film end credits are sometimes extraordinarily long (seven minutes is quite normal), while TV end credits tend to be relatively brief.

2. As a British writer, my examples will all be of programmes that show on British channels and while there are a large number of fictional shows among U.S. imports, there are relatively few factual and current affairs programmes. I therefore have a more limited knowledge of how music works in such programmes in other countries.

3. Diegetic or source music is music that can be heard by the characters. It may issue from a CD player or television somewhere in the scene or be played or sung by a character, but it is real to the characters as it is to the audience, unlike underscore or non-diegetic music which is only audible to the audience.

4. The various online message boards and chatrooms of the *Star Trek* fan community were alive with negative reactions to the music when the show first aired in 2001.

5. This theme started life as Jerry Goldsmith's main title for *Star Trek: The Motion Picture* (1979).

6. A notable exception to this rule is the use of specially composed songs for Australian soap operas.

7. My thanks to Stacey Abbott for drawing out this point.

Part 3

Constructing Cult TV: The
Broadcast Industry and
Cult Television

13 The *Star Trek* Franchise

Lincoln Geraghty

tar Trek is the epitome of cult television. From its very inception as a
short-run, late sixties science-fiction serial to it becoming a worldwide
syndicated series with four spin-offs and ten feature films (with one more on
the way), the mother of all television franchises has gained a multinational
fanbase devoted to its utopian ethos. Aside from giving us the television series
and films, *Star Trek* has successfully crossed over into other related media
and popular culture forms including novels, comics, computer games, toys
and merchandise, conventions, collectibles and memorabilia, the Las Vegas
Experience, world Exhibition tours, the Internet, and music. Within these
disparate areas, the franchise continues to attract fans while maintaining its
connection to Gene Roddenberry's vision of how the future could and should
be. The television series or the marketing and entertainment ephemera,
whether related to space stations or starships and whether set in the future
or in the past, are all part of Roddenberry's tradition. This means that the
entire franchise, including all five series and ten feature films, can be looked
at as one – as a gestalt entity greater than the sum of its parts.

The original series lasted three seasons, from 1966 to 1969; after a second
letter campaign failed to save it, the fans were left to rewatch the 79 episodes
on syndicated television. The series narrowly survived cancellation in 1967
when fans organised a letter campaign to 'Save *Star Trek*'. The response was
long thought to be a spontaneous campaign organised by hard-core fans
such as Bjo Trimble. Co-authors Henry Jenkins and John Tulloch described
these contemporary mythic accounts as contradictory in that 'their focus
on the intensity of the audience's commitment to the programme displaces
the established mechanisms by which NBC and other networks measured
audience response: the Nielsen Ratings' (Jenkins and Tulloch, 1995: 9). As
identified by Jenkins and Tulloch, far from being a 'spontaneous uprising of
average television viewers', many of the letter writers were hardened science-
fiction authors and readers who had a history in American science-fiction
fandom (10). Roddenberry was well aware of how he could use these fans
and their letters as a tactic to strategically harass the network to renew the
series and indeed bring it back as a movie in 1979. The ten-year period after
Star Trek's cancellation was a defining moment both in franchise history and
in the history of cult television. More and more fans started to watch the series
for the first time in the early seventies, expecting a supply of new episodes

when the 79 ran out. During this period, fans began to write and distribute fanzines and organise conventions to contact fellow enthusiasts. The first convention was held in New York in 1972. Fans could write stories and for the first time meet up with other fans from around the country (soon to be from around the world) to discuss their favourite episodes and buy merchandise. Out of this growing fan culture grew a renewed call for more *Star Trek*; what was originally going to be a second series starring most of the original cast became *Star Trek: The Motion Picture* (Robert Wise, U.S., 1979), released as a big-budget movie to counteract and benefit from the hype created by *Star Wars* (George Lucas, U.S., 1977). During the early eighties, the almost yearly film versions of *Star Trek* kept fans absorbed and helped the franchise remain ever-present in the media. The only thing that was missing was a weekly series on television.

In 1987, Roddenberry, acting as executive producer, introduced fans to *Star Trek: The Next Generation* (*TNG*). This series was initially received with some trepidation because fans were unhappy that a new crew was aboard the famous Enterprise; however, it would run until 1994 when it eventually jumped to the big screen and spawned four movie sequels. *TNG* was the embodiment of glossy American science-fiction of that period. New ships, sets, uniforms, and alien characters breathed life into a well-loved yet marginalised franchise. Its success in maintaining a mainstream audience without the backing of a major network intimated that audiences wanted more series that offered weekly snapshots of distant worlds and intergalactic exploration. Although distinctly *Star Trek* in its ethos, the new series differed in many ways from the original, which was entirely located in a Cold War context and was influenced by a distinctive 1960s visual aesthetic. Whereas the original replicated the New Frontier philosophy of John F. Kennedy through the figure of Captain Kirk, *TNG*'s Captain Jean-Luc Picard (played by Patrick Stewart) represented a more reserved kind of diplomacy. Most episodes focused on the relationships between crew members. After seven seasons, this meant that the fans had become very familiar and attached to individuals, with some characters such as Troi, Riker, LaForge, Crusher, and Worf also having families introduced in storylines to help flesh out their back stories. The android Data offered huge scope in stories dealing with humanity and notions of mortality; episodes devoted to his character mirrored attempts by Gene Roddenberry to discuss the human condition through Spock, albeit in far more detail.

In 1993, *Star Trek: Deep Space Nine* (*DS9*) started its run. Contrary to the continued adventures of the original and new Enterprise, *DS9* was set on a space station. Producers broke the mould by having an African-American actor play the lead role and it offered a third dynamic setting in which a core group of characters could meet and become a close-nit family: '*DS9* bears a striking resemblance to a soap opera since it incorporates narrative structures very similar to those used in soap television such as complicated and involved character back-stories and interwoven story arcs, plus the highly developed historical [*Star Trek* mythos]' (Geraghty, 2007: 134). Even without Roddenberry's involvement – he died in 1991 – *DS9* continued to espouse the original series' themes of utopianism and self-improvement within a supportive community. It did not remain standalone for long as the fourth *Star Trek* series, *Star Trek: Voyager* (1995–2001), hit TV screens with a female captain of the eponymous ship. Returning to familiar format of exploring space, *Voyager* encountered mixed reviews on its seven-year run; many fans welcomed the conflicting characterisation of femininity onboard the starship (between Captain Janeway and Seven-of-Nine) but others grew tired of the constant rehashing of old plots and storylines (including the constant reappearance of The Borg). Such rehashing would reach its zenith with *Star Trek: Enterprise* (2001–2005), where the series revelled in depicting events and characters previously established in the famous 'future history' of the *Star Trek* universe. The new ship and crew were the pioneering forerunners to Kirk's first five-year mission screened in 1966, only this time fans would get to see how the Federation and humankind first encountered the popular and important Vulcan and Klingon species. Following another campaign to stave off cancellation in 2004, the series finally came to an end after only four seasons. *Star Trek*'s status as most popular science-fiction TV is under threat as series such as *Lost* and *Battlestar Galactica* attract new cult fans who eagerly anticipate new plot twists and story arcs on Internet blogs and discussion boards. What's more, some consider the darker and more paranoid tone of newer series to be more appropriate for television post 9/11.

Whether or not the series remains what it once was, the format of *Star Trek*, as a long-running and potentially infinite television series, proved a highly suitable vehicle through which stories based on common science-fiction narratives such as space or time travel, alien contact, or alternate worlds could be screened. The potential to attract devoted cult TV followers increases as series grow in narrative complexity and introduce more characters: 'Seriality, textual density, and, perhaps most especially, the nonlinearity of multiple time frames and settings that create the potentially infinitely large metatext of a cult television text create the space for fans to revel' (Gwenllian-Jones and Pearson, 2004b: xvii). As a cult series *Star Trek* provided its fans a taxonomic and labyrinthine universe in which they could and still can immerse themselves. The mythos, its narrative future history, is used even as a positive blueprint or life template for a number of fans who have encountered particular hardships such as divorce, war, illness, bereavement, and disability. The stories and characters have captured imaginations and offered life lessons based on the reworking and retracing of human history – albeit an American version of history: 'In effect, the series have mapped out a chronology within which fans can further engross themselves, a fictional universe complete with its own documented history ripe for Jenkins' [textual poachers]' (Geraghty, 2007: 33).

Perhaps the huge success of the *Star Trek* franchise is attributable to the utopian ideals espoused by Roddenberry over 40 years ago. As a form of political and historical allegory, all five series have been praised for the part they have played in providing social commentary; even those who doubt the legitimacy and cultural impact of television's first interracial kiss between Kirk and Uhura in the 1968 episode 'Plato's Stepchildren' (3:12) credit *Star Trek* for offering a different view of what the world could become if racism and prejudice were overcome. Some critics believe it is too hard a task that the 'franchise could ever be convincingly reduced to one coherent and comprehensive "reading"' (Hills, 2004b: 197), yet this has not stopped countless academics and cultural observers from trying to offer a definitive explanation for *Star Trek*'s popularity and place amongst the cult TV elite. For sure there are multiple different readings of the television and film texts, and there are equally plenty of studies which concentrate on the various audiences and cult fan practices concurrent to the whole franchise, but despite the varied foci and interpretations all these analyses intimate that *Star Trek* has a life outside of the television set, free from the constraints and changing trends of contemporary broadcasting. Although *Star Trek* is a product of American network television and, as a franchise, is consumed and enjoyed by millions of people who would not consider themselves 'die hard' fans, it maintains its cult status because it has gone beyond the very public forum of its medium. Its fictional narrative and universe has the potential to offer its fans a very private and personal experience, separate from the lucrative franchise aspects.

Reflecting on the various self-confessed experiences, memories, and actions of the fans, I would argue that the *Star Trek* franchise can be characterised by the necessary function of Matt Hills' idea of 'affective play' and its fans' imagined subjectivity rather than through the tropes of the science-fiction genre and the textual parallels to U.S. history and politics. Affective play 'deals with the emotional attachment of the fan' and 'suggests that play is not always caught up in a pre-established "boundedness" or set of cultural boundaries, but may instead imaginatively create its own set of boundaries and its own auto-"context"' (Hills, 2002: 112). The fans' relationship with the fictional text – that which is created and sustained in the collecting of merchandise, buying of repackaged DVDs, attending conventions, interacting with networks and communities on the Internet – is more important than the actual text itself. The interrelated, constantly expanding universe of *Star Trek* is a playground for testing personal identity, improving social relations, and acquiring subcultural capital. The series and related cultural ephemera are reread and appropriated within the contexts of contemporary life experienced by fans using new media technologies such as the Internet to connect with fellow enthusiasts in the *Star Trek* community, competing with each other over their grasp of trivia and sharing their thoughts on how it has impacted on their lives.

14 Cult TV and the Television Industry

Catherine Johnson

I t is perhaps paradoxical to include in this book on cult television (that is, programmes that have generated fan audiences) a chapter from the perspective of the television industry. Perhaps one of the defining features of a cult text is that it becomes a cult through its context of reception rather than through its context of production. It is not possible to produce a cult text. Ultimately texts can attain the status of a cult only through the activities of their fans. Yet, this does not mean that one cannot offer an industrial history of cult television. In fact, as cult television becomes an increasingly important feature of the contemporary television landscape, it becomes pressing to examine the reasons why the television industry's attitudes towards cult television and fan audiences have changed.

The history of cult television from an institutional perspective is quite different from the history of television programmes that have gained fan followings. From its early years television programmes generated fan audiences. However, between the 1940s and the 1970s, the notion of cult television was not culturally dominant and was certainly not a concept of particular significance to the television industry. It is only over the 1980s that the concept of cult television began to gain significance to the television industry and with this shift the place and nature of cult television changed. This chapter will examine these changes and offer a history of cult television from the perspective of the television industry. In doing so, it will focus on the case of television drama and will look primarily at the US. This is not to suggest that other forms of television (and in particular sport) do not attract fan audiences and cannot be understood within an industrial history of cult television. However, televised sport has quite a different status from televised drama. In particular, sport on television is the transmission of an event created elsewhere and relayed through television. By contrast, drama is largely produced specifically for television. As such, the case of drama is particularly revealing for understanding the ways in which broadcasters have changed their production practices over time. It is this shift in production practices which has had such an impact on cult television and which has ultimately altered its status within the industry from insignificance to an important strategy in an increasingly competitive and fragmented marketplace.

Pre-cult Television and the Importance of Syndication: The Case of *Star Trek*

It may seem strange to propose *Star Trek* as an example of pre-cult television. The series has generated an active and vociferous fan following since its initial broadcast in the US in the second half of the 1960s, and it has subsequently been the subject of numerous studies of the active fan, making it a seemingly clear example of a cult text. Yet within its context of production *Star Trek* is quite different from the cult television of more recent years, such as *Buffy the Vampire Slayer*. In fact, when *Star Trek* originally aired in the US (and in the UK) 'cult television' was not a particularly widespread concept. Rather, television was understood, within both the industry in particular and society in general, as a mass medium, a medium of nation-building, a medium that brought people together. The idea of 'cult' television, with its connotations of exclusivity and specialness, would seem to run counter to the aims of television broadcasters at this time to produce programmes that appealed to consensus national audiences. Whether in the UK context of public service broadcasting, where television had a specific remit to address the British public as one nation, or in the US, where the three national networks fought to gain the highest ratings for their programmes, a primary aim for television broadcasters in the 1960s and the 1970s was to attract mass audiences for their programming, particularly in prime time. It was not uncommon at this time for successful prime time terrestrial programmes in the UK to gain audiences of over 20 million viewers, and prime time networked US programmes to gain audiences of up to 90 million (Brown, 1998: 155).[1]

In the 1960s and 1970s, while in the UK, competition for ratings was muted by the public service requirements of the BBC and ITV, in the US high audience figures were essential for the success of a network. By the mid-1950s there were three national networks broadcasting in the US: NBC, CBS, and ABC. These three networks had an oligopoly on national broadcasting and competed fiercely for audiences. Audience ratings determined the amount that a network could charge for an advertising spot. The highest-rated programme in a time slot could earn 50 per cent more than the programme rated third in the same time slot. The network that came top of the average ratings could consequently make $20–30 million more than its closest competitor, and ratings also affected the price of the network's shares on the stock market (Brown, 1998: 154). This funding model had a direct impact on programme production. The networks wanted to commission those programmes that would rate the highest and that would compete most effectively for audiences against the other networks. One common strategy for this was to attract audiences with variations on existing successes, attempting to create something 'similar but different' to existing network fare. *Star Trek* is a clear example of this strategy. Roddenberry sold the idea of *Star Trek* to NBC as much as a re-working of the Western genre as an example of television science fiction. The Western genre had been particularly successful on US prime time television over the late 1950s and early 1960s. However, by 1965 the genre was in decline with the number of Westerns on network television in prime time reduced from 31 in 1959 to 7 in 1964 (Newcomb, 1997: 289). Roddenberry pitched *Star Trek* as '*Wagon Train* to the stars', offering to re-invigorate the once-successful Western genre by transposing it into the setting of a futuristic space voyage at a time when episodic fantasy and space voyage series were not common on US television.[2] The programme, therefore, took a successful genre (the Western) that was beginning to lose it freshness and invigorated it by drawing on elements of the science fiction genre. This combination also avoided some of the elements of science fiction that the network feared would alienate audiences. In particular, NBC's research indicated that science fiction did not appeal to female viewers. As a consequence, in the production and marketing of *Star Trek* they placed a clear emphasis on the construction of believable and appealing characters over futuristic or scientific technology, specifically attempting to widen the appeal of the programme to the broadest possible audience (see Johnson, 2005a).

To some extent the network's strategy with *Star Trek* was a success, and the programme certainly proved popular with both female and male viewers. However, the programme failed to gain the large audiences that the network expected of a prime time series. Its first episode gained a respectable rating of 19.8 per cent and a 40.6 per cent share, but the series was not able to sustain these figures, falling regularly below a 30 per cent share (NBC's measure of a successful series) and finishing 52nd among all series in its first season (Pounds, 1999).[3] In its second season, it was moved from its Thursday evening slot to a Friday evening slot where another action/fantasy show, *The Man from UNCLE*, had rated well. However, audience numbers continued to decline and after another move in the schedules for its third season the show was cancelled. The fan audience for *Star Trek* did complain about the series' cancellation and some have claimed that the letter campaign mounted by fans at the end of its second season saved the show from cancellation at that point (see Tulloch and Jenkins, 1995: 8–10, and Whitfield and Roddenberry, 1991: 345–347). Yet the presence of a vociferous and active fan audience was not enough to keep the show on air. Without the high ratings expected of a prime time series, *Star Trek* was potentially losing the network money, preventing it from being able to charge the prices for its advertising slots that a higher-rated show would allow.

In most instances, *Star Trek* would have then disappeared from our screens. For a series to be picked up for syndication (and hence for re-runs on non-network channels), it would need to have run to at least 100 episodes and *Star Trek* was cancelled after only 79 episodes had been made. Without syndication, *Star Trek* was unlikely to be repeated and would probably have emerged a few decades later in nostalgia shows as a vaguely remembered moment in television history. It is possible that its existing fan audience would have kept the series alive through fan fiction and other fan activities and may have been able to encourage the network to bring the show back when fantasy television had a revival in the 1990s. Yet, speaking of a time before the home video recorder, it is important to stress the significance of syndication for the longevity of a programme. Without syndication it would have been impossible for viewers to have re-watched episodes of the programme, effectively removing the possibility for audiences to experience and re-experience the show. This is particularly significant when one considers the importance of re-watching to fan activities and to the initiation of new fans.

The unusual story of *Star Trek*'s successful syndication despite having only 79 episodes points to some of the reasons why cult television would go on to be so important to network television in the US over the subsequent years. Kaiser Broadcasting took the unusual step of negotiating the syndication rights for *Star Trek* in 1967 during its first season and two years before the series was cancelled. Their interest in *Star Trek* as a show for syndication stemmed from their status as a non-national broadcaster that could not hope to compete with the national networks for audiences in prime time. Therefore, they developed a strategy of differentiation, offering alternatives to the programming provided by the national networks at specific times of the day. Rather than scheduling *Star Trek* against other action-adventure drama series, they placed it against their competitors' news programmes at 6 pm and ran the series daily, rather than weekly, repeating the entire series a number of times. *Star Trek* was particularly suited to such a strategy, and although it failed to gain a large enough mass audience to satisfy the national networks, it performed perfectly for the syndication market in the 1960s and the 1970s.[4] The regulatory changes to syndication introduced in 1970 further boosted the syndication market. The Financial Interest and Syndication Rule (known as the fin-syn rule) prevented the networks from engaging in domestic syndication (that is, from selling or distributing networked programmes to local stations after their initial network run) or owning the programmes that they aired. This significantly opened up the syndication market, and its consequent growth over the 1970s certainly contributed to the elevation of *Star Trek* to cult status by providing a wide and profitable market through which it (and other series) could be re-run over the decade. In particular, the fin-syn rule enabled production companies to retain the syndication rights to the programmes that they produced, vastly increasing the potential profits that they could make from programme production.[5]

The strategy adopted by Kaiser Broadcasting with the syndication of *Star Trek* was one of niche marketing. They knew that they could not gain the large audiences of the networks and so wanted their programming to serve a different function from the networks' programmes. While the networks were chasing large audiences regardless of their demographics, Kaiser Broadcasting (and other syndication outlets) favoured programmes that generated loyal viewers and repeat viewing. The two qualities that made *Star Trek* successful in syndication are the two qualities that Matt Hills (2002) has associated in particular with cult media texts – hyperdiegesis and an endlessly deferred narrative. *Star Trek*'s narrative is based on the central and endless question of what lies beyond the Earth in the far reaches of space. This narrative question is effectively open-ended (even if each episode brings its narrative to a close), allowing space for audience interpretation and engagement. Over and above this, *Star Trek*'s futuristic fictional world is highly distinctive (both visually and aurally), densely imagined, and only partially revealed within the series' 79 episodes. This hyperdiegetic fictional world offers a trusted, coherent, and safe space for creative speculation on the part of the fan. These textual attributes that Hills argues are characteristic of fan texts, invite viewer participation in the text, and reward repeat viewing. Although these were qualities not particularly sought by the US national networks in the 1960s, they were ones that were particularly suited to the scheduling and viewing patterns of syndication which were based on repetition and familiarity. However, as the industry changed over the next two decades, these attributes would become increasingly favoured, not just in the syndication market but also in the national networks.

From Consensus Television to Niche Television

The first change within the US television industry that has led to the shifting fortunes of cult television is the rise of interest in demographics. Over the late 1960s and early 1970s, advertisers sought more detailed information about the audiences for television programmes and became increasingly interested in the kinds of viewers tuning in to particular programmes. While they still wanted to buy advertising slots within those programmes gaining the largest ratings, they were also keen on selling to those audience members most likely to purchase their goods. The kinds of viewers most likely to buy the goods advertised on television were reasonably affluent, well-educated, urban, 18–49-year-old consumers. Advertisers became increasingly interested in programmes that appealed to this particular demographic bracket, and the networks shifted their programme production accordingly. For example, in the early 1970s CBS transformed its sitcom production from rural comedies such as *The Beverley Hillbillies* to urban comedies (often with young female leads), such as *The Mary Tyler Moore Show* and *All in the Family.* This shift has been understood as the emergent point for 'quality television', television produced specifically to appeal to an up-market audience likely to be interested in purchasing the kinds of products advertised on television (see Feuer et al., 1984). Yet at this point in the history of US television, brute ratings still remained central, and a show appealing to the quality demographic but failing to gain large ratings was still unlikely to remain on air.

The first indication that this strategy might be shifting came in the early 1980s with the production of *Hill Street Blues*, where significantly ratings were not the driving force in determining the programme's fate. Produced by MTM, the same production company that had made a name with quality sitcoms and dramas such as *The Mary Tyler Moore Show* and *Lou Grant*, *Hill Street Blues* was a cop drama that made extensive use of an ensemble cast and multiple, interweaving, and continuous storylines. The series did not rate well in its first season, yet it was a critical success gaining excellent reviews and numerous Emmy nominations and awards.[6] Rather than cancelling the series, NBC commissioned a second season which went on to gradually draw in an audience through word of mouth by viewers aware of the critical hype behind the series. Although the ratings for *Hill Street Blues* were never huge (the series never made it into the top-20 rated shows in its seven-year history, peaking at number 21 in its third season), it did generate a regular, loyal audience and continued critical success. Significantly, the series also attracted a valuable audience demographic. As Paul Kerr states,

> *Hill Street Blues*, for all its relatively low status in the overall ratings, actually rates first among men of all prime-time programmes in the crucial consumer category of 18–49 year-olds, as well as rating third among women in the same age group. (Kerr, 1984: 157)

The series' popularity with urban viewers was also valuable for NBC. Not only did advertisers prefer urban viewers (who were more likely to buy their products), but also the five stations that NBC owned were all in large cities. Although NBC lagged behind in the national ratings, its flagship station WNBC-TV, based in the largest and richest market in the US in New York City, ranked first in prime time in 1983 (Kerr, 1984). Finally, *Hill Street Blues* also performed well in homes with cable (most of which were based in urban locations). As the threat of cable began to loom in the early 1980s, this made the series an attractive offering to NBC.

The case of *Hill Street Blues* points to a gradual shift that was taking place in the US television industry at a time when the demographic make-up of the audience was becoming as important (if not more) as the brute ratings that a show might generate. *Hill Street Blues* had many of the attributes one would associate with cult television. It was overtly different from cop shows on air at the time; it was discovered by loyal audiences who appreciated its difference and spread interest in the show through word of mouth. However, while the network did allow *Hill Street Blues* to gradually build up an audience, the series was not deliberately constructed and promoted as a cult show. Rather the network took the relatively unusual step of taking a risk and hoping that the series' critical praise would generate an audience for its second season. This risk was bolstered by the particular demographics that the programme attracted and by the critical success it continued to receive. In fact, it was not until the early 1990s that the US networks actively attempted to create television programmes specifically targeted at fan audiences, and this emerged largely because of the next shift in the industry – increased competition from cable, satellite, and new national networks.

While cable and satellite channels had started to gain some success in the early 1980s when *Hill Street Blues* was produced, the networks still retained their oligopoly on national broadcasting. Yet this was soon to change. The first half of the 1980s saw the deregulation of cable television and the end of anti-monopoly regulations in the telecommunications industry. These changes enabled conglomerate takeovers of the three national networks and allowed new media conglomerates to enter network television broadcasting for the first time in 30 years (see Barnouw, 1990 and Balio, 1998). This effectively signalled the end of the three-network oligopoly that had dominated US television from the mid-1950s. In 1986, Rupert Murdoch's News Corporation media conglomerate bought the Metromedia group and developed it into a fourth national network which started broadcasting in 1986 and became profitable by 1989. Other media conglomerates followed suit with the WB and UPN networks emerging in 1995. The emergence of new networks, combined with the rise of cable and satellite television, significantly fragmented the US television industry. While in the 1960s the three national networks commanded around 90 per cent of the total television audience, by the 1990s this had been reduced to around 60 per cent (Caldwell, 1995: 11). The national networks could no longer hope to gain the large mass audiences that they had competed for in the 1960s and 1970s, leading to a shift in the way that the networks measured the popularity and success of their programmes. The networks could no longer regularly deliver audiences of 70–90 million to advertisers, and so they shifted to a strategy of niche marketing, producing programmes targeted to specific audience groups that would be attractive to particular advertisers. Economic profitability no longer resided in the total number of viewers tuned into a particular programme but increasingly depended on the type of viewer watching, so that the price for advertising spots within network programmes came to be measured by audience demographics rather than by brute ratings. These changes led to a shift from consensus television, based on creating programmes to appeal to the largest possible audience, to niche television concerned with attracting specific audience segments that are desirable to both networks and advertisers.

141

Within this new era of niche television, the fan audience emerged as an attractive audience segment. Fans are loyal viewers who watch and re-watch episodes of their favourite programmes (as the success of *Star Trek* in syndication demonstrated). Fans are also consumers of ancillary products associated with their favourite shows. The new networks such as Fox and WB were owned by media conglomerates with a number of holdings in different media companies. A successful show that appealed to a fan audience could generate additional income for the conglomerate through the sale of ancillary merchandise produced by the conglomerate's other media holdings. An early example of this new strategy can be seen with the television series *The X-Files*. *The X-Files* was produced by the Fox network. When Fox started broadcasting in 1986, it couldn't hope to gain the broad mass audiences of the established networks and so commissioned programmes targeted specifically at the upper-income audiences that were more attractive to advertisers. Initially, Fox focused on the 18–34 demographic and had some success with its half-hour comedies and teen series such as *The Simpsons* and *Beverley Hills 90210*. *The X-Files* was part of the network's attempt to widen its demographic to the 18–49 bracket, so that it could more effectively compete with the other national networks. However, in doing so, it did not attempt to replicate the programming of the established networks. While CBS, NBC, and ABC were attempting to retain their audiences under the new threat of competition from cable and satellite, Fox was attempting to break into the network market and build a new audience, and this demanded a different strategy in its commissioning of hour-long prime time drama. This different strategy involved specifically attempting to produce a 'cult' drama that would encourage fan audiences.

It was, therefore, Fox's nascent position as a new national network that led it to develop a new form of quality/cult television in the production of *The X-Files*. As Reeves, Rogers, and Epstein (1996) have argued, there were two types of cult television before *The X-Files* was produced in 1993. The first were network shows such as *Star Trek* that failed to gain large audiences when initially transmitted, but which had gained cult followings through syndicated re-runs. The second were cable and satellite shows such as *Mystery Science Theater 3000* specifically produced for small niche audiences on channels that could not hope to gain the large audiences of the national networks but valued the small loyal fan audiences that cult television could attract. *The X-Files* differed from such earlier cult television in two ways. First, unlike the niche cult shows on cable, this was a network series produced by a new network attempting to compete with NBC, ABC, and CBS. Second, rather than being a network series produced for a consensus audience that was 'found' by fan audiences and subsequently gained the status of a cult, *The X-Files* was actively produced by Fox as a cult series designed to attract the fan-consumer taste market. As such, Fox took a strategy used by cable television and adapted it to the needs of network television at a time when niche marketing was becoming an increasingly important strategy for the networks.

Fox targeted the fan audience for two reasons: because audience loyalty is particularly important at times of increased competition, and because fan audiences have a reputation for being conspicuous consumers of both television programmes and the ancillary merchandise associated with them. As part of a large media conglomerate, Fox could exploit *The X-Files* across a number of different media platforms (including film, toys, and publishing) in order to increase the revenue gained from one product. At a time when audience share was diminishing, looking beyond advertising for sources of revenue became a valuable strategy – one that was particularly successful with *The X-Files*. For Fox, targeting the fan audience with *The X-Files* was effectively a means of minimising risk and maximising profit. The network still hoped to produce a high-rated show that would compete effectively with the national networks and allow them to charge high prices for advertising spots within the programme.[7] However, they were also spreading the risk by creating a product that was designed and marketed to appeal to a specific fan audience made up of loyal consumers of both television programmes and their ancillary merchandise.[8]

While this strategy went on to be used successfully by other national networks (e.g., WB adopted a very similar strategy with their production of *Buffy the Vampire Slayer* [see Johnson, 2005a]), over the last decade new networks and new technologies have further transformed the production strategies used by the US television industry. Subscription networks, in particular HBO, have emerged as profitable sectors in the television marketplace by developing strategies geared towards creating loyalty in the 'quality' audience (see Johnson on HBO and *The Sopranos,* and Brown on cult channels in this volume). Meanwhile, the older national networks have begun to exploit the possibilities of new media technologies to encourage audience participation and engagement with their shows. Perhaps the most high-profile example of this has been ABC's *Lost*. The marketing strategy developed for *Lost* was specifically designed to encourage the kind of active participation with a programme that is traditionally attributed to fans of cult television. *Lost* was commissioned by ABC at a time when the network was struggling in the ratings. The series' co-creator Damon Lindelof claimed that ABC's poor performance fostered a culture of risk-taking that led to the commissioning of *Lost*:

> ABC wanted something different and it wanted to make a noise. It also responded to the potential for this [*Lost*] to have mass appeal – it isn't sci-fi, or romance, or action, or procedural, but all of those rolled into one. (Damon Lindelof, cited in Campbell, 2005: 21)

143

While *Lost*'s generic mix certainly offers the potential of something 'similar but different' and the possibility of appealing to a wide-ranging audience base, its narrative structure and densely layered fictional world demand an engaged and loyal form of spectatorship. *Lost* begins with a plane crash-landing on a desert island and follows the experiences of the survivors as they attempt to escape and realise that the island is certainly not all that it seems. The series' narrative is essentially based on a puzzle to be solved; replicating in an extreme version Hills' endlessly deferred narrative characteristic of cult texts. This puzzle narrative invites an active speculation on the part of the audience, and its multiple characters and extensive fictional world (or hyperdiegesis, to use Hills' terminology again) offer possibilities for audiences to create and develop their own stories around *Lost*'s diegesis.

Over and above these textual attributes, however, was a highly innovative marketing strategy for *Lost* that encouraged audiences to participate actively with the series' deferred narrative and hyperdiegesis. This included a number of fictional websites based on companies that appeared within the series' diegesis – for example, a website was created for the airline Oceanic (whose crashed plane begins the series' narrative) which appeared to be 'real' by offering the kinds of functionality one would expect from a real airline website. However, if you accessed a page displaying the seating plan of an aircraft and clicked on the seat numbers using a mysterious sequence of numbers that appeared within the narrative of *Lost,* you would access a secret page that gave you highlights of the second season. This website, therefore, extended the diegesis of the series into the everyday world of the viewer, while also encouraging participation and knowledge of the series on the part of the audience – effectively rewarding fan activity in its viewers.[9]

From an industrial perspective, such strategies demonstrate the shift in cult television from the 1960s to the present day. Increasingly, network US television has actively attempted to create cult television with programmes and marketing strategies designed to encourage and reward loyal viewing and active participation. As such, cult television and fan audiences are no longer understood by the industry as marginal, atypical, or simply irrelevant. As the example of *Lost* demonstrates, the networks appeal to the 'fan' in all viewers, encouraging fan activity and loyalty as a part of television spectatorship in an era when multi-media participation is increasingly becoming the norm.

The Different Context of the UK

Thus far, our discussion of the impact of the television industry on cult television has largely focused on the US. I want to end with a few reflections on the different context of the UK. As with the US, the UK television industry has been through a number of changes since the 1960s, when BBC1 and BBC2 formed a duopoly with the commercial public service broadcaster ITV. The 1980s saw the emergence of new terrestrial channels, first with the arrival of Channel 4 (followed in 1997 by Channel 5), and second with the growth in up-take of cable, satellite, and later digital television. Within the UK, however, the history and place of cult television is quite different. Despite the rise of cable, digital, and satellite television, public service broadcasting remains at present the defining feature of the UK terrestrial television landscape. With increased competition from non-terrestrial providers, the audiences for these broadcasters have certainly declined over the past 10 years[10]; while the public service requirements of ITV have diminished, ITV1 and BBC1 remain largely conceptualised as mixed programme channels for consensus audiences. As a consequence, the notion of 'cult television', with its implications of exclusivity and specialness, goes against the very remit of these two main terrestrial channels. While the public service requirements of BBC1 (and to a lesser extent ITV1) to provide specific kinds of programmes (such as religious programming or children's television [see Wood in this volume]) could be understood as a form of niche broadcasting, BBC1 would not be free to pursue the kind of niche targeting adopted by the US networks. However, this does not mean that cult TV has no place on British television. Programmes understood as cult are much more likely to find a home on BBC2 with its status as a 'minority audience' channel, on Channel 4 with its remit for diversity and alternative programming, or increasingly on one of the terrestrial broadcasters' new digital channels such as BBC3 or E4. This is the case even with cult US television transmitted in the UK. For example, *Star Trek* was initially transmitted in the UK early on Saturday evenings on BBC1, but it later found its home on BBC2 as part of a series of re-runs of classic cult series from the 1960s targeting niche fan and youth audiences. When *The X-Files* was first transmitted in the UK, it was on the minority channel BBC2 and was moved to BBC1 in its second season only due to the high ratings it initially generated (see Brown on *The X-Files* in this volume). Even the NBC series *Heroes*, the latest US cult offering to find its way on to UK screens, appears on BBC2 rather than on BBC1.

The scheduling of US cult television programmes on the minority public service channels is partly due to the status accorded in the UK to US television, which is not seen as part of the remit of public service broadcasting to preserve and encourage British culture. The centrality of the mixed programme schedule to the ethos of public service broadcasting also has an impact on cult television in the UK. Since the 1950s, the prime time US television schedules have contained a central core of drama series made up of seasons of around 26 episodes. Furthermore, as argued above, the importance of the syndication markets for the profitability of networks and producers has also placed an emphasis on series that run to over 100

145

episodes. Within the UK, drama production is more varied. Since the 1950s, continuous series have formed a significant part of the schedules; these series now constitute the central core of BBC1 and ITV1's prime time programming. However, other serialised dramas tend to be shorter – usually one, two/three, or six episodes in length. Occasionally series will be produced in half-seasons of 13 episodes, often with a particular eye on the overseas market.[11] This greater variety in drama production has an impact on the ability of UK television drama to generate a cult following. In the current crowded and fragmented multi-channel television environment, it is difficult for a television programme of only a few episodes length to have enough impact to generate a cult following. Furthermore, shorter series are more likely to be serialised, bringing their narratives to a conclusion and hence lacking the open-ended narratives characteristic of cult texts in general.

Yet this does not mean that UK television is incapable of producing cult dramas. The US examples, such as *The X-Files* and *Lost,* demonstrate that shows that are produced with elements of cult and that use tactics to encourage fan activities in their audiences can still generate large mass audiences, both in the UK and in the US. There have been a number of attempts to build on the success of these US series in the UK. The successful BBC1 series *Spooks* (re-titled *MI5* for the US market), which is produced in seasons of 13 episodes, also regularly gains a loyal audience of 6 million in its prime time slot, while being the test bed for the BBC to try out new media applications designed to appeal to the fan audience (such as web games and interactive content). Meanwhile, Russell T. Davies' revival of *Doctor Who* appeals to cult fans and family audiences alike, generating regular audiences of 8 million and above and a very successful 40 per cent share. Furthermore, its combined appeal to fan and child audiences makes it a valuable property to be exploited through merchandising and it has also been used by the BBC to develop a range of interactive content clearly designed to appeal to the fan audience associated with the programme (see Richards in this volume). As such, it displays precisely those attributes that have made cult television so important to the US market – attributes that appeal to a loyal audience also likely to purchase the ancillary merchandise that can provide broadcasters with additional income.[12]

As Matt Hills argues, 'there can be no final and absolute classification of the media cult' (2002: 131). Certainly, from an industrial perspective, producers may attempt to create cult television, but programmes can become cult texts only through the activities of viewers and not through their mode of production. Yet, looking at the history of US (and UK) television, there is a clear shift in the status and place of cult television and the fan audience. While the US networks had an oligopoly and the UK terrestrial channels had a duopoly on broadcasting in the 1950s, 1960s, and 1970s, the fan audience was not a particularly important audience segment for producers. However, since the fragmentation of the audience over the 1980s and 1990s, audience demographics have become increasingly important and, with it, the fan audience has emerged as a valuable taste market. With this shift, broadcasters have actively attempted to create cult status around their shows, encouraging all audiences to engage in the kinds of activities associated with cult fandom. Although the precise place of the fan audience differs in the UK and in the US, certainly loyal audiences who are active consumers with disposable income are valuable to broadcasters in both contexts. As digital television becomes more widespread and as we move to digital switch-over in the UK, the current distinction between the mainstream terrestrial/network channels and the more niche, specialised digital channels is likely to weaken, and the audience to fragment further. The television industries will certainly look for new strategies to maintain and attract audiences and, with it, the place of cult television is likely to shift again.

Recommended Reading

Johnson, Catherine (2005) *Telefantasy.* London: BFI, 2005.

Reeves, Jimmie L., Marc C. Rogers, and Michael Epstein (1996) 'Rewriting Popularity: The Cult Files', in David Lavery, Angela Hague, and Marla Cartwright (eds) '*Deny All Knowledge': Reading The X-Files.* Syracuse and New York: Syracuse University Press, 22–35.

Rogers, Mark C., Michael Epstein, and Jimmie L. Reeves (2002) '*The Sopranos* as HBO Brand Equity: The Art of Commerce in the Age of Digital Reproduction', in David Lavery (ed), *This Thing of Ours: Investigating The Sopranos.* London: Wallflower: 42–57.

HBO and *The Sopranos*
(1999–2007)
Catherine Johnson

The HBO network began broadcasting in 1972 as a subscription cable channel specialising in the broadcast of premium sports events and films. Over the 1980s and 1990s, it moved into original programme production, competing more directly with the national networks. As such, HBO was part of the fragmentation of the US television industry in the 1980s and 1990s during which the production of cult television emerged as an industrial strategy. In fact, HBO was particularly successful in its production of cult television, and this stems in part from its different status as a pay-TV network. Audiences pay indirectly for the programming on the national free-to-air networks by buying the products advertised between programmes. By contrast, there are no adverts on HBO; the audience pays directly for the programmes aired through a subscription to the channel (see Rogers, Epstein, and Reeves, 2002). This different relationship between audience and channel has a number of consequences that contribute to the importance of cult television as an industrial strategy for HBO. As HBO audiences subscribe to the channel it is not subject to the FCC's requirements regarding violent, sexual, and language content. HBO exploited this by producing programming that could not be shown on other networks, in terms of both subject matter and its treatment. Furthermore, while viewers can discover and sample programmes offered by the free-to-air networks, they cannot chance upon HBO programming or view it before committing to paying a subscription for it. As such, HBO needed to develop programming strategies that would entice audiences to pay for the channel in advance of seeing the programmes that it aired. Over the 1990s, HBO focused on creating an aura of prestige around its original drama production and produced a number of critically acclaimed programmes (including films, documentaries, sports programmes, and dramas) in an attempt to create a reputation as the home of quality television in the US. In doing so, HBO was attempting to appeal to an audience likely to have the disposable income to be able and willing to pay its high subscription.

This is exemplified in the strategy developed by HBO in the late-1990s to make its Sunday evening schedules the home of original quality drama in the US, beginning with *The Sopranos* in 1999. *The Sopranos* was a drama series about a New Jersey mob leader, Tony Soprano, and his relationship with his two families: his blood family and his mobster family. *The Sopranos* exploited HBO's exemption from the FCC's regulations regarding profanities, nudity, and violence to offer a representation of mob life that confronted the realities of this violent, macho world. This contributed to its aura of prestige and quality in that *The Sopranos* offered a vibrant, realist, and rounded portrayal of modern gangster life (see Rogers, Epstein, and Reeves, 2002). In addition, the series was densely plotted, focusing on exploring the complexities and contradictions of its characters' moral landscape, and never allowing its audience to take an easy position in relation to the storylines and characters. *The Sopranos* initiated HBO's creation of an appointment to view on Sunday nights and was soon followed by other dramas such as *Six Feet Under* (set in a funeral home and beginning each episode with a graphic death) which offered serious and complex treatment of adult themes. By 2000, the network had enough original programming to allow it to schedule a number of different original series throughout the year on Sunday evenings. Both *The Sopranos* and *Six Feet Under* were publicised as being authored by a 'creator' given freedom by the network. *Six Feet Under* was created by Alan Ball who secured a reputation for quirky quality drama with the huge success of his film *American Beauty* (Sam Mendes, US, 1999), while *The Sopranos* was written by David Chase who was given the space to take long breaks between seasons, exemplifying HBO's promotion of itself as a network where creativity comes before commercial demands. HBO's production of *The Sopranos* is indicative of the attempts by the US networks in the 1990s to explicitly create cult television, developing programmes that aimed to construct loyal relationships with viewers, that were positioned as distinctly different from existing television fare and that were authored by creators given well-publicised freedom from the constraints of commercial demands. Through this strategy HBO constructed a brand identity as the 'quality' channel in the US, inviting viewers to identify themselves with the channel and to construct a loyal and personal relationship with it (see Johnson, 2007).

While this strategy was successful in securing HBO's reputation for quality drama. In the years following 1999, there was a gradual slowdown in its subscriptions and it began to depend on other forms of revenue, such as DVD sales and theatrical movies, which made up 20 percent of the network's revenues in 2004 (Higgins and Romano, 2004: 6). These ancillary markets enabled HBO to extend its products to viewers not prepared to pay the subscription rates for its series. However, they are also markets that appeal to fan viewers who want to own and re-watch their favourite programmes and buy products associated with them. HBO also exploited the emergence of new media platforms, developing a website that has pages for each of its programmes, often offering interactive games, the sale of merchandise,

149

and information about interactive experiences, such as a tour of sites used in the production of *The Sopranos*, all of which invite active participation on the part of viewers (see Johnson 2007). HBO's dependence on these non-broadcast markets further indicates the importance of the fan for contemporary US television, where profits depend not just on advertising revenue or subscriptions, but also on the ability to persuade audiences to engage in a relationship with the programme beyond its initial broadcast, a relationship typified by the practices of cult television fans.

The *Quatermass* Serials
Catherine Johnson

Many historians identify the televising of the Coronation of Elizabeth II in Westminster Abbey on 2 June 1953 as the moment when television came of age (see Crissell, 1997). Yet, just two months later, a very different broadcast from Westminster Abbey (albeit a model of this historic building) gripped viewers, this time seeing the Queen supplanted by an alien organism taking root in Poet's Corner and threatening to destroy all humanity on Earth. This television broadcast was the culmination of a six-part drama serial entitled *The Quatermass Experiment* (1953) and written by Nigel Kneale and produced by Rudolf Cartier, which told the tale of the fated consequences of the first manned space flight engineered by Professor Bernard Quatermass. The audience reaction to *The Quatermass Experiment* and its two sequels in the 1950s (*Quatermass II*, 1955, and *Quatermass and the Pit*, 1958–1959) was pronounced and all three of the serials are often fondly remembered (primarily for being extremely frightening!) by audiences today. By the third serial in 1958, the *Quatermass* programmes had become a cultural event, with *Variety* reporting 'a motion at one local council that business shouldn't start until after the *Quatermass* transmission had ended' and adding that 'cinema exhibs testify to the pull of the program by saying that they had one of the worst evening's biz in a long, long time' (cited in WAC (BBC Written Archives Centre), T5/2, 306/1, 13 March 1959).

There are a number of reasons for the reaction caused by the 1950s' serials. The serials were relatively unusual in their use of science fiction and horror narratives, genres that did not feature heavily on television at this time. Furthermore, the *Quatermass* serials firmly located their fantastic narratives within the present day, tapping into contemporary fears and anxieties about new technologies, social change, and so on. For example, in *Quatermass II* a government experiment to create synthetic food is being used as a cover for aliens planning to take over the world, tapping into fears about government secrecy and the exploitation of science. The use of the newly constructed Shell Haven Refinery in Essex as the location of the alien base only served to reinforce the proximity of the story to the everyday reality of the viewers. Over and above this, the serials made significant use of the conventions of horror and the domestic location of television to frighten their audiences. For example, at the end of the first episode of *The Quatermass Experiment*, the surviving astronaut staggers out of the crashed space rocket and falls directly into the camera, his terrified expression visible in extreme close-up before the fade to black. Here *The Quatermass Experiment* deliberately set out to shock and surprise its audience by exploiting the effect that the sudden close-up could have. Such techniques had all the more impact at a time when there was anxiety about the place of television in the home, and the *Quatermass* serials were particularly effective at frightening their audiences because they challenged the homely address of much of the BBC's television output (Caughie, 2000: 32). The *Quatermass* serials were also significant for their use of spectacle. At a time when television screens were small with low resolution, there was a strong sense that television was not suited to visual spectacle (see Jacobs 2000). The *Quatermass* serials challenged this by building up to spectacular sequences in which the fantastic was on display to the audience, such as the climax to *The Quatermass Experiment* when the alien organism was shown towering over Poet's Corner in Westminster Abbey. Such moments of spectacle were particularly impressive when considering that they were largely created live in the studio. As such, it was not simply the storylines which resonated with audiences in the 1950s, but also the treatment of those stories to engage audiences emotionally with the drama through the use of innovative techniques to create fear and awe.

The cultural impact of the 1950s' *Quatermass* serials is also evident in their longevity. All three serials were adapted into films by Hammer over the 1950s and the 1960s and Kneale's scripts for the 1950s' serials were published in book form in 1959 and 1960. In the 1970s, *Quatermass* was revived as a drama that was produced simultaneously as a film for cinema release entitled *The Quatermass Conclusion* and as a four-part television series entitled *Quatermass*. Still written by Nigel Kneale but this time directed by Piers Haggard, *Quatermass* retained its interest in using science fiction to explore contemporary concerns. This time Professor Quatermass was an old man disillusioned by a world in which the structures of society (in particular law and order) were breaking down, and the young generation were drawn into cults in which they 'dropped out' of society and rejected science and rationalism. However, *Quatermass* did not have quite the impact of the original *Quatermass* serials, perhaps because it lacked their stylistic innovation.

Following the radio serial *The Quatermass Memoirs*, in 1996, *Quatermass* was revived again for television in 2005 as part of BBC4's 'TV On Trial' season. Rather than a new story, this was a reconstruction of the first serial, *The Quatermass Experiment*. As only the first two episodes of the original still exist in the archives, the remake of *The Quatermass Experiment* offered the opportunity for audiences to see how the story developed in the missing episodes, tapping into both the fan audience and those who would have remembered watching the serial when it was initially transmitted. Although the serial was also remade live, mimicking to some extent the original mode of production, it actually ran 20 minutes under time, indicating the extent to which the skills of live television drama production had been lost in the intervening years. The BBC's choice to remake *The Quatermass Experiment* as part of a season of retrospectives of British television history attests to the cultural resonance of the original series. They are also one of the few existing programmes of the 1950s to be released by the BBC on DVD. Although, as Lez Cooke (2003) points out, it is difficult to assert definitively the extent to which the *Quatermass* serials were stylistically innovative as so little of 1950s' television drama remains in the archive for us to compare it with, the series' cultural resonance with audiences and continued longevity points to their importance as an early example of cult television.

Notes

1. Although at this time the three major US networks (CBS, NBC, and ABC) and the two major terrestrial channels in the UK (BBC1 and ITV) were able to generate such large audiences in prime time, not all television channels at this time were able (or aiming) to garner such large audiences. As we shall go on to see, the non-networked channels could not expect to generate the large audiences of the national networks in the US, and in the UK, BBC2 was established in 1964 with a specific remit to provide minority programming.

2. *Wagon Train* (NBC, 1957–1962 and ABC, 1962–1965) was the second highest rated programme on US television from 1958 to 1961 and the highest rated programme in the 1961–1962 season. When Roddenberry pitched *Star Trek* to NBC, most science-fiction and fantasy series were anthology series or aimed at children.

3. Ratings measure the audience for a particular programme as a percentage of all households that own a television. Share measures the audience for a particular programme as a percentage of all households watching television when the programme was aired. Both statistics are estimated from a sample of households measured.

4. The success of *Star Trek* in syndication revived network interest in the show. NBC produced a cartoon spin-off of the original series which ran from 1973 to 1975, possibly attempting to exploit the propensity that the series had had in its initial network run to attract audiences of children and teenagers. The series was then made into a series of film spin-offs over the 1980s and the 1990s and spawned a number of television spin-off series as well.

5. See Feuer et al. (1984), who argue that the fin-syn rule effectively enabled companies such as MTM to be able to afford to produce series at a deficit during their network run, as they reaped most of their profits through the syndication market.

6. *Hill Street Blues'* pilot episode gained at 15.2 per cent rating and a 26 per cent share, dropping to an 11.5 per cent rating and a 19 per cent share in its second episode. It stayed in the low 20 per cent share for the rest of its first season and was ranked 83rd out of 92 series in its first year (Gitlin, 1983: 307). Despite these very low ratings it won eight Emmys in 1981, a record number in one season for a series at that time.

7. *The X-Files* rated well for Fox, peaking at an 8.8 per cent rating and 16 per cent share in its first season. It maintained ratings of around 10 per cent over the decade. It is worth noting, however, that the ratings and share for *The X-Files* are lower than those gained by *Hill Street Blues* in its first season, indicating how audience figures had dropped and how much lower the measure of success (particularly for a new network such as Fox) had become.

8. Fox's attempt to move into a broader demographic from its original 18–34 niche was not always successful; over the 1990s, it was often programmes produced targeting the more narrowly defined youth audience (such as *The Simpsons*) that rated most highly (see Perren, 2003).

9. Channel 4 devoted £1million to marketing *Lost* when it bought the rights to screen the first season in the UK and developed a website with an on-line game, and clues

and puzzles that enabled the player to access information about the characters and narratives of the series (Campbell, 2005: 21).

10. In December 1996, the audience share for BBC1 was 31.6 per cent and for ITV1 it was 35.4 per cent, while all the non-terrestrial channels combined had 10.2 per cent (*Broadcast*, 20 December 1996: 23). In the week ending 20 April 2003, the combined share for all non-terrestrial channels exceeded that for the main terrestrial channels for the first time, with BBC1 gaining a 23.9 per cent share, ITV1 gaining a 23.8 per cent share, and the non-terrestrial channels gaining a 26.1 per cent share (*Broadcast*, 2 May 2003: 1). While it is worth noting that the share for non-terrestrial television was bolstered in this week by the high ratings for Sky Sports' football coverage, this trend has continued with the terrestrial channels gradually losing audiences to the non-terrestrial channels with the rise of cable, satellite, and digital.

11. Clearly it is beyond the scope of this chapter to go into the history of serialised drama in the UK in depth and certainly the form of UK serialised dramatic output has varied. For example, in the 1960s, ITV screened a number of drama series produced in seasons (such as *The Avengers*) that were also targeted towards the lucrative US market (see Johnson, 2005a and Chapman, 2002a).

12. In addition, it is worth noting that both *Spooks* and *Doctor Who* have been sold abroad, and the overseas market is clearly an additional means of generating income for both US and UK television producers.

15 Cult Channels: Showtime, FX, and Cult TV

Simon Brown

Writing about Comedy Central and its signature spoof news programme *The Daily Show*, Jimmie L. Reeves, Mark C. Rogers, and Michael M. Epstein argue that *The Daily Show* is a prime example of how 'quality television operates as an economic strategy' (2007: 83). They claim that although its topicality prevents syndication and to date has not translated successfully into DVD sales – two potentially lucrative additional markets – the show has bestowed a mark of respectability on the channel whose most famous previous hit was the potty-mouthed but inspired *South Park*. Although *South Park* generated vast sums in merchandising and subscriptions, it delivered, they argue, 'cash, not cachet' (97), the latter being offered by *The Daily Show*'s insightful political satire. This cachet has assisted in branding Comedy Central not only as the home of cutting-edge low comedy, but also as the home of accessible high-quality satire, increasing its brand equity in the marketplace. This, they argue, has helped Comedy Central find its niche, a niche driven mostly by advertisers seeking what they call the 'quality demographic group' of 18–49-year-olds (94).

However, in addition to being quality, there is an essential cult-ness to *The Daily Show*. Though Jon Stewart satirises politics, politicians, and the issues of the day, so too, in its own way, does *South Park*. The two shows occupy similar territory attracting different yet overlapping audiences. Each adds to the brand identity of Comedy Central, but they are arguably both quality and cult in very different ways. If quality is about branding, so too is cult, and I will examine this using the example of two networks who brand themselves with cult credentials.

Firstly it is necessary to outline what I mean by the slippery concept of cult. Roberta Pearson in this volume quotes herself, Mark Jancovich and Nathan Hunt in saying that cult TV should be defined not by searching for features shared by individual shows, but rather by identifying similarities in the ways in which audiences respond to them. This could be, as Mendik and Harper point out, 'a ritualistic form of near obsession' which sees audiences responding with a form of 'intense physical and emotional involvement' (2000: 7) or a definition of a text by audiences as being 'in opposition to the mainstream' (Jancovich and Hunt, 2004: 27), offering supportive viewers a chance to distinguish

155

themselves from the majority and thus encouraging a certain amount of ownership of the material. These two forms of cult audience are not, of course, mutually exclusive. Although there were fans of *The X-Files* who 'crave(d) information the way mutant flukes craved human flesh' (Reeves, Rogers, and Epstein, 1996: 23), part of the reason for the show's phenomenal success was an army of regular viewers who simply thought the show was different/good and watched it each week, creating what Mark Frost, co-creator of *Twin Peaks*, has described as a 'coalition of viewers' (cited in Collins: 338).

The X-Files' success marks a blurring of the lines between cult and quality television, as the latter has increasingly come to be seen as an alternative to the mainstream networks' output of reality shows and sit-coms, an extension of Robert Thompson's definition of quality TV as 'not "regular" TV' (1996: 13). Whereas cult TV could once be labelled by its generic affiliation and the ritualistic devotion of its fans – SF, *Star Trek,* and Trekkers being stereotypical examples – the notion of being cult now needs to be redefined using the quality criteria of being an alternative to the mainstream, and in terms of the viewing practises of quality audiences. In 1996, Thompson listed 12 criteria for quality TV (1996: 13–16). Although the changing nature of the field since then means that these are still under debate (see McCabe and Akass, 2007), for the purposes of this chapter many of Thompson's criteria are still valid, including a high standard of writing and production values, the addressing of serious issues and the challenging nature of their presentation, the ensemble casts, and serial narratives. This shift away from genre as a defining cult identifier has allowed the new quality-as-cult to have both cult and mainstream viewer appeal, thus achieving not so much a coalition but a merging of the loyalty of the avid cult fan and the numbers of the more casual appreciative viewers.

This merging of cult practises and mainstream appeal is reflected in the increasing significance of synergy in relation to quality TV as TV shows, like films, become links in a chain of merchandising products. The most high profile of these is the DVD box-set which is itself an example of the mainstreaming of quality-as-cult TV, offering as it does to the conventional home video market the kind of contextual material which hitherto had been sought by cult audiences on niche formats such as laser disc. Furthermore the DVD box-set extends to viewers the notion of both literal and metaphoric ownership of a text which can enhance its identification as 'their' show. This does not however stop with individual series since, as Catherine Johnson has argued, the DVD is another key to the concept of branding a network, not only providing 'a valuable alternative source of income but also [allowing] the programmes to convey the [network] brand to an audience of non-subscribers' (Johnson, 2007: 11).

This new emphasis on branding picked up both by Johnson and by Reeves et al. is an extension of the targeted marketing practises which emerged with the sudden proliferation of cable channels in the early 1980s. As Johnson has argued elsewhere in this volume, prior to the 1980s the benchmark of TV success was the ratings – the number of people watching translating into higher advertising charges and larger revenues. As a result of deregulation in the 1980s and the rise of new channels, the networks had to change how they measured success. They could no longer deliver to advertisers the huge numbers of viewers because with an increase in choice audiences were more thinly spread across more channels. This led to a rise in the importance of demographics alongside ratings. In the 1980s, in addition to the *number* of people watching, what also became important were the *types* of people watching, who could then be targeted by specific advertisers. As a result, the networks aired both programming and accompanying advertising aimed at particular niche viewers, which became an important factor in the emergence of quality TV. Indeed the original definition of quality TV was an appeal to up-market audiences likely to be interested in purchasing the kinds of products advertised on TV, and the networks targeted them with intelligently written complex dramas such as *Hill Street Blues* (see Johnson on the industry and cult TV in this volume).

In this respect, quality was cult, since it lay outside mainstream programming by the networks and was designed to attract a niche audience, but a very different one to that traditionally seen in the cult arena. This larger, quality audience was mostly middle class, adult, relatively wealthy, and possessed of discerning taste; Robin Nelson refers to them as ABC1s: educated professionals with little time to watch TV who when they do watch are likely to prefer quality programming which 'challenges as well as entertains' (2007a: 27). As a result what was aimed at them was intelligently written, adult-themed entertainment which dealt with serious issues in an uncompromising fashion. This was taken up by Fox with *The X-Files*, which represented a hybrid of more mainstream themes (the investigative procedural) with generic cult concerns (conspiracy theories and SF), effectively offering a mainstream drama with cult appeal but leaning more towards the mainstream than, for example, *Twin Peaks,* with its less surreal tone and its stand-alone episodic structure interspersed with the serial conspiracy narrative.

However the cult-ness of *The X-Files* derives in part from its affiliation with cult genres. Targeting the emerging potential of the new ABC1s, the link between quality and cult has been exploited in recent years by a number of smaller cable channels, less preoccupied with garnering the kind of vast audiences expected by the major networks. Seeing the potential of building a loyal fan base, they have abandoned cult genres and instead sought to produce programmes whose cult status is linked instead to quality by an adherence to provocative plotlines and/or aesthetics. These shows deliberately set themselves apart from 'regular TV' through a quirkiness, an edginess, or a general boundary-pushing fearlessness in their subject matter but do so within essentially mainstream rather than cult genres. In doing so, they offer product designed to foster the loyalty of cult viewing practises without being so niche as to alienate casual viewers. Furthermore, the formula for these shows, once successful, is repeated in a move designed to sell the channel-as-brand as well as the shows themselves, to encourage viewers to treat the channel as the home of their favourite type of programming and to keep coming back to see what else is on offer. In 1999, Margaret Loesch, president of the Odyssey Network, said 'acquisitions and movies bring people in, but it takes a well-done original series to keep them' (cited in McAdams, 1999: 24). In the world of the smaller cult channel, it takes not just one but a whole slate of series.

The model of the cult channel is HBO, a subscription service which does not carry commercials. In the late 1990s, under the tagline 'It's Not TV. It's HBO', the channel sought to differentiate its product from that available anywhere else – in other words as alternative to the mainstream – through being at the vanguard of what Janet McCabe and Kim Akass have called 'a darkening of tone, deepening of subject matter [and] complexity of structure' (2005: xviii). This came partly through the quality of the writing, direction, acting, and production values, and partly through pushing the boundaries of what was acceptable on television in terms of sex, violence, language, and subject matter in *Sex and the City*, *The Sopranos*, *Six Feet Under,* and *Deadwood*, while the high level of seriality in the shows demanded loyal viewing. Though it sold its product as quality and never used the word cult, HBO fostered the notion of its programmes as quality-as-cult to sell subscriptions. What HBO did was to take the kind of changes to television being made by the networks with shows such as *Hill Street Blues*, and later *The X-Files*, and go a step further (see Johnson on HBO and *The Sopranos* in this volume). In recent years, just as HBO went further than the networks, so the mantle of HBO has been challenged by younger channels keen to push the boundaries to attract new viewers.

In March 2002, the Fox-affiliated FX channel was struggling after its slate of bought-in, previously aired, quality series *Buffy*, *Ally Mcbeal,* and *The Practice* delivered ratings well below predictions. The move was designed to attract existing viewers of these tried and tested successes to the channel in time for the debut of FX's new in-house shows, the most high profile of which was *The Shield*, described as 'FX's first attempt at bringing HBO-style fare – complete with foul language, nudity and violence – to basic cable' (Romano, 2003: 16). *The Shield* reinvented the cop show by offering a desolate picture of contemporary urban American inner city life. Its ensemble cast of cops, detectives, and captains are dysfunctional, Machiavellian, and helpless, and the show presents in a bleak realistic fashion the LAPD drowning in a cesspool LA rife with drugs and gangs. The first episode begins with corrupt detective Vic Mackey (Michael Chiklis) shooting dead an undercover internal affairs cop who is about to expose him. In spite of this, we are drawn to the character due to the fact that his nemesis, Captain Aceveda, is even more sleazy and corrupt than Mackey. The week that *The Shield* aired in March

2002, *Broadcasting and Cable* noted that its big challenge was to do for FX what the bought-in shows had failed to do – find an audience (Romano, 2002: 16). It did. *The Shield* first aired to a basic-cable record rating of 4.8 million viewers, while Michael Chiklis' subsequent Emmy award for best actor was a basic-cable first (Stambler, 2005: 57). It is a measure of the impact of HBO that the less controversial bought-in titles should be unsuccessful while this controversial first in-house production should succeed so well and FX quickly learned this lesson. The success of *The Shield* changed the fortunes of FX and encouraged it to commit to similar product. Four years later, FX was riding high with a slew of challenging series, including *Nip/Tuck, Rescue Me*, *Over There,* and *Starved,* joining *The Shield*. The opportunity to push the envelope of what was acceptable in terms of subject matter and treatment attracted talent to the channel. Peter Tolan and Denis Leary took their potentially controversial drama dealing with the sensitive issue of New York fire-fighters post 9/11 to FX after being promised creative freedom. At FX, said Tolan, 'I can point to that product and say, "That's the show I wanted to do, and I am doing it exactly the way I want to do it"' (cited in Stambler, 2005: 58). As Michael Chiklis, star of *The Shield*, stated, on his previous show, *The Commish* the attitude was 'It's a cop drama, but it's family oriented, and we're never going to go in certain directions', whereas on FX 'there's none of that. We're just going, "What's the best story?"' (58). Equally significant is that this new creative energy, led by FX's desire to produce challenging quality work, translated into profits, with FX being worth approximately $3 billion in 2005 (56).

But if FX was challenging the boundaries of what could be addressed in serious drama, another channel was pushing the limits of good taste in comedy drama, for the same reasons and with the same effect. While FX's slate of productions tackled serious political issues – *The Shield* explored police corruption and inner city crime, *Over There* the Iraq War, and *Nip/ Tuck* America's obsession with beauty and image – Showtime sought its comedic content in the headline-grabbing world of sex, drugs, and murder. Part of CBS Corporation since CBS' split with Viacom in 2005, Showtime is a subscription channel which began broadcasting in 1978. In 2000, Showtime found success with the American version of *Queer as Folk*. In 2002, along with MTV, it was involved in plans for the formation of a gay channel called Outlet. The plans were put on hold in July 2003 ostensibly due to budgets, but the same month Robert Greenblatt was hired as Showtime's head of entertainment. Greenblatt had worked for Fox and HBO on *The X-Files*, *Six Feet Under,* and *The Sopranos*, and his hiring signalled a change in direction which may have had something to do with the shelving of Outlet. Greenblatt was keen to move away from niche shows like *Queer as Folk* to produce 'some shows that everybody wants to watch. I want to try some things that aren't immediately conceptually pigeon-holed' (cited in Romano, 2004: 30). Greenblatt wanted to maintain Showtime's loyal gay following and so promised that Showtime would not abandon targeted drama such as *The L Word,* but at the same time he sought a broader audience by mixing the quirky and the challenging aspects of *Queer as Folk* and *The L Word* with more mainstream material and concerns, something Showtime chairman Matt Blank describes as 'more commercial, broader in appeal and a little hipper' (cited in Romano, 2007: 23). Blank may claim that 'good programming generates more subscribers' (23), but Showtime, as a subscription channel not included in many US basic cable packages, faced a much greater challenge. As Robert Thompson puts it, in the case of Showtime, 'It can't just be must see TV – it has to be must-call-cable-company-so-I-might-see TV' (Thompson, cited in Anon, 2007a). Subscription costs money, which again meant the targeting of that ABC1 group with their disposable income and challenging tastes. The first breakthrough for the new formula was *Weeds* in 2005, telling the story of a suburban mom who turns to selling pot to make ends meet after her husband's death. Unlike the gay environments of *Queer as Folk* and *The L Word, Weeds'* suburban school-mom milieu was pure American apple-pie, given a comically vicious citrus twist. While its subject matter and language were challenging, it echoed the witty writing, edgy characterisations, superior acting, and suburban shenanigans which characterised ABC's runaway success *Desperate Housewives. Weeds* was *Desperate Housewives* plus one, a little more outrageous, a little more vulgar, a little more subversive – a little hipper in Blank's terms – and loud enough to attract the attention of fans of the network show and encourage them to try something new. As *Weeds* writer Jenji Kohan said at the time the first episode aired, 'Showtime was on a mission to make noise. This is a noisy premise' (cited in Wax, 2005: 17). Showtime certainly did make some noise, placing in August 2006, just before the second season premiere, a giant billboard in Times Square showing star Mary-Louise Parker sitting on a throne-shaped armchair under the words, 'Her Highness'. This is a clear example of a high-concept advertising campaign, the tagline drawing upon the irreverent humour of the show while the visuals capitalised upon Mary-Louise Parker's star image both from film and from *The West Wing.* If, as Johnson argues, branding is a set of relations between producers, writers, networks, texts, and viewers, then this campaign was clearly offering the promise of nudge-nudge naughty fun to those willing to participate (2007: 20).

As *Weeds* was *Desperate Housewives* plus one, *Dexter,* Showtime's next big hit, was *CSI* plus one, once again inserting a cult ingredient – cult due to its challenging nature – into a mainstream genre. It takes the standard format of the police forensic procedural drama, including the wide cast of characters and quality aesthetics, and mixes it with the deeply subversive element of the lead character being both forensic specialist and serial killer, likeably portrayed by Michael C. Hall, who had previously played David Fisher in *Six Feet Under*. *Emmy* magazine reported in 2007 that 'Showtime ... for years has sought the type of acclaim achieved by rival HBO ... *Dexter* might just be the one that seals the deal. Its first season finale broke ratings records for a Showtime series ... and subscriptions for the channel are rising' (Griffiths, 2007: 129). The final episode of the first season was watched by 1.1 million viewers and became the most watched original series shown on Showtime in two years (Anon, 2006b). The second season quickly broke this record. The premiere attracted 1 million viewers, setting the record for 'the most-watched season premiere for a Showtime series' (Nordyke, 2007), the eighth episode, aired on 18 November, attracted 1.23 million viewers, becoming the most watched episode of a Showtime series in the channel's history, a record broken by the second season finale which delivered 1.4 million (Anon, 2007c; Anon, 2007b). This remarkable success came despite, or perhaps because of, the upping of the ambiguity factor by having Dexter deny his murderous impulses and be investigated by the FBI, pushing viewers into the uncomfortable position of actually wanting him to get away and to start murdering people again.

The series may have won acclaim but what is most important is that the cult appeal of *Dexter*, as well as *Weeds*, has translated into higher viewing rates and more subscriptions, up to 15 million by 2007, having been stagnant around 14 million for several years (Romano, 2007: 23). Equally popular has been the 2007 premiere, *Californication*, starring David Duchovny, who brings with him the cult appeal of his starring role in *The X-Files*. *Californication* effectively signals Showtime's move full-circle. It merges the sexual explicitness, frank dialogue, and outrageous content of *Queer as Folk* (the series opens with a dream sequence of the lead character getting a blow job from a nun in front of an altar), but unlike *Queer as Folk* it remains rooted in the mainstream with its story of Hank Moody, a struggling writer and father, trying to resolve his problems and re-insert himself into American society within a modern-twisted nuclear family unit of one child and unmarried but stable parents. Partnered with *Weeds* on Monday nights, *Californication* was picked up for a second season almost immediately, in part because, as *Variety* reported, it was actually gaining viewers from episode to episode, rather than following the more traditional path of losing viewers after a strong premiere, and it achieved ratings figures higher than even those of *Dexter* (Adalian, 2007). Crucially, *Californication* was also holding on to 90 per cent of the audience who tuned in for *Weeds*, Showtime's most consistent hit, clearly indicating that the audiences were sticking with the channel to enjoy similar fare.

What is significant about all three series is that despite their outrageous premises, each is deeply rooted in fundamentally mainstream moral codes. Dexter may be a killer, but his bloodlust is not his fault and he kills only those who escape justice, making him more Batman than Hannibal Lector. Mary-Louise Parker's suburban mom deals drugs not for power or riches, but to keep her family together, while in *Californication* the sexual permissiveness of the characters hides a fundamental need for a stable relationship. Not only is Hank's aim to restore his post-nuclear family, his agent's wife gives up her nascent lesbianism and her husband his proclivities for S&M to reunite once more as a contented sexual couple. These are shows which push taste boundaries in terms of dialogue, imagery, content, and theme, but not, crucially, in terms of morality. As such they offer, like a horror film, a dip into a dark nether world from which mainstream viewers are able to emerge unharmed.

As with HBO, for smaller channels such as FX and Showtime, abandoning the family audience imperative has not only allowed creative freedom but has also deliberately positioned them as attractive to a younger, niche audience keen to follow material outside the mainstream. However in many ways it is the success of HBO which has set the benchmark in terms of quality aesthetics and also viewing figures, effectively meaning that while FX and Showtime seek to emulate HBO, the HBO product represents the mainstream side of cable quality TV. As a result, although the cult shows on FX and Showtime attract viewing figures which pale in comparison to HBO's mainstream successes – the finale of *The Sopranos* attracted 11.9 million to HBO, compared to *Dexter*'s 1.1 million viewers for Showtime – to the cult channels, this kind of comparison is less important. Comparatively speaking *Dexter*, *Weeds,* and *Californication* are big successes, and it is the very size of the audience, coupled with the commitment of the channel to constantly repeat the boundary-pushing elements of the shows themselves, that make the channels cult. In the new media landscape, therefore, cult does not mean attracting small and fanatical audiences, it means seeking a new band of loyal viewers prepared to stick with 'their' show from episode to episode and season to season and also to stick with 'their' channel from show to show.

Recommended Reading

Johnson, Catherine (2007) 'Tele-Branding in TVIII: The Network as Brand and the Programme as Brand', *New Review of Film and Television Studies* 5:1, 5–24.

Nelson, Robin (2007) 'HBO Premium: Channelling Distinction Through TVIII', *New Review of Film and Television Studies* 5: 1, 25–40.

Reeves, Jimmie L., Mark C. Rogers, and Michael Epstein (2007) 'Quality Control: The Daily Show, the Peabody and Brand Discipline' in Janet McCabe and Kim Akass (eds) *Quality TV: Contemporary American Television and Beyond.* London and New York, I.B.Tauris, 79–97.

The X-Files (Fox, 1993–2002)
Britain and the Emergence of a Cult Classic
Simon Brown

Fans of cult TV in Britain today have little opportunity to determine their own cult TV programmes from the raft of cult US imports. Shows such as *Lost*, *Dexter,* and *Pushing Daisies* make their satellite and terrestrial debuts dragging behind them the weight of cult connotations and Stateside success. Their debuts attract column inches and high viewing figures born of marketing campaigns highlighting their cult connotations and appointment-to-view status. Famously Channel Four took the unusual step of promoting already-established cult juggernaut *Lost* with a cinema advertising and billboard campaign, emphasising its unusual narrative and American popularity (see Grainge 2009 for a detail discussion of this marketing campaign). The American cult show is already defined before it reaches British shores, making its emergence into British popular culture hard to chart. It can, therefore, be illuminating to return to a simpler time and trace how an American import could make its own way in the UK market without the weight of expectation upon it.

On Wednesday 19 January 1994 at 8 pm, Sky One debuted a new American TV show. The debut was neither noteworthy nor auspicious. *Satellite Times* billed it as a new drama series 'based on chilling documented reports and true accounts', in which 'two FBI agents ... try to get to the bottom of some truly bizarre incidents' (*Satellite Times*, January 1994: 143). The *Radio Times* called it 'the casebook of two FBI agents whose mission is to solve the unsolvable' (*Radio Times*, 15–21 January 1994: 79). It rated barely a mention in both *Starburst* and *TV Zone*, the two essential readers for all things cult and sci-fi in the United Kingdom, although after a few weeks on the air, *Starburst* noted that the show seemed to be an interesting cross between *Kolchak: The Night Stalker* and *Dragnet* (*Starburst* 186, February 1994: 35). This opening was a far cry from the established image of *The X-Files* as a bona fide global phenomenon, which isn't surprising. When *The X-Files* premiered on Sky One, it was languishing in America on the Fox network on a Friday night – traditionally a TV graveyard – and averaging 102nd place out of 118 shows in the ratings (Thomas, 1996: 10). In the United Kingdom in January 1994, it was, therefore, a cheap imported show appearing on a satellite channel which comparatively few people actually subscribed to or watched. During its run on Sky One, it averaged 0.2 million viewers with the season one finale attracting 0.35 million, approximately the same figures received by the short-lived drama *The She-Wolf of London*.

The fact that *The X-Files* made little impact in the United States also made it a cheap acquisition for the BBC (McCabe, 2000: 151) who launched it on its art-house niche BBC2 channel on Monday 19 September 1994. By this time the second season of *The X-Files* was already underway in America and its following was growing, so *Radio Times* could now announce it as a 'new cult American drama series about the investigation of strange paranormal phenomena' (*Radio Times* 17–24 September 1994: 80). The decision to debut *The X-Files* on BBC2, as *Radio Times* pointed out, labelled *The X-Files* as 'the latest in a line of eerie American dramas with a touch of *Twin Peaks* and *Wild Palms*', two recent American imports which also found their home on BBC2 (*Radio Times* 17–24 September 1994: 71). However, the *Radio Times* sought a more mainstream viewer base for *The X-Files* by highlighting its links to the science-fiction genre. It did this by running an article by Richard Johnson on TV SF entitled 'Back to the Future' (*Radio Times* 17–24 September 1994: 28–31). SF was popular among BBC2 audiences at the time, thanks to the success of imports such as *Star Trek – The Next Generation*, *Quantum Leap*, and *Red Dwarf*. For the BBC, therefore, *The X-Files* was niche rather than cult, its cult affiliations coming more through its genre than anything inherent within the show. As it turned out, *The X-Files* proved unexpectedly popular, averaging 4.9 million viewers in its first season. In early November, the *Radio Times* described it as 'BBC2's most popular programme' (*Radio Times*, 29 October–4 November 1994: 98). *Starburst* reported in December 1994 that despite being 'largely unnoticed on Sky One ... BBC2's real sucess [*sic*] story of the year, as consistently high ratings testify, was *The X Files*' (*Starburst Special*, 22, Yearbook 94/95: 5) while by the end of the run in February *Broadcast* was able to report that 'no domestic series performed as well for BBC2 as *The X-Files*' (*Broadcast*, 10 February 1995: 29).

The popular status of the show hid a groundswell of cult interest among the viewers which would continue to grow during 1995. *TV Zone* published its first letter about *The X-Files* in November 1994, describing it as 'the greatest thing to happen in the world of Sci-Fi since Gene Roddenberry put pen to paper and wrote the words "Star Trek"' (*TV Zone* 60, November 1994: 13) and the following month it offered its first full *X-Files* article, a season one episode guide. When season two debuted on Sky in February 1995, its ratings soared to 0.89 million, second only to *The Simpsons*. *TV Zone* suggested that it was the success of the BBC2 broadcast which enabled Sky One to achieve such large viewing figures, and it maintained a consistent average of 0.82 million through its run (*TV Zone*, 66, April 1995: 4).

The debut of season two on BBC2 in September 1995 reached 4.82 million and season two quickly dominated the BBC2 ratings. Inspired by this success, the BBC made the decision to switch *The X-Files* to BBC1 after the Christmas hiatus. For its first episode on the more mainstream channel, the BBC elected to change the order of the second season and start the BBC1 run with 'Humbug' (2:20) rather than 'Fearful Symmetry' (2:18) which was considered to be weaker and less likely to appeal to the mass audience which BBC1 were hoping for (*TV Zone*, 75, January 1996: 4). 'Humbug', set within a community of freak show performers, can be read as more palatable for mainstream audiences, featuring as it does a scientific-based resolution and a playful comic tone, while 'Fearful Symmetry' is more in keeping with the cult aspects of the show by revolving around the abduction of zoo animals by aliens. The choice of episode for the BBC1 debut clearly delineated the show as 'quirky' rather than 'cult' in an attempt not to put off casual viewers less inclined to accept the alien mythology.

The gamble paid off. The first two BBC1 broadcast episodes both achieved ratings of around 9 million, up 1.5 million from the BBC2 high point of 7.53 in mid-December 1995, making it the highest-rated programme on UK television for its timeslot (*TV Zone*, 76, March 1996: 5). When season two ended in February 1996 with the cliffhanger 'Anasazi' (2:25) getting an audience of 9.95 million, the BBC was inundated with calls demanding that the opening episode of season three be shown immediately. Sky One ran 'Anasazi' simultaneously in preparation for the launch of season three the following week; although 'Anasazi' achieved less than 0.5 million viewers, the season three premiere the following week achieved their highest audience figure of 1.35 million for *The X-Files*. In response, the BBC elected to abandon plans to show selected *X-Files* episodes and instead repeated the entire first season, while the video of *The Unopened File* – a compilation of 'Anasazi' plus the first two episodes of season three, 'The Blessing Way' (3:1) and 'Paper Clip' (3:2) – which had been released in January went straight to number one in the video charts with sales of 345,000 copies (*TV Zone Special* no 23, Yearbook 1996: 5)

By December 1995, *TV Zone* confirmed that *The X-Files* had 'crossed the boundary between cult hit and mainstream TV phenomenon' (*TV Zone*

165

Special, 19, December 1995: 6). What is interesting about this journey in Britain is that it seems that *The X-Files* went from unknown American import to niche success and then to popular success, both responding to and being led by its scheduling over Sky One and the two BBC channels. The cult status of *The X-Files* it seems underpinned rather than led this progression, the fanatical fandom running parallel to mainstream popular success.

16 Through the Oblong Window: The Regulated Duopoly and the Creation of a Cult Children's 'Canon' in Britain

Tat Wood

When the word 'cult' was first applied to British television, it was children's series with unexpected adult followings that earned the title. It came from advertising: the Leo Burnett agency's audience research found in 1972 that otherwise unrelated series had similar followings that did not fit into pre-set generic categories. If adults were rushing home from work to see *The Magic Roundabout* in 1965 then something more than straightforward nostalgia was already at work. Why the period 1967–1980 is seen as the golden age of such programmes requires a book to itself; I'm going to try to sketch in some institutional, aesthetic, and practical considerations that served to make the programmes from this period more durable than any before or since. Durability is, in many cases, the primary criterion for their present cult status. These programmes are staples of a British childhood but antithetical to the present environment.

A few signposts through this period might be helpful: the BBC television service ran from 1936 until the outbreak of World War II in 1939, then again from 1946. In 1948 a Film Unit was established and in May 1951 the pokey Alexandra Palace studio was supplemented with an old film studio at Lime Grove (the opening ceremony included the first major children's TV star, Muffin the Mule). September 1955 saw the start of commercial television (or 'Independent', as it styled itself), with the nation divided into regions and each region originally given two franchises. In February 1957, under pressure from the commercial lobby, the Postmaster General (the communications minister) revoked the prohibition of transmission for an hour in the early evening (the 'Toddlers' Truce'). The BBC and local ITV stations continued to expand their regional coverage and by 1962 most of the United Kingdom was able to receive transmissions. 1962 also saw a government-backed but independent review, under Lord Pilkington, on the nature of television in the coming years. This reprimanded the more rapacious practices of the ITV companies and, unexpectedly, granted the BBC the permission to get a second television channel for experiments on UHF transmissions for colour broadcasting and less overtly populist programming. This phase of British broadcasting is generally called the 'Regulated Duopoly' and lasted until November 1982 and the start of Channel 4.

The cliché is that the BBC's output, particularly pre-Pilkington and especially for children, was stuffy and staid and as soon as any ITV alternative was provided the viewers swarmed over to it because their programmes were hipper and slicker. Closer examination complicates this story. In fact, the regional ITV companies showed very little that was intended purely for children (as they lost money on every minute shown when advertising restrictions were in place) but put out broadly (if accidentally) child-friendly programming throughout prime-time. The many animated ads with jingles were so popular with children that further regulation was introduced. US imports and the swashbucklers intended for export (*The Adventures of Robin Hood* [ATV 1955–1957] can stand for dozens) had simplistic storylines (they were aimed at the US market, after all), with frequent climaxes where ad breaks could go, and were made to be transmittable in almost any order. Whatever its flaws, Umberto Eco's discussion of *Casablanca* (Curtiz, US, 1943) provides an agreed starting-point for any definition of 'cult'. In his handy spotter's guide for a cult film, this segmentability is a necessary, almost sufficient, condition of cultishness (1986). Set-pieces and incidents can be isolated from the whole and discussed with fellow-*aficionados*. However, five years before ITV, the BBC's Film Unit had chanced upon the same thing when *Andy Pandy* (BBC 1950) began. In making short filmed programmes for children, programmes with a great deal of redundancy and ritualised elements, the team of Freda Lingstrom (incoming head of Children's Television) and Maria Bird virtually created cult television as we know it. Until *Andy Pandy*'s 13 original episodes began to be repeated, television programmes were almost all live: a successful drama was re-staged and re-performed later in the week. Even if the programmes were telerecorded for posterity, a second showing was an event in itself. *Andy Pandy* was then followed by *Flower Pot Men* (BBC 1952) and soon a hefty repertoire of similar marionette shows were in continuous rotation until the film physically wore out. The working week was divided up among five of these series, under the general heading *Watch with Mother*. The ludic nature of the programmes was a marked shift in BBC thinking. The previous slot, *For the Children*, had been aimed more at school-age televiewers and was emphatically pedagogic – the first main programme was *Children's Newsreel*. The original head of the department, Richmond Postgate, was an evangelist for the tutelary power of television (he later helped set up the Open University).

Perhaps the most fundamental point, one Eco addresses almost in passing, is that the audience feels proprietorial (1986). In the case of children's television, this is inevitable with the schedulers and continuity-announcers proclaiming the 'private'/'ghetto' status of the programmes and each cohort within this overall audience claiming or rejecting specific programmes, like siblings sharing a room and chalking lines on the wall. *Andy Pandy* and the others, in being designated as for pre-school children, were the first programmes to be 'owned' by an apprentice viewer. This sense of 'territory' and 'exploration' connects children's television with an older current in British children's fiction but brings us up against 1950s politics and child psychology.

There are two debates underlying this curious period: one is over the nature of childhood, the other is over the duties of public-service and commercial television. The positions of the two sides are not as clear-cut as might be expected. The BBC was periodically under the control of people who saw children as trainee citizens and who were desperate to maximise audience share. These people, notably hairshirt Marxist Stuart Hood (then controller of BBC Television), saw the privileging of imagination and play as 'too bloody middle-class' (see Buckingham et al., 1999). Throughout this period, the BBC would alternate between a construction of childhood as a state-in-itself and the Lockean perception of the child as an incomplete adult. The former camp (we might term them 'Romantics') were allowed to get on with it between 1950 and 1957 and again in the years 1967–1980 (and sporadically thereafter). The ITV companies may have begun by seeing children as potential consumers but, after the excesses of the late 1950s, were more stringently regulated than the BBC and were fearful of having their franchises revoked if they were perceived to be irresponsible. Some of these companies saw the lack of 'quality' children's programmes in their potential markets as an export opportunity, as we will see.

Television offered places to explore and new worlds to see: *Play School* (BBC2 1964–1988) offered round, square, or arched windows to look through, whereas television was a rectangular one to *climb* through. This 'exploration' began with *Andy Pandy* but became the standard narrative of first *Watch With Mother*, then children's non-fiction, and eventually most adult non-fiction television of the late 1950s (e.g., *Tonight* or *Zoo Time*). *Play School* bucked the trend in live-action programming for children in not stressing the factual but exploring the possibilities. Whilst the prevailing orthodoxy (Piaget's theories) said that children under five could not empathise with someone else experiencing something, almost all programmes made by the BBC for this age-group assumed that they could (ITV caught up later, as we will see). Both networks made programmes (and ads) where viewers were invited to second-guess what was coming ('Peekaboo!'). It is now thought that this allows a degree of anticipation and control for the child viewer to 'master' a narrative by prediction (the present-day justification for apparently tedious items in *Teletubbies* or *In the Night Garden...* and the like), but the studies that confirm this thinking happened only when *Sesame Street* began (CTW, 1969–). For the early makers of British children's programme, at least the 'Romantics', these guessing-games were part of the ritual of entering a place that existed behind the glass of the screen. Bird and Lingstrom were not working on the Piaget/Bruner principles, they were making a relatively cheap 15 minutes wherein the little darlings could tire themselves out and then be told it was time to go to bed. The timing of the broadcasts, as with *Listen With Mother*, the radio original, was strategically planned for parental convenience, coinciding with the recommended nap-time.

Following nineteenth-century children's literary tradition, the child viewer was invited into a world. That world generally existed when others (adults in general and one adult in particular, such as the Gardener in *Flower Pot Men*) had left. Curiously, *Andy Pandy* included a commentary on this trope, almost like a variation introduced for more experienced viewers, despite being the first to use it. After a few minutes of Andy and Teddy hopping about, they would go out of shot and Andy's doll, Loobie Loo, would come to life just as Andy and Teddy had. The point was that the viewers knew but Andy and Teddy did not. This exclusivity and bond of silence between the tots watching and the puppets was taken to almost *omerta*-like extremes by Bill and Ben (the eponymous flower-pot men). The inclusivity was reinforced here by the characters speaking 'Oddle-Poddle', just about comprehensible, so that the return of the Gardener was a threat to the existence of the game-world *and* the child's grasp of a new lexicon. Lingstrom and Bird, and their eventual successors Monica Sims and Anna Home, relied on exploration of an 'inscape' or consensual fantasy environment rather than on instruction. Jacqueline Rose (1984) points out that children's literature in Britain has perpetually run into this debate, often setting up didactic indoctrination as uniquely American (ergo 'bad') and non-utilitarian fantasy-play as the indigenous tradition, always under threat. Oddly, after the BBC closed it's children's department (in 1964), play was what the ITV companies encouraged.

The easiest way for a child to continue the game after a programme has ended is to have toys, books, puzzles, or clothes. *Muffin the Mule* had been made by people who had commercial sense working *with* the BBC, not *for* it, and had spawned a merchandising bonanza five years before America's *Davy Crockett* fad and ten years before 'Dalek Christmas', 1964 (the not-for-profit corporation's most notable cashing-in). Muffin had been almost the only puppet before *Andy Pandy* but rapidly became, for salesmen seeking to persuade parents to buy sets, what television was 'for'. Enamel 'screen-savers' were placed over display sets showing Muffin and Annette Mills. However, it was with fantasy dramas that this approach really paid off. Following Lew Grade's lead, the Corporation was making family drama (*Doctor Who*, BBC 1963–1989) whilst Grade himself was financing *Thunderbirds* (ATV 1965–1966). Grade's 1950s film series had been fairly infantile and, with the Spy boom and puppets-in-space, he found a way to sell not only programmes but entire worlds, via models and comics. Grade's 'kidult' entertainment prompted many of the BBC's hardy perennials into spawning annuals and books for Christmas (*Blue Peter*'s is still going), and for the very young there were now magazines such as *Playhour* with strips based on the *Watch With Mother* shows.

After a restructuring of BBC television in 1961, there was no drama made explicitly for children – the Lockeans were in the ascendant again – and *Play School* was commissioned mainly to do something with the fledgling BBC2. The Pilkington Report halted the reckless ratings land-grab (companies had to provide for all audiences, not just chase big ones) and the reformed ITA became a mirror-image of the BBC – well, almost so. Commercial television was *not* monolithic. It was, by this stage, 14 separate companies, competing with one another for air-time and with the BBC for audiences. Whilst the Big Four (ABC, Rediffusion, Granada, and ATV) still carved up prime-time to suit themselves, the smaller regional companies specialised. Companies such as Anglia, HTV, and, notably, Southern found that they had a better chance of getting a show networked if it was unlike anything anyone else was making. Adventures for children had fewer competitors, especially with no indigenous drama on BBC at that time. They persisted well into the 1990s but it was the smallest companies that had the most ingenious ways of maintaining viewer loyalty. *The Moon Stallion* (BBC, 1978) might be objectively 'better' than *Into the Labyrinth* (HTV 1980–1982) but the latter (deservedly) has the cult following.

The programmes we have inherited are, inevitably, unrepresentative of the whole allocation for children at any given time. Much has been wiped or was never recorded, including the bulk of the dramas that were the staple of programming for older children prior to 1967. Later book adaptations fared better as the subject of cults partly for their fantasy elements (e.g., *The Owl Service*, Granada 1969) but mainly because they were made entirely on film. Hitherto, up two-thirds of the BBC's children's output had been sustained narrative drama, often serialised novels. Their main source of drama now was imports, such as the French *Robinson Crusoe* (BBC 1965) with its thrillingly anachronistic spy-movie music and lavish location filming (significantly, the soundtrack CD outsold the DVD). This and others like it were repeated every summer. The repeatability and availability for video/DVD reissue of a series reinforces cult status but does not create it.

The import that altered the BBC's policies was *The Magic Roundabout*. Serge Danot's animated puppet series *La Manege Enchantée* was a satire on the Common Market, with national stereotypes embodied by animals or old men. Eric Thompson, seeking to account for the events on screen for British audiences, redubbed the dialogue with entirely new stories and characters. This added an entirely new dimension that adults enjoyed, with the Hancock-like Dougal alluding to topical concerns usually miles over the heads of the official audience, and the characters occasionally acknowledging the show's position as the last programme on before the news bulletin. Like the many French series that followed it to Britain, with notably less success, the original Danot series was very obviously a parable. Thompson's rendering, however, was undidactic showing how these various British character-types reacted matter-of-factly to surreal events, firmly in the Lewis Carroll tradition.

The success of *The Magic Roundabout* meant that this time-slot became the second most desirable market for quasi-independent producers such as FilmFair or Q3. These and many other companies had cashed in on the sudden spurt of commissioning when the BBC relaunched the Children's Department in 1967, requiring new filmed shows in colour. Perhaps the most significant thing is how similar these programmes were. Given commissions in batches, so there was little direct influence, this cottage industry employed craftsmen who made utopian microcosms that simultaneously hearkened back to their own childhoods and used whatever was current (children, they hoped, saw no contradiction between steam-trains and spaceships). They were by and about people making wonders out of odds and ends (see Wood on *Bagpuss* in this volume).

The DVD of *Crystal Tipps and Alistair* (BBC/Q3, 1972) brazenly announces that there are fifty 'wacky' episodes and makes veiled hints that it might be enjoyed (and have been made) with chemical assistance. 'Everybody knows' that all British children's television in the 1960s and the 1970s was laced with coded acid-head humour. As this series was from the makers of *Fingerbobs* (BBC/Q3, 1973), this might be true; children (anecdotally) found the whimsical inconsequentiality a bit dull. Now we can appreciate the production values (bespoke scores for every episode), the art-school Dadaism, and hints of kinkiness; however, at the time, it was watched, if at all, because it was the last programme that day offered to children. Scarcity bred gratitude, not love. The stoner humour associated with *detourning* children's shows began with the adults watching *The Magic Roundabout* noticing the large numbers of sugar-lumps and Dylan the Rabbit's hazy demeanour. The adult following is a function of the slot in which it was placed, as they were settling down to the news after coming home from work.

Many of the programmes shown in this period were scheduled on an empirical basis, as if they were hoping *something* would work. The ones that did are fondly recalled and seem perfectly natural; the ones that were less successful now seem downright freakish. It now seems bizarre that so much of the scant allocation of time for children on BBC1 was given over to Czech cartoons about armed robbery (*Boris the Bold* TX 1972), nightmarish East German fairy-tales (*The Singing Ringing Tree* UFA 1955, TX BBC 1965–1973), or whatever *Ludwig* was (BBC/Q3, 1975). ITV companies tried the same approach, giving rise to *Danger Mouse* and other near-forgotten sports ... *dozens* of them. If the 'canonical' shows of that era occasionally seem like the work of drug-crazed weirdos, it's fortunate that nobody remembers *Yak* (Yorkshire, 1972).

The perplexity of German and American researchers over *Teletubbies* reflects not only those nations' lack of the Carroll/Wordsworth tradition (to British eyes this series is a compendium of 'Greatest Hits' from the previous 40 years) but also the extent to which the assumptions the 'Romantics' worked under have been assimilated in the United Kingdom. It is a tradition derived from children's literature (coinciding with both the expansion of the market for Children's Lit and the publication of many 'modern classics', especially by Puffin Books under Kaye Webb). Much of this programming was made both for children and *about* childhood, at a time when this was a state of being lauded by most adults in the arts and broadcasting (and, of course, pop music: John Lennon and Syd Barrett made sure of that).

The children's TV 'canon' ticked every box in the modern scholar's checklist for a cult series. Programmes made for *Watch With Mother* or shown in its wake share the following distinguishing marks of Cult TV:

- Each was known *about* by a lot of people but loved passionately by a select few (under-fives with access to tellies).
- Attempts to change it were met with alarm by concerned viewers (or their parents).
- There was a hefty fantasy element.
- Each series evoked a world with its own rules and invited the viewers to participate in sustaining it.
- The series looked like nothing else on the screen (except something made by the same company for the same slot).
- There were moments of generic instability (e.g., inserted animation or addressing the audience) and discontinuous signifiers (anachronisms, abrupt switches from fairy-tale to everyday, unexpected musical items)
- It came apart into segments, both as a series and in individual episodes. It had repeated phrases that could be quoted out of sequence and songs that acted as shibboleths.
- The story-world continued extradiagetically (especially through merchandising).

So the status of children's television in Britain by 1970 was almost unrelated to how many children enjoyed the programmes. The BBC and many regional ITV franchise-holders were staking a lot of their corporate image on their children's output and there was a sense that innovation for its own sake was to be encouraged. The form of 'golden age' programmes might have begun from a tried-and-tested norm and diversified as part of the arms-race for the available slots, but today's programmes tend *towards* accepted conventions and are, thereby, more homogeneous worldwide. That CTW reformatted *Sesame Street* in 1993 to be almost identical to *Play School* speaks volumes. Their website proclaims that 'this is what the experts tell us children need'. Note 'need' rather than 'enjoy'. Most children now have a different relationship with television to that undertaken by the 1970s British kids. They have umpteen channels, all day. Despite there being far fewer children now than at any time since World War II, Britain's under-fives are a much more significant market and a lot more rides on the success or otherwise of a costly new children's programme. Research also shows how to make the raucous, lurid products of commercial television in America (or made to their models) more effective at delivering child-audiences who will demand the products attached to the programmes. A higher than average proportion of what British producers made between 1967 and 1980 had inbuilt cult-friendly tendencies that were derived by guesswork but are now scientifically proven to make better children.

Mind you, a lot of it *was* crap.

Recommended Reading

Buckingham, David, Hannah Davies, Ken Jones, and Peter Kelly (1999) *Children's Television in Britain.* London: BFI Books.

Lemish, Dafna (2007) *Children and Television, a Global Perspective.* London: Blackwell.

Bagpuss

(BBC 1974)

Tat Wood

Bagpuss demonstrates how cults can be formed through managerial negligence. Created for the BBC's *Watch With Mother* strand (although this was being 'rebranded' as *See-Saw*), the 13 quarter-hour episodes were shown repeatedly until 1987. Then the Corporation's experts decided that modern children would not enjoy the series, despite all the evidence, and let the rights lapse. In 1994, Channel 4 showed *Bagpuss* and *The Clangers* in the noon slot where *Sesame Street* had been transmitted, alongside other former BBC hits such as *Roobarb* (1975) and the colour episodes of *The Saga of Noggin the Nog*. Later it was broadcast in a seemingly unlikely semi-regular position at 4 am on Sundays in 1998–1999. In 1998, the BBC ran one of their cynical 'Nation's Favourite' polls, with the incentive that the talking-heads documentary would announce the winner and show a complete episode of whichever series won out of the 10 for which viewers were permitted to vote. They allocated five minutes for this, hinting heavily that *The Magic Roundabout* should triumph. Embarrassingly, *Bagpuss* won, a fact always mentioned whenever the series is reported on. With this status as National Treasure confirmed, Universal Pictures secured the rights to the series, together with *The Clangers* and the colour remake of *Ivor the Engine*. (The merchandising rights were owned by Licensing By Design, itself recently bought by children's intellectual property consortium Coolabi.) These three programmes were thus promoted on video and DVD for parents to share with their own children and have been transmitted almost constantly ever since. Being a division of a global media outlet ensures a long 'tail' for such apparently ramshackle productions.

Bagpuss was the eleventh of 16 series made by Peter Firmin, Oliver Postgate, and their various associates, under the working name 'Smallfilms'. It was the second to be made in colour, the first being *The Clangers*. It was the ninth to be made on film. Firmin, the designer and illustrator, and Postgate, writer and chief voice-artist, had nearly 20 years' experience in fast, low-cost animation of various kinds. They averaged two minutes of footage per day of shooting, twice what more 'professional' outfits managed. Their first major commission, the initial run of *Ivor the Engine*, earned them 'about ten pounds a minute' (Postgate, 2003). With no large sums of money riding on their success or failure, Postgate and Firmin concentrated on making something that appealed to them (a huge consideration when moving stuffed

175

creatures or pieces of card incrementally about 3,000 times a day) and told interesting stories. Whereas their earlier animations had been done as serials, both *The Clangers* and *Bagpuss* can be seen in any order, although there are visual clues that suggest possible sequences. Smallfilms seems not to have been concerned about whether their series would be shown within the *Watch With Mother* slot (which tends towards self-contained episodes) or at other times where sustained narrative is more appropriate. Whereas most animators specialise in stop-motion, rostrum-camera, animatronics, or Norman McLaren-style 'pixilation', Smallfilms had attempted all of these and mixed them promiscuously within their films. Thus the apparent gulf between the spontaneity and improvisation their stories champion and the meticulous craftsmanship needed for animation is bridged.

Each episode of *Bagpuss* begins with the ritual introduction: *faux* Victorian photos show a girl in period garb, playing with her toy cat, who supposedly runs a 'shop' that is a lost-and-found curio emporium. On finding something suitable, Emily recites a rhyme that wakes Bagpuss (whereupon the picture becomes full-screen and colour), who then wakes his toy chums in sequence; the last of these, the scholarly woodpecker Professor Yaffle, steps down from his bookend to investigate and at this point we go into the new material. Each object is dilapidated, so Yaffle's first assessment is tentative until the Mice clean it up and a more positive identification is attempted. Bagpuss, aided by one or other of his thinking-caps (an appropriate hat for each genre of story – this was Firmin's first notion for the series), tells a story about it (in rostrum-animated paintings, where everything hitherto has been stop-motion). Gabriel, the banjo-playing toad and ragdoll Madeleine, aided by the Marvellous Mechanical Mouse-Organ, find old songs about the object and, thereby, restore it to its pristine state. The worth of Emily's finds is in how many stories they contain, not their scrap-value. *Bagpuss*, with props, models, and camera-rigs constructed from odds and ends, is clearly the work of people who share this view. The episode ends as Bagpuss goes back to sleep and the rest return to inanimate sepia. The relatively slow pace is mitigated by unpredictability: within the regular set-up described above, there are many variations and abrupt changes of genre. Child viewers have to accept each step into a new story-level. Bagpuss may be *Primum Mobile* but it is Yaffle who speaks for the audience. The others sing or tell stories but Yaffle tries to make sense of it all, questioning whether each unlikely development is 'fiddlesticks and flapdoodle'. He is authoritative but wrong. Making chocolate biscuits with breadcrumbs and butterbeans is, as he says, preposterous, but so is a bookend saying so in a voice like Postgate's parents' friend Bertrand

176

Russell (Postgate, 2002). (Bagpuss himself has an honorary degree from the University of Kent at Canterbury.)

The filming followed the recorded soundtrack. Although Firmin's visual ingenuity gave the stories their starting points and character, Postgate and the cast treated the voice-work as radio. Vernon Elliott, their usual composer, had worked with Benjamin Britten and scored the stories for woodwind and in minor keys (in contrast to *Bagpuss*'s mandolin/accordion brightness and I-IV-V chord progressions). This homespun melancholy is at odds with the brashness of most children's television but entirely in synch with the hand-made quality of the films and the timeless bucolic of the settings. *Bagpuss* seems different, using folk music researched by Sandra Kerr (who also voiced Madeleine Remnant) and being set in a shop, yet the roots of the music, the shop setting, and the Smallfilms ethos are still, in a sort of William Morris approach, exalting the past as a source of value. Even when set in space, or in Wales, their films are resolutely English pastoral. Even on first transmission, the music was nostalgic for adults.

The 13 series not in the Universal/Coolabi deal are in the hands of fans. In the last years before his recent death, Postgate cultivated links with 'The Dragons' Friendly Society', whose membership comes from the same folk-music/pacifist/canal restoration circles in which he and Firmin moved. The Internet, perhaps contrary to expectations, fits Postgate's home-brew and handicrafts ethos. The distribution of these neglected series uses the techniques of small-scale activism pioneered by the Arts and Crafts movement in an attempt to secure this portion of childhood from political interference by resisting overt commercialisation. The Society (the name is from *Noggin*) has custom-made graphics by Firmin and is almost the archetypal cottage industry. They have been transferring the contents of Postgate's film-cans, including the suppressed serial *The Pogles* (Smallfilms/BBC 1965), to DVD and circulating them online or in shops. Ads for the recently restored *Noggin* series appeared in the broadsheet papers, where page upon page of reminiscences by celebrity admirers were published after Postgate's death on the 8 December 2008.

177

17 Cult TV and New Media

Denzell Richards

'We've also got a DVD extra saving the universe'
'Yes, well it's bound to happen eventually isn't it?'

David Tennant & Steven Moffat,
Doctor Who Confidential 3:10 *'Do You Remember
the First Time?'* (BBC Three, 9 June 2007)

The nature of television is currently undergoing substantial change and redefinition, with implications for how programmes are produced, disseminated, accessed, and viewed, as the United States and Europe plan to cease electronic analogue broadcasting and replace this with digital transmission. At the time of writing, much of continental western Europe has already switched to digital broadcast, the United States switched over in 2009 (http://www.dtv.gov), and analogue transmitters began to close down in the United Kingdom in 2008 with a projected final digital switch-over by the end of 2012 (http://www.digitaltelevision.gov.uk). At the same time, the number of different media formats ('delivery platforms' or 'technologies') on which television can be received and/or viewed continues to expand. A full list is impossible to make since new technologies continue to develop, but such platforms include the following: cable/satellite video-on-demand (VOD) and pay-per-view (PPV); interactive digital services (such as BBCi or Sky Interactive in the United Kingdom, accessible via the red button on a digital TV box remote control); digital versatile, Universal Media, and Blu-Ray discs (DVD, UMD, and BD respectively); hard disc drive (HDD) recorders, also known variously as digital or personal video recorders (DVR/PVR) (well-known examples being TiVo in the United States and Sky+ in the United Kingdom); video-equipped mobile phones and MP4 players (such as Apple's iPod); and internet broadband streaming video (including BBC's iPlayer service).

The television broadcast industries have reacted to these developments with some uncertainty, occurring as they have within the context of a multi-channel environment which has already seen the decline and fragmentation of the television audience and advertising revenue (Gomery and Hockley, 2006: 27). While some of these technologies can benefit broadcasters by enabling them to re-sell their back-catalogue to consumers (especially DVD), devices such as PVRs have caused industry concern with predictions that viewers will use the technology to avoid commercials altogether (Boddy, 2004: 104–107). The industry has responded to this with an increased use of so-called 'virtual' advertising and closer co-operation with corporate sponsors in programme production, as well as by experimenting with greater viewer interactivity to maintain audience interest and loyalty (143–149). What is particularly significant in the context of 'cult' television programmes, however, is the increasing need for broadcasters to create strong and clearly identifiable 'brands' through marketing particular 'hit' shows which can both maintain audience loyalty and be effectively exploited across all the proliferating digital platforms (Griffiths, 2003: 89–93). While this strategy is not exclusive to cult franchises (as the popularity of *Big Brother* [Endemol, 1999–] as a worldwide brand testifies), cult programmes are in part defined through their accumulation of particularly 'invested' fan audiences who not only regularly consume the text but also actively participate in the dissemination of franchises through what John Fiske calls 'enunciative' and 'textual' productivity (1992: 37–42). Broadly defined, this includes contributions to discourses surrounding the text (whether in person or online) as well as creative acts such as the production of fanzines, websites, art, fiction, and videos, all of which are circulated within and occasionally beyond the fan community. These interactive practices are often in turn encouraged by programme-makers who produce additional secondary or 'satellite' texts that are aimed primarily at a fan audience and, in the realm of fiction at least, have led to cult programmes leading the way in terms of television/new media innovation.

Digital Television as New Media

All the new television platforms described above are examples of what is referred to variously as 'new', 'digital', or 'computer' media. Unlike older analogue formats which always possessed physical referents (celluloid film, video tape, etc.), new media is essentially 'virtual', having been either 'digitised' from its original physical form or captured digitally in the first instance, and exists only as computer code. This has a number of important implications for analysing new media texts, which Lev Manovich (2001) has explored. Of his categories, the most pertinent for a discussion of television as new media are 'programmability', 'automation', and 'variability' (in particular considering the 'database' as a cultural form).

'Programmability' refers to the fact that new media texts are constructed purely from code which can be 'subject to algorithmic manipulation' (27), allowing viewers to adjust various aspects to suit their preferences (such as changing the image resolution to match their internet connection when watching streaming video online). Since most viewers are not equipped to manually adjust the code themselves, some measure of 'automation' is built into the digital box, DVD, PC, or other human-computer interface (HCI) so the viewer need only select their preferences for the artificial intelligence (AI) to adjust the settings appropriately according to its programming (32–36). Such programmability and automation extends to media content as well, with PVR users able to create customised television schedules which are time-shifted and stored on the hard drive to watch at their convenience. Some PVRs such as TiVo even feature AI that 'learns' its user's preferences over time and records not only the viewer's own selections but also other similar programmes for them to sample.

Automated programmability of this type means that while there may have once been an original 'base' media object, it now exists in a range of personally customised variations (36–37). Moreover, digital television exists as code which can be stored on a computer server or hard drive, forming a digital archive which if connected to the internet could be accessed remotely and instantaneously from anywhere in the world. This means that digital television programmes are not only textually variable at the point of reception but also representative of the potential for what Boddy refers to as 'the end of simultaneity' (2004: 102) where it can no longer be taken for granted that viewers are watching the same programme at the same time. Instead viewers increasingly have a greater opportunity to select what they want to watch, in the way they want to watch it, at the time they want to watch it, from a database of content stored across a range of new media platforms.

This new wider access to, and customisation of, an archival database of television programmes from which viewers can select has important implications for existing critical and industrial understandings of the television audience and viewer practices. Specifically, the concept of broadcast 'flow' (see Williams, 1974; and Ellis, 1982) has traditionally held that television does not consist of discrete self-contained programmes so much as it is divided into sequential narrative segments which have no definitive beginning or end and can be joined and left by a viewer at any time. While the viewer may switch channels to one of several alternative broadcast flows they have no actual control over what each contains. However considering television as a database of programmes spread across various platforms radically alters this conception of broadcasting by allowing viewers to circumvent the flow. This has considerable implications for television producers, broadcasters, and advertisers, whose traditional conception of passive media consumers has become increasingly threatened by a view of audiences as active and discriminatory users of interactive digital technologies (Boddy, 2004: 106–107). Jenkins has considered this shift in industry/audience relations in terms of a newly emerging paradigm of media 'convergence', or 'the flow of content across multiple media platforms, the cooperation between multiple media industries, and the migratory behaviour of media audiences who will go almost anywhere in search of the kinds of

181

entertainment experiences they want.' Under this new paradigm, he argues that increasingly 'old and new media collide, ... grassroots and corporate media intersect, [and] the power of the media producer and the power of the media consumer interact in unpredictable ways' (2006: 2).

Cult Television's Use of New Media

Television's redefinition as a form of new media and its dissemination across multiple digital platforms is particularly relevant to a consideration of cult television programmes for several reasons. First, owing to their frequent positioning within science-fiction, fantasy, and horror genres, cult programmes are likely to already require new media technologies (such as computer graphics) in their production. Indeed it is often innovation in style facilitated by such technologies which helps assure a programme's cult status. *Babylon 5* is a good example, not only for its pioneering use of computer graphics and virtual set technologies, but also for effectively 'future-proofing' itself by shooting in the 16:9 high-definition image aspect ratio from the beginning of season one. More importantly however, new media (especially the internet) can also greatly facilitate interactive viewer practices and discourse, not only within the active fan community but also between invested viewers and programme-makers via official websites and in weblogs such as *Whedonesque* (http://whedonesque.com), where *Buffy the Vampire Slayer, Firefly,* and *Dollhouse* creator Joss Whedon regularly posts.

Partly to encourage this active fan community as well as to more firmly establish their franchise across multiple media platforms, particular cult series frequently provide additional secondary or satellite texts made available as special features on DVD releases, via interactive TV services and online. Such texts can be distinguished from fan-produced works by the official involvement of the production team and their dissemination through commercial channels. This in turn lends them additional authenticity, providing canonical status in the case of fiction and a sense of 'authoritativeness' where providing an account of the series' production. The new *Battlestar Galactica* (*BSG*) and *Doctor Who* (*DW*) both provide good examples of the use of new media technologies in this way to strengthen their respective franchises, with *DW*'s initial executive producer and show-runner Russell T. Davies very candid about the increasing commercial necessity of providing such wide-ranging media content across a variety of platforms (see his interview with Mark Lawson, 2008). Most notably both series have produced additional video texts which expand on the main series' narrative, an approach first pioneered online by the web series *Homicide: Second Shift*, a spin-off to *Homicide: Life on the Street*. This is part of the process Jenkins refers to as 'transmedia storytelling', where narrative elements which contribute to the overall fictional universe of any given series are disseminated across a variety of media platforms, encouraging and rewarding increased audience engagement and interaction with the franchise as invested viewers actively seek these out (2006: 21).

The *BSG* expansion series *The Resistance* is a 10-part mini-episode serial which takes place during the Cylon occupation of New Caprica between the end of season two and beginning of season three. Made available in 2006 as streaming video 'webisodes' from the official website (http://www.scifi.com/battlestar) and later included on the U.S. DVD release of season three (Universal Studios, 2008), *The Resistance* includes several cast members from the parent programme and ties directly into the continuing *BSG* narrative, setting up several story points which are resolved during later episodes. The producers subsequently released a further series of seven webisodes on a weekly basis leading up to the premiere broadcast of the television movie *Battlestar Galactica: Razor* in November 2007. Set during the final stages of the first Cylon War, 20 years prior to the events depicted in the parent series, these webisodes were intended to build anticipation ahead of *Razor*'s broadcast, including the revelation that old-style Cylon Centurions from the original *Battlestar Galactica* (1978–1979) would feature. Viewers of these webisodes would later discover that footage from them would also feature as flashbacks in the film itself (further confirming their canonical status), while the complete web series was also subsequently made available on the DVD release (Universal Studios, 2007).

DW's first new media expansion video meanwhile was 'Attack of the Graske', made available on the interactive BBCi television service after broadcast of 'The Christmas Invasion' (2:X) in 2005. This 15-minute adventure featured David Tennant as the Doctor encouraging the viewer to make either/or selections at appropriate moments to determine the course of the narrative; it remains one of the few examples of television fiction yet to utilise such direct interactivity with respect to story content itself (Fig. 17.1). Later during series two, 13 one-minute videos were also released weekly to accompany each new episode broadcast. These *Tardisodes* (2006) could be downloaded to mobile phones or viewed online via streaming video from the official website (http://www.bbc.co.uk/doctorwho), and although not as narratively integral to the parent series as *The Resistance,* they still referred to story events, occasionally including the participation of characters from the main narrative. *DW* expansion videos have not been limited to new media platforms alone, however, with two mini-episodes broadcast as part of the BBC's annual *Children in Need* appeal (untitled, 2005; and 'Time Crash', 2007) and another incorporated into the first *Doctor Who Prom* held at the Royal Albert Hall in July 2008 ('Music of the Spheres'). Following the commercial logic of media convergence, this latter episode was also made available simultaneously to non-attendees via streaming video from the official website during the 25-minute interval. (For a more detailed analysis of the transmedia storytelling techniques

Fig. 17.1   David Tennant as the Doctor in Doctor Who

utilised by *Doctor Who*, as well as further consideration of some of the *DW* and *BSG* expansion series referred to here, see Perryman, 2008.)

In addition to their fictional expansion series, both *BSG* and *DW* make available a number of 'behind-the-scenes' features in a variety of formats across multiple new media platforms. Such audio, video, and other textual materials demonstrate Manovich's database in action, since often the same source materials will be re-edited to suit different platforms and their particular mode of exhibition, highlighting his variability principle. For example, audio commentaries by *BSG* executive producer Ronald D. Moore and others were initially made available as downloadable podcasts from the official website following the broadcast of 'Tigh Me Up, Tigh Me Down' (1:09) and thereafter. These same audio commentaries were then transferred across to the subsequent U.S. DVD release of season one, while earlier episodes feature newly recorded commentaries (Universal Studios, 2005). Downloadable audio commentary podcasts were also made available on the *DW* official website from 'The Christmas Invasion' onwards; in the case of the subsequent DVD releases of series two to four, the majority of these were, however, replaced with newly recorded alternatives (BBC Worldwide, 2006–2008). *DW* also has a dedicated documentary crew following its production, footage from whom can be found in a variety of re-edited formats as the following: the BBC Three series *Doctor Who Confidential* (BBC Three, 2005–) which is 30–45-minute long; *Doctor Who Confidential Cut Down* (BBC Three, 2005–) re-edited to 15 minutes and included on the DVD boxsets; extracts incorporated into the CBBC series *Totally Doctor Who* (BBC1, 2006–2007); and as 5–10-minute-long video podcasts downloadable to mobile phones, or as streaming video from the official website. As with the choice of alternative episode commentaries, these 'making-of' videos will also often feature content exclusive to one or another version of the material, providing an incentive to access these across several different platforms and rewarding viewers who do so.

BSG and *DW* are by no means unique amongst cult television series in their production and dissemination of secondary texts across various new media platforms. Other examples of fictional expansion videos include *The Animated Alias* 'Tribunal' included on the DVD release of *Alias* season 3 (2004), the 13-part *Lost: Missing Pieces* mobile phone series (2007, see http://abc.go.com/primetime/lost/missingpieces), and the three-part *Heroes: Going Postal* (2008, http://www.nbc.com/Heroes/Webisodes). Meanwhile virtually all programmes with an official website and/or DVD release make some kind of 'behind-the-scenes' material available (see, for example, http://www.cwtv.com/cw-video/supernatural, where interviews with *Supernatural* cast and crew members and even selected episodes are available to watch via streaming video). As I have argued elsewhere specifically with regard to DVD releases (Richards, 2007), such 'behind-the-scenes' materials give the impression of an inclusive dialogue between the producers and fans of the programme, strengthening these viewers' support of and investment in the continuation of the franchise, while also establishing an official over-arching meta-narrative of its production. Following Craig Hight (2005), this involves the establishment of particular 'interpretative frames' which cumulatively suggest the 'appropriate' contexts within which viewers are invited to consider and discuss the programme's creation, typically de-emphasising points of contention and concentrating on actual production issues rather than commercial concerns such as financing. Considered alongside expansion series such as *The Resistance* and *Tardisodes*, this means that while access to all aspects of any given series is increasingly fragmented across multiple platforms, the net result for invested viewers likely to seek out such official secondary sources is that the franchise's overall fictional universe is actually rendered more coherent, and a meta-narrative of its production is particularly well-established and disseminated throughout the fan community. In this sense, it might be possible to expand Jenkins' concept of 'transmedia storytelling' to incorporate all 'transmedia narratives' (plural) established for any given series, to also include official accounts of the programme's production.

Audience Appropriation

While Jenkins argues that the successful circulation of media content in this emerging 'convergence culture' 'depends heavily on consumers' active participation... [where they] are encouraged to seek out new information and make connections among dispersed media content' (2006: 3), the variable aspect of digital media (essentially that it is one giant database of media objects which

185

can be remotely accessed and easily manipulated through automatic processes by its various users) means media producers cannot particularly control what operations the audience will actually perform on and with these texts. This is especially the case with invested fan audiences, who, Jenkins has argued, are 'consumers who also produce, readers who also write, [and] spectators who also participate' (1992b: 208). In particular, fan appropriation of material ('textual poaching' to use Jenkins' terminology, 1988) is greatly facilitated by such a database of existing texts, where new works such as fan videos can be created from the digital archive of already existing materials. Indeed, where examples of this textual productivity by fans were once only 'narrowcast' to a relatively small network of correspondees and convention-goers (Fiske, 1992: 38), thanks to the internet, such user-generated material (UGM) is now broadcast more widely on video-sharing websites such as YouTube (http://www.youtube.com).

It is not only the creation and dissemination of fan works which are facilitated by convergence culture and the database form; issues of access, broadcast, and intellectual property rights are also raised more generally. A clear example of this was the internet 'leak' in March 2005 of 'Rose' (1:1), the first episode of the new series of *DW,* three weeks before its planned broadcast (Lyon, 2005: 132–134). The easy transfer of and remote access to digital materials also threatens traditional national television markets, with old, small-scale, and comparatively slow fan tape-trading groups replaced by mass-traffic online peer-to-peer (P2P) networks and file-sharing websites such as RapidShare (http://rapidshare.com), effectively eliminating any international time lag for new episodes. National broadcaster attempts to limit the 'global' fan community/market to domestic users – for example, the BBC restricting users without U.K. IP addresses from accessing video materials on their web domain – has had only a small measure of success. This risks being counterproductive when attempting to disseminate particular brands as widely as possible, however, potentially leaving non-U.S. *BSG* and non-U.K. *DW* fans frustrated at being unable to view, for example, the *The Resistance* and *Tardisode* expansion series.

Future Developments

While the current transition of television from an analogue to a digital, new media form will undoubtedly bring changes in, and a redefinition of, practices of production, exhibition, and reception, it is important to avoid a teleological or technological determinist view of these developments. This is a field which continues to evolve; just because the technology is capable of being used in particular ways, such as circumventing the broadcast flow with a PVR, does not mean that television viewers will actually use it for this (indeed TiVo's own research suggests they do not; see Boddy, 2004: 129–135). Boddy and Manovich both stress the need to situate current television and new media developments within their appropriate historical and cultural contexts. Manovich has pointed out the strong influence nineteenth–twentieth-century visual codes (especially cinematic 'realism') have on new media texts (2001), while Boddy has drawn attention to the unrealised (and remarkably consistent) utopian predictions and fantasies which have accompanied every emerging media developed in the twentieth century, from broadcast radio onwards (2004). In similar terms, Jenkins has highlighted some of the more revolutionary promises made by early advocates of digital media which also failed to materialise (2006: 5–6). For specific examples of how these issues apply within the current television/new media context, consider that, although reasonably successful in Europe, interactive television in the United States has to date been a comparative failure (see Boddy, 2004: 136–143). UMD also failed as a popular media format (Arnold, 2006); and despite heavy promotion, the number of people who downloaded the *DW Tardisodes* to their mobile phones eventually fell well below levels anticipated by the BBC (BBC Annual Report 2006/2007 pt2: 30; for some possible explanations for this failure, see Perryman, 2008: 32–33).

From the industry's perspective, a major issue which has so far prevented the proliferation of original, made-for-the-web cult series remains the lack of any proven commercial system for effectively exploiting these texts online. Any such system would ideally enable the programme authors to continue taking advantage of an audience of active, invested viewers to strengthen their franchise (with all the accompanying interactive fan practices this entails), while maintaining firm control of intellectual property rights and making a profit. So far attempts to achieve this have been somewhat mixed. *Sanctuary* (2007), originally an independently produced webcast science-fiction drama made available on a paid-download basis, was partially re-shot and retooled as a television pilot for a continuing series broadcast on the U.S. Sci-Fi Channel (2008–). Star and co-executive producer of the webcast, Amanda Tapping, explained in an interview with *SFX* magazine that 'the monetary business model doesn't quite work for the internet in the way we'd hoped', highlighting in particular that the video was quickly disseminated across the web for free from a variety of sources, rather than viewers coming to the official website to pay to download it (cited in Edwards, 2008: 24).

By contrast, different tactics were adopted by Joss Whedon for his three-part *Dr. Horrible's Sing-Along Blog* (2008). Presented free over the course of one week from 15 July 2008 via streaming video from the official website (http://www. drhorrible.com), the episodes were then made available as paid-downloads from Apple's iTunes online store until the end of July, before eventually being released on DVD with additional extra features. The success of the free video stream was immediately apparent – at one time averaging around 200,000 hits an hour, according to writer Jed Whedon, and necessitating a server upgrade after the website crashed due to user demand (Dr Blog Bot, 2008). Similarly the

187

first episode became the most commonly downloaded television show within 24 hours of being made available on iTunes, with all the episodes remaining in the top ten downloads for the next week (http://www.apple.com/itunes/store/tvshows). It remains to be seen whether this level of success will extend to the DVD release as well, however; if it does, then this system of limited tiered releases on different platforms following a media convergence model (where each subsequent release brings with it new options for user interactivity while also acting to build anticipation for the next) may well become highly influential. As Sanjoy Roy observes, however, the success of *Dr. Horrible* is likely due to a confluence of factors including Whedon's cult-auteur status as much as the method of web distribution employed, so the extent to which such success could be replicated remains unclear (2008). From a wider industry perspective, it is also by no means certain that the independent production practices employed on *Dr. Horrible* (themselves inspired by the Writer's Guild of America strike during Winter 2007–2008) could be successfully replicated commercially, and it is still unclear to what extent the venture has actually proved to be profitable (Littleton and Miller, 2008).

Even if made-for-the-web series do become increasingly successful, however, long-held audience viewing habits mean that, despite continuing new media innovations, the vast majority of programmes continue to be produced for, and received by, viewers in a context of traditional television broadcasting. While this shows definite signs of developing as television continues to redefine itself as a digital, new media format, it would be precipitous to judge exactly what this will mean for our current critical and commercial understanding of the industry and its audience. Regardless of this, it can be demonstrated that current cult series' use of new media across multiple platforms to establish closer links with their invested viewers is already having an effect on interactive fan practices; although this can be of benefit to the shows, it is also problematic for broadcasters attempting to maintain control of access to their franchises and of their exploitation. Furthermore, it seems likely that cult programming will continue to represent a major site of experimentation and innovation in the potential application of newly emerging digital media technology.

Recommended Reading

Boddy, William (2004) *New Media and Popular Imagination*. Oxford: Oxford University Press.

Jenkins, Henry (2006) *Convergence Culture: Where Old and New Media Collide*. New York: New York University Press.

Manovich, Lev (2001) *The Language of New Media*. Cambridge, Massachusetts: MIT Press.

18 *Doctor Who*
(BBC, 1963–1989, 2005–)

Miles Booy

Doctor Who, which began transmission in November 1963, was finally cancelled after it ran for a little over 26 years and was returned in 2005. The program garnered the United Kingdom's largest cult fanbase as it oscillated between being a mainstream UK hit, a solid-but-unamazing part of the BBC schedule, and a niche cult. It is perhaps the only show ever to generate its own publicly circulated cliché about its viewing position (it was always watched from 'behind the sofa'), not to mention its own sub-genre of programming (since *The Tomorrow People*, *Sapphire and Steel*, and *Primeval* are all shows consciously created and marketed as 'ITV's answer to *Doctor Who*').

One sign of the presence that the programme maintained in the centre of culture was the number of behind the scenes staff who were, however briefly, in the public spotlight. Writer Terry Nation became a mini-celebrity as creator of the Daleks. By the early eighties, Matt Irvine was the semi-official face of the BBC Special Effects department, a frequent guest on magazine programmes showing off technical tricks and props. As such appearances suggest, although *Doctor Who* lacked the prestige of costume dramas, it was consistently used by the BBC, just as historical serials were, to promote the imagination and skills of their design and costume departments. This reached its peak with the Radiophonic Workshop – the branch of the BBC dealing with electronic music and non-naturalistic sounds – which in the mind of the British public became so associated with the programme that the rest of their broad range of work was neglected and under-appreciated. This was most famously the case of her majesty Queen Elizabeth II, who, when introduced to the staff of the Workshop in the early seventies, said 'Ah, Doctor Who' (Briscoe and Curtis-Bramwell, 1983).

From the beginning there were signs of extreme devotion amongst certain viewers (what we'd now calls fans). The fourteenth episode (broadcast 22 February 64) is one of the 108 missing from the BBC's archive, having been wiped in the early seventies when black and white TV was no longer thought to be of interest. However, that episode (like the 107 others) survives as an audio soundtrack, recovered from tape recordings made by enthusiastic viewers – people who had decided, as early as February 1964, that this programme was something special, something worth recording with the only equipment to hand. Nor was this enthusiasm just a passing fad – those recordings survived for decades before being donated to the BBC.

Possibly the oddest thing about this fan commitment is that early *Who* offered almost no continuity from story to story. Backstory and a detailed fantasy environment, often thought to be crucial to cult success, are almost wholly absent. The Doctor's origins are the subject of mystery, and the stories (at this point anything from four to seven episodes in length, and very, very occasionally longer) a series of unconnected landings, linked only by one common set – the TARDIS control room – and the regular characters. When the Daleks return, their second story contradicts the first in important ways, and the third has nothing of the rich post-nuclear themes of the original. There are no details of an imagined world for fans to immerse themselves in. When, in the eighties, continuity did manifest itself in terms of an obsession with the program's own history, the programme shed viewers – perhaps not a complete co-incidence.

What the show possessed was strangeness. Even those with no time for the show acknowledged its haunting theme tune as important. It is a cliché to say *Doctor Who* scared you as a child, but some people who say that are just talking about the abstract imagery and weird electronic sounds of the title sequence! Though overshadowed by the titular villains, the expressionist sets of the Daleks' first story are striking even today. No-one would suggest that all the design work reached that standard – some of it was laughable – but its visual and aural icons entered British culture. Towards the end of its initial run, the design became perhaps more literal than it had initially been. Compare, for instance, the famous Tom Baker title sequence. Though invariably referred to as a 'time tunnel', it is really only a graphic pattern. Deciding it is a time tunnel involves a massive interpretative leap. The later sequence, which adorns Sylvester McCoy's episodes, is simply mundane imagery of the TARDIS in flight. Had the show lost its knack of making abstract imagery and pop art palatable and resorted to more literal representations? This sort of reading of what was special about the programme – its experimentation with sound and vision – is at the centre of the *About Time* books, a fine fusion of academic and fan paradigms (Wood and Lawrence, 2004–2007). I like it. It seems true to my experience; since the Queen associated the Radiophonic Workshop with *Doctor Who,* perhaps it was true to hers as well. Readings of *Doctor Who* will continue to proliferate, but there will surely be few which receive royal endorsement.

Recommended Reading

Briscoe, Desmond and Roy Curtis-Bramwell *The Radiophonic Workshop – The First 25 Years.* BBC Books, 1983.

Wood, Tat and Miles, Lawrence *about Time: The UnAuthorised Guide to* Doctor Who. Mad Norwegan Press, Des Moines. Six Volumes. 2004–2007.

19 Writing Tie-ins

Nancy Holder

have been a rabid fan of every TV show for which I've written tie-in material. They include *Highlander, Buffy the Vampire Slayer, Angel, Smallville,* and *Wishbone* (a wonderful PBS show that presented the classics to children with the help of a Jack Russell terrier). Like other fans, I invest heavily in the reality of 'my' programs, going so far as to spin fantasies about 'what-if' relationships and additional adventures for the characters. I get frustrated or disappointed over character arcs and plotlines that don't go the way I want. And I worry that a wrongheaded turn of events will result in cancellation.

But I watch even my most beloved series with a detached, professional eye that puts me at a constant distance. My mandate is to serve the show as it exists, not to change or alter its reality. So I'm taking notes, physically or mentally, to try to get a bead on the reality the creators/producers are trying to present, and how they do it – their style, their voice. Then I seek to replicate that as closely as I can. I can't depart from the intentions of the creators even if I would prefer to see things go another way.

Recently I listened to an interview on National Public Radio with Spanish actor Javier Bardem. When asked which of the characters he has portrayed is most like himself, he replied that his job as an actor requires that he stop being himself in order to fully embody the character he is playing. That's a good analogy for what I do when I'm writing tie-ins. The more I love a show, the more I try to assimilate what I think makes that show so special and dear to me. Then I attempt to leave myself out of the equation and embody the characters, applying whatever storytelling skills I have acquired over the years to do justice to the work.

Everything I write in the service of the show has been vetted and approved by an editor (or editors) at the publishing company, the creator of the series or someone in his production company, and the copyright holder – in the case of *Buffy the Vampire Slayer*, for example, that would be Twentieth Century Fox. In the usual course of events, the person who invites me into the sandbox is the editor of the publishing company who has bought the license to publish material based on the show. These licenses can run into the millions of dollars, and one might assume the pressure would be on the tie-in writer to help the publisher recoup his/her investment.

That's true only to an extent. Usually, the licenses are spread out over many different projects, written by more than one author. Unless an author's sales figures are significantly better or worse than those of the overall program, the success or failure of the program is attributed to the editor, the marketing department, or the original intellectual property – the TV show or movie itself. If the books aren't selling, the publishing company may review their approach to the material. In the case of *Buffy the Vampire Slayer,* the young adult line was dropped because even younger fans were reading the 'adult' books. Cover art was revamped a number of times. But if such efforts go for naught, the publishers may suspect that the franchise is losing steam and reassess whether or not they want to renew their license. This was the case with *Buffy* after its first-run broadcast ceased. Simon and Schuster slowed interest and then eventually abandoned the book-publishing program.

Sometimes the rights to material devolve naturally to a specific publisher because both entities are owned by the same conglomerate; other times, publishing houses bid on the rights at auction. At most large publishing houses, there is an editorial group in charge of the media tie-in program; the editors in those groups acquire a stable of authors like me, whom they commission to write material for them. (In turn, many of us belong to the International Association of Media Tie-in Writers, where we discuss our work and on occasion share market information with each other.)

Authors gain status when they get a contract to write work based on commercially successful movies or TV shows, or properties that may not be 'big' but are perceived as cool. The jobs attached to high-profile movies and TV shows generally go to high-profile tie-in authors, which naturally raises their stature even higher. There is jostling and competition for various 'franchises.' A recent plum was *Supernatural;* another, *Ghost Whisperer.* As soon as I read about Joss Whedon and Eliza Dushku's plan to create a new series titled *Dollhouse,* I emailed my old *Buffy* editor. My entire message, *'Please*?' Invited authors pitched original *Firefly/Serenity* novel ideas, but publishing plans for an initial order for three original novels never came to pass. I also campaigned for *Joan of Arcadia* and *Veronica Mars* (neither of which ever developed into a publishing program.)

There are three main types of book tie-in material: original fiction, novelised versions of extant episodes, and nonfiction works. In the case of *Buffy the Vampire Slayer,* I have written original novels, short stories, and novellas; novelisations; and companion guides; with my co-author, Chris Golden, I created an ersatz Sunnydale High School Yearbook. Other nonfiction ephemera can include quiz and trivia books, biographies of the stars, spell books, encyclopaedias, 'field guides', 'the making of' books, and the like, as well as script books containing photographs in collectable form.

Editors, producers, and copyright holders are more hands-on during the first couple of seasons of a show's run. During the first season especially, the producers must find an audience and keep it; so everyone with a stake in the project's success wants to ensure the quality of ancillary merchandise (everything from lunch boxes to novels). Alas, for the tie-in writer, pioneers can be the unfortunates with arrows in their backs. I know of more than one instance where the debut author of a series of tie-in novels was abruptly (and sometimes very publicly) dismissed and replaced. 'Now that I know what I don't like,' a producer once told me, 'I can tell you more clearly what I want.'

So giving 'them' what they want can be a moving target for a tie-in writer. That pressure extends to pleasing the fans as well. Cult fans are as proprietary of their image of a show as the producers are. They also 'plug in' by positioning themselves as the true fans, the original fans, the real fans. They make distinctions of fan seniority – who has been a fan longer; whether someone has met writers, cast, and/or crew; visited the set; gone to a posting board party, etc.; and whether they can pinpoint errors of fact or interpretation in a tie-in author's work. To assert their status, they will give themselves titles and responsibilities, for instance, using e-signatures such as 'Keeper of Spike's Duster' (Spike being a popular character on *Buffy*).

They will also establish themselves as heads of offshoot mini-cults who are privy to what's 'really' going on a show. For example, there is a group of fans who firmly believe Joss Whedon has paired teenage Buffy the Vampire Slayer and her Watcher (mentor), the middle-aged Rupert Giles, as a romantic couple. While Whedon has never mentioned this in any interview or DVD commentary, they point to his invitation to 'bring your own subtext' as code that he is not being 'allowed' by his masters at Twentieth Century Fox to overtly portray this core relationship.

Fan influentials become so proprietary that they will also regard themselves as keepers of the true flame if a series changes direction away from their perceived view of 'accepted' reality. If they see what they perceive as errors, they are quick to point them out. I have known things about 'my' shows that the 'civilian' fans do not and cannot know about until later in that season or even a few years down the road. There's also the case of what is termed 'continuity drift', where the producers deliberately cause their own canon to alter. This occurs for all sorts of reasons. Certain characters are more popular or compelling than expected (in the case of *Buffy,* Angel, Spike, Anya). Sometimes actors are replaced, as with *Bewitched* and *The Waltons*, with new actors who play the same characters, with no explanation offered for the substitutions.

The unfolding of an arc may require some continuity retrofitting (the arrival of a new character, such as Buffy's magically created little sister, Dawn; or the loss of a character who 'goes off to college') and, dare I say it, in the blinding speed with which episodic TV is made, sometimes canon is unintentionally violated.

It takes six months or more for a manuscript to become a book on a shelf; in that time, an entire season of new episodes might air. A lot can change as the episodes go into production, and not all those changes are communicated to the publisher and, therefore, to me. In the case of *Buffy*, a popular character (Oz) didn't have a last name for a very long time; and it was a complete surprise to me to discover that Buffy's vampiric boyfriend Angel was not named Angel at all. That was his nickname; his real name was 'Liam.' But by the time a book comes out, the fans have already seen the episodes containing the new information. So some fans count coup by informing the rest of the tribe of the perceived blunders that I have made in print.

There are also fans who are jealous that I am in the sandbox, while they are not. Every tie-in writer I know has had reviews written by jealous fans who wonder aloud (all over the Internet) why such a hack was allowed to write a novel in that show's universe, asserting that the fan could do a better job because s/he is a 'real' fan. Fans such as these view each publication that is not theirs as a lost, wasted opportunity, and so it necessarily must be found lacking.

I understand and sympathise, although professional courtesy at the very least prohibits me from saying so. I haven't gotten all the tie-in assignments I've auditioned for and have watched plums go to other tie-in writers. I was in the running to write a novelisation for a comedy-horror movie; I was such a geeky fan of the 'franchise' that I went straight from the airport after a flight from Japan to see the theatrical release of the most recent film. Another author got the job, in part because he had tie-in credits on his resume, while I, at that point, did not. When I professed my envy, he offered to let me ghostwrite it for him (for half his advance) because he had no real feeling for the material.

I recently failed to get another job I wanted badly because the producers specifically requested for writers without tie-in credentials. In another recent case, I was solicited for a children's picture book for an animated film, only to be told that one of the producer's wives had decided to write the book herself.

I got my first tie-in gig – *Highlander* – not only because I was a *Highlander* fan but also because I had already written and sold a lot of novels. Some fans don't appreciate that sheer love of their show won't get them a writing assignment. But here's the rub – I wasn't a *rabid* fan when the editor and I made first contact. I liked the show and I was excited by the idea of writing a novel for it. But I was not a cult follower.

After the editor told me I had a shot at writing a book for her, I watched three years of episodes in a week. I *became* a rabid fan, and I think that showed in the 13 story ideas I faxed to her on day eight.

As soon as I got the green light, I met with the producer (the late Bill Panzer) in Los Angeles – the first and only time I have been asked to 'take a meeting' for a tie-in – and we hashed out exactly what Mr. Panzer wanted.

He told me he 'didn't want the book to sound like an episode.' I took that to mean he wanted more character development, subplots, etc. But it turned out that in my masked ball scene, he wanted 300 guests instead of a handful of extras; there were some scenes he had always wanted to show in the series but couldn't afford in his budget.

It was at this point that I understood that a tie-in writer acts much like a scribe, putting on paper the ideas of the show/movie's creators. Fanfic writers don't have to operate under the same strictures; they tend, precisely because of their love of the show, to imprint themselves on the material. I am compelled to 'Bardemise' myself, that is, to present the show as it exists as closely as I can rather than to represent it through the lens of my own ego.

I am fascinated by the dialogue the Internet has created among producers, fans, and 'cultural workers' such as myself. Show writers put in 'shoutouts' for fans – on *Buffy,* for instance, the inclusion of a Polgara demon was for a fan whose screen name was Polgara (who is now, I believe, the webmistress for former Whedon writer Jane Espenson). I mentioned Jazzercise in *Buffy* novels and then heard Buffy's mother, Joyce, shout it out it in an episode. When 'VIP's' post on fansites, it adds to the status of the site owners and the participants. It also lets the fans know that the VIP's are aware of them and of their wishes. If VIP's respond to those wishes, through shoutouts or perceived alterations in the creative property – TV episodes, movie sequels, subsequent novels – the recursion/feedback loop creates a sense of community and belonging.

I think this gives these properties breath and life. The reality of the 'universe' extends past the experience of watching someone else's imagination at work and integrates, at varying levels, into the viewer's daily 'mundane' life. I look to the exploding amount of web content on official show websites as evidence of this, combined with crawls at the bottom of the TV screen of email messages from fans or the 'secret' URL's that viewers can access either during or after a broadcast, which contain yet more content.

I've done shoutouts to fans and fan-friends by using their names or variations of their names in books, or by including material only a true keeper of the flame might know about, such as mentioning once-cult-now-mainstreamed actor James Marsters' band, Ghost of the Robot, or alluding to characters who have come and gone. On occasion I've been criticised as having too many shoutouts or references to other episodes, as if I'm trying too hard to prove that I'm in the club.

There may be some truth to that; that may be ego or sheer fan-love of the show. Most likely it's a combination. Sometimes the victory of getting the job does, embarrassingly, translate into showing off. And the energy of loving at a cult level has to go someplace. It's best spent when it translates into becoming as invisible as possible, so the beloved – the show – can be venerated by other cultists. For a tie-in writer, the honour lies in the attempt.

Film is slightly different. There's less give-and-take between creators and fans, but it's not wholly absent. In the case of *The Golden Compass* (Chris Weitz, US/UK, 2007), the producers fed tidbits of information and solicited opinions from influential fans via websites such as bridgetothestars. By the time a novelisation author is brought in, the story is set, but the discerning author may realise that the producers and fans have a number of concerns s/he would do well to address. And although there may be a number of individual recapitulations aimed at different age groups, there is only one story to retell. This actually makes it easier to step aside and serve as the movie's scribe.

A set of authors is usually hired to work on these demographically different novelisations; other authors may be working on the official 'the making of' book, quiz books, colour books, and the like. Often, writers have very little time to write these books – sometimes as little as three weeks – and there appears to be a trend to hire authors who live in Los Angeles, who can come into the studio to read the script in an office rather than receive a copy of the film. Sometimes the novelisation writers are even forbidden to take notes, and authors have complained of being allotted as few as three hours to read the script, never to see it again.

Novelisers rarely get to see the finished film – it's usually still in production – and there are stories of realising quite late in the game that they have been sent the wrong copy of the script. Nevertheless, if the movie is a hit but the novel sells poorly, the blame is usually heaped on the author.

Occasionally, a 'franchise' is developed that expands past the individual film into sequels, and then beyond the original 'universe' of that film. K.W. Jeter actively sought out writing the sequel to *Blade Runner* (Ridley Scott, US, 1982) in hopes of increasing his sales figures – which he did – and has gone on to write two more, although there have not been two more film sequels. There are *Alien Versus Predator* novels, created after the two franchises (*Alien* and *Predator*) joined forces first in a comic book and then in a film and a sequel. The original novelisation author might be brought on board to write additional material if the franchise has 'legs' – more novels, short stories, comic books – or, in my pioneer model, s/he might be left out entirely.

In such cases, editors and fellow tie-in writers will give the one who was booted some tea and sympathy and exhort him/her to get back to work on something else. In other words, not to take it personally. Again, it's necessary to quell one's ego – and that makes for a strange exercise in quasi-Buddhist detachment. Difficult, perhaps, but that is what the Force is for. A cultist fanfic writer can keep going, but once the publishing program is over or my services are no longer required, it really is time to fall in love with something new.

That's much easier to do in the film world, where there's an implicit understanding that the number of adventures of a beloved character/universe is limited. There are only three *Matrix* movies and, so far, only three *Pirates of the Caribbean* movies and only two *Hellboy*'s. Fans accept that the movie franchises they love may not make it back to the big screen for a few years, if ever, due to the huge production costs in time and money. There was a series of films planned for *The Rocketeer* (Joe Johnston, US, 1991), but the first one did badly and the rest were never made.

But the visits to a beloved TV show's world can number in the hundreds. There's more to talk about in chat rooms, more to ponder as a writer – in short, more to love. More to grieve when it's over. On the night of the broadcast of *Buffy the Vampire Slayer*'s last episode, I didn't watch it. Instead, I watched the clock as I put together a Barbie puzzle with my daughter, counting off the acts, then sitting quietly for a moment when I knew it was over. It felt like a death.

With the arrival of DVDs and the Internet, shows can enjoy a sort of life extension. But thus far, this hasn't translated into more opportunities for tie-in writers to share the love professionally, as it were. Though some of us are hired to work on web content and, on occasion, on ancillary merchandise such as comic books and graphic novels, it really is time for us to accept that it's over and start dating again. It's strange to let go of one franchise and become infatuated with another, become committed ... and then disappear in the service of the beloved. But somehow, we tie-in writers keep managing it.

I was talking to someone who worked for Joss Whedon and he said, 'People ask me when I'm going to get a life. My life is here. My family is here.'

Then he got fired. I've always wondered how he moved on. When involved in a franchise at a production level – at the level of a tie-in writer – one does feel a sense of belonging. Not only do I love my franchise, but that love is reciprocated – in the form of discussions with my editor, set visits and cast parties, presents from producers, and relationships with show runners and actors that sometimes last beyond my formal association with the show.

But at some point, most of the headiness and the perks fade; unless I'm careful, I can sound like an old soldier recalling her glory days. It really is time to fade off into the sunset ... until I find another job.

20 *South Park*
(Comedy Central 1997–)

David Simmons

O riginally, the creation of enfant terribles Matt Parker and Trey Stone, Comedy Central's hugely successful cartoon series follows the adventures of four young boys: Kyle, Stan, Cartman, and Kenny, as they go about their day-to-day lives in the fictional town of South Park, Colorado. While ostensibly following the traditional sitcom format (like other contemporary animation successes such as *The Simpsons*), the show is best known for its highly irreverent and subversive nature, both in terms of stretching the boundaries of the sitcom format through its formal innovations and in wilfully mocking many of the 'politically correct' discourses that typically surround institutions such as the family, the police, celebrity, and the religious, political, and educational systems of America.

The genesis of the show is well documented. Though originally trying to sell the idea of a series based on the transgressive concept of a friendly, talking piece of faecal matter titled *The Mr Hankey Show*, Parker and Stone redeveloped the idea to focus on the four young boy characters, capitalising on the cult success of a video Christmas card they had created (*The Spirit of Christmas: Jesus vs Santa*) to get a deal with the nascent Comedy Central. The first episode of the re-titled *South Park* aired on 13 August 1997 attracting an audience of approximately 65,000 households; by the following year, *South Park* was getting the highest ratings for *any* program in 'basic cable' history.

The critical and commercial success of *South Park* demonstrates the popularity of 'cultishness' as a selling point in the contemporary era. The series actively courted a niche audience with its consciously crude animation style (actually now produced on the latest computer software) and frequent taboo-breaking, scatological humour. In spite of or perhaps because of this niche aesthetic, the show went on to achieve immense mainstream popularity, appearing on numerous magazine covers, spawning a host of merchandise (estimated to have raised over half a billion dollars to date), creating a feature film (1999's Oscar-nominated *Bigger, Longer, and Uncut*), and seeing the bigoted, self-centred, character of Cartman being voted the tenth most popular cartoon character of all time.

The huge commercial achievements of *South Park* as a media product raises interesting questions surrounding the supposed cult status of the series and similar contemporary cartoon 'breakthrough' hits such as *The Simpsons*, *Beavis and Butthead,* and *Family Guy*. Can such shows be considered as 'cult' when they appear on the cover of *Time* magazine and win Emmy awards? In many ways, *South Park* exemplifies the innate conflict of interests between the creatively irreverent, anarchic attitudes expressed in cult shows and the antithetical need to adhere to the conformist practices of a capitalist system such as network television.

The relative aesthetic, ideological, and financial freedoms of the cartoon form certainly seem to gift such series with greater satiric and parodic possibilities than their 'live action' cousins. Throughout the 12 seasons of *South Park* to date, the characters have been kidnapped by aliens, befriended a talking poo, morphed into mechanised monsters, led to indulge in cannibalism, and met by a host of famous individuals including Tom Cruise, Britney Spears, Michael Jackson, Saddam Hussein, Jesus Christ, and Satan. Indeed, *South Park* has courted controversy with its handling of celebrity-based scandals. Episodes' dealing with accusations that Michael Jackson was a paedophile ('The Jeffersons', 8:7) and Steve Irwin's untimely death ('Hell on Earth 2006', 10:11) provided column inches for the tabloid newspapers. Perhaps more significantly, the now infamous 'Trapped in the Closet' (9:12) episode, which mocked Scientology and many of its more prominent celebrity followers, raised the ire of both Isaac Hayes (one of the show's voiceover artists who resigned as a result of the program) and the Church of Scientology, who allegedly threatened Comedy Central with litigation should they repeat the episode. The subversive nature in which *South Park* deals with celebrities points to another facet of the show's appeal to niche audiences; the series' embracing of the postmodern techniques of referencing and self-reflexivity, exemplified in episodes such as 'Simpsons Already Did It' (6:7) and 'Cartoon Wars: Part I' and 'Part II' (10: 3–4), satiates a contemporary cult audience's desire to seek out complex cultural references and attempt to decode them.

Yet, the permeation of *South Park* into the mainstream arguably occurred as a result of the process of merchandising rather than through an appreciation of the creative and frequently cultish content of the show. Such was the high media profile of *South Park* during the late 1990s that Comedy Central was able to divorce much of the show's iconography (most notably its four central characters) from the taboo-breaking extremities of its episodes. Thus merchandise targeted at audiences that would probably be (largely) unfamiliar with much of the actual content of the show, such as children's tee-shirts and plush dolls of the characters, found a great deal of success with minors in particular. This overt commercialism caused many fans to begin to criticise the show for what they perceived as its overly aggressive merchandising. Indeed, many felt betrayed when Parker and Stone apparently relented to allow bringing the popular character of Kenny back to life in order that Comedy Central could make more Kenny merchandise.

This tension between commercial and cult interests manifested itself also in the ongoing battles between Comedy Central and many of the show's more creative fans over the issue of intellectual copyright. Many commentators have suggested that a great deal of the early buzz surrounding the series was created through the Internet, and more specifically through a host of fan-made websites that sprang up following the show's broadcast, offering original artwork using *South Park* characters. Perhaps, some semblance of an amicable agreement has been reached concerning this issue with the recent official publishing of *South Park* episodes online by the show's creators for fans to download for free. Nevertheless, Comedy Central's tight grip on the marketing and merchandising offshoots of the show means that, for many of its original audience, *South Park* has lost much of the anarchistic subversiveness that once made it such required cult viewing.

Part 4

The Cult in Cult TV:
Audiences, Fans, and Fandom

21 *Dark Shadows* (ABC, 1966–1971)

Stacey Abbott

Collinsport Maine, a town haunted by ghosts, werewolves, witches, alchemists, and most famously vampires, is an unlikely setting for a daytime soap opera, let alone a successful one. Yet in 1966 Dan Curtis launched what would become the first cult daytime soap opera and therein lays *Dark Shadows*' uniqueness. In terms of its serial format, the volume of episodes, and its emphasis upon unfolding, often duplicitous relationships, *Dark Shadows* is a soap to its core. Within that format, however, the shows' creators flooded the daytime TV screens with storylines and monsters adapted from the classics of horror literature, including *Dracula, Frankenstein, Dr. Jekyll and Mr. Hyde, The Turn of the Screw,* and even the work of H.P. Lovecraft. This hybridity gave the show tremendous cross-generational and cross-gender appeal, as it not only maintained the soap opera's traditional 'housewife' audience but also developed a huge teenage fandom, making it the show that everyone 'used to run home from school to watch'.

First aired on 27 June 1966, the show began its life as a fairly conventional soap, replete with secrets, deceit, sex and violence, but presented with a Gothic twist. The isolated coastal town, the old Collinswood Manor house, and the young heroine, Victoria Winters, newly arrived in Collinsport, situated the series within traditions of Anne Radcliffe's *Mysteries of Udolpho*, Charlotte Bronte's *Jane Eyre*, and Daphne DuMaurier's *Rebecca*. Faced with poor ratings and potential cancellation, Curtis inserted a ghost into these Gothic surroundings and the ratings began to rise. Following this success, Curtis introduced an even more supernatural creature in the form of vampire Barnabus Collins (Jonathan Frid), a character that both Curtis and Frid acknowledged was supposed to appear only briefly, terrorising the town of Collinsport before a stake was eventually driven through his heart. The rest is the stuff of TV legend. The fan letters began to pour in, the ratings soared, and Barnabus, now considered a form of anti-hero, was saved from an untimely staking, instead becoming one of the first 'reluctant vampires', killing only out of physical need, plagued by guilt and consumed with self-loathing for his cursed existence. In this regard, *Dark Shadows* prefigures a long tradition of reluctant vampires: from Louis in *Interview with the Vampire* to Angel, and later Spike, from *Buffy the Vampire Slayer* and *Angel*. Unlike these later examples, however, Barnabus' reluctance was never entirely planned. Frid himself says that it was largely the creation of the fans who saw something in his performance that hinted at a deeper sentiment (cited in Berkvist, 1968: 17). When they began to write to Frid and explain how they related to the character's sense of isolation and loneliness, the actor and writers responded by incorporating it into Barnabus' characterisation, going so far as to have him search for a cure to his vampirism. So even at this very early stage, the fans played a crucial role in the show's mainstream success.

But how can this successful soap opera – that at its height drew in 20 million viewers, made stars of its cast, and lead to a merchandising boom that was unprecedented for daytime TV – be considered cult? It did so initially by breaking the rules. While the content was clearly unusual for soap operas, the format of the series was equally challenging. Curtis insisted that something scary happen every episode, a format that defied soap convention in which storylines are slowly developed so that audiences can easily catch up on the plot (cited in Berkvist, 1968: 17). Instead *Dark Shadows* demanded *constant* attention, a fact reinforced by the introduction of lengthy flashback narratives set in the eighteenth and nineteenth centuries. Initially introduced in order to provide Barnabus with a backstory to his vampiric condition and to fuel the audience's reading of him as a victim of circumstance, the flashbacks took on a life of their own, sometimes lasting for months in which the modern narrative would be paused while the past narrative took over. To spare the cost of replacing the cast, the show developed an ensemble tradition in which each actor would take on multiple characters from different time periods. Later they even began to explore parallel universes, in which the actors would play alternate versions of their modern-day characters, all of which required the audience to distinguish between each of the actors' different personas. Furthermore, this approach to narrative positions *Dark Shadows* as the prototype for the cult TV text, whose seriality, according to Gwenllian-Jones and Pearson, permits and facilitates 'non-linear narratives that can go backward and sideways as well as forward, encompassing multiple time frames and settings to create a potentially infinitely large metatext' (2004b: xii). *Dark Shadows'* complex storytelling not only requires commitment from its audience but also anticipates within its very text the form of metatext that would evolve around the entire *Star Trek* franchise or would be built into much later cult series such as *Babylon 5* and *Buffy the Vampire Slayer*. In *Dark Shadows*, the writers created a complex narrative universe in which the fans could insert their own 'interpretations and inventive reformulations' of the narrative, a characteristic considered by many to be a key component of cult TV (Gwenllian-Jones and Pearson, 2004b: xii).

Dark Shadows' cult status is also enhanced by the series' simultaneous brevity and longevity as well as by the context of its production. As a soap opera, *Dark Shadows*, lasting only five years, was comparably short. As a cult series, however, the text, with 1,245 episodes, is vast. Rewatching the show is no small commitment on the part of fans or scholars. Also, the low budget and the live-to-tape format meant that the series sported a host of much loved gaffes and flubbed lines. While contemporary cult series such as *Alias* and *Supernatural* include outtakes as a pleasurable addition to the DVD experience, *Dark Shadows* embeds all of these painfully comic moments within the show itself and, as a result, engenders the affection of the fans for these strained moments of early television.

More significantly, while soap operas, pushing ever forward into the future and never inviting the reviewing of past episodes, are considered the most ephemeral of television, *Dark Shadows* was the first soap opera to be sold into syndication as early as 1975. This desire to revisit and re-experience the world of the Collins family was renewed again when MPI Publishing decided to release the series on video, later on DVD, with high-profile advertising campaigns in horror and science-fiction magazines, appealing directly to the children who grew up with the show by featuring the tag line 'Remember when you ran home from school to watch *Dark Shadows*. Relive every fang-filled moment from the Grand-Daddy of the soap operas'.[1] The kids who watched it in the late 1960s form the fan community of today, still keeping the love of the show alive through fan magazines, fan fiction, conventions, and festivals. Although less visible than *Star Trek* fans, *Dark Shadows* fandom rivals the Trekker community for its commitment and endurance, reminding the modern cult TV scholar that longevity remains the ultimate test of cult fandom. *Dark Shadows*, like its vampire-hero Barnabus Collins, has stood the test of time.

Notes

1. See *Cinefantastique* 21:2 (1 September 1990).

22 Television and the Cult Audience: A Primer

Hillary Robson

Television and the cult audience are often linked, perhaps due to the fact that no other media form has produced such devoted fans, with some displaying an array of seemingly bizarre behaviours perceived as socially unacceptable to 'normal', mainstream society. Historically, fans have been known to act a bit odd: consider the sports fanatic who dresses in the team's colours and refuses to miss a game – no matter what else is scheduled, including work or familial obligations. Or, the music fan who travels cross-country to watch his/her favourite band play in 20-plus cities, singing along to every song in trance-like, devoted fashion. And, then there's the television fan who reschedules activities around airings of their favourite series, haunts the internet for interviews or the latest casting news, and knows each episode title and storyline by heart.

These behaviours may seem obsessive, odd, and eccentric to the non-fan, and occasionally the cult fan can commit acts that catapult them from harmless eccentrics to what is best termed as mentally disturbed behaviour. Consider Edward Seidel. In 1979, the 15-year-old jumped to his death from an overpass bridge after learning that his favourite television series – *Battlestar Galactica* – had been cancelled (Snopes, 2006). The story was chronicled in regional newspapers and had national appeal; Seidel went from a disturbed teenager to urban legend as Americans across the country learned of his death. Seidel epitomises the modern understanding of the crazed, obsessed fan who defines himself based on his object of fandom: the 'cult' fan – the one that your parents warn you about and that society often makes into a laughingstock. He is the Trekker, the Friday night SF geek who stays home to watch *Stargate SG-1* and spends a fortune buying the perfect costume for Comic Con.

But the so-called cult fan is more myth than reality, a definition based on a skewed understanding of audience behaviour that is largely outdated. The term 'cult' suggests something that is outside of the mainstream, an organised group of abnormal rebels chafing against the norm, and invariably has a religious connotation, one that suggests a certain prescribed ritual, a degree of ceremony, and a process of initiation. Beyond the religious implications, the idea of the cult also carries a negative weight, especially when heard in conjunction with the words 'deviant', 'abnormal', or 'obsessive.' Certainly, the largest body of fan scholarship has focused upon the dysfunctional or 'pathological' fan, perhaps most evident in an observation made by scholar Lisa Jensen, who commented on the invariable 'linking of fandom, celebrity, and mass media [as] an unexplained constant in commentary on fandom'. In a chapter of Jensen's *The Adoring Audience*, theorist John Caughey discusses how the modern celebrity functions as a role model and argues that a fan's fixation on a celebrity or star where there is an 'intense fantasy relationship with a celebrity figure' can prove dysfunctional (cited in Jensen 11). Through the 1980s and the 1990s, this concept of the 'dysfunctional' fan was highly popularised by the media, suggesting that 'cult' is always a negative term, resulting in mass suicides à la Heaven's Gate, brainwashing, polygamy, spousal abuse, or religious sacrifice. Another connotation associated with the term relates to size – cults are usually a small (albeit organised) group of people sharing similar beliefs, ideals, or practices in a way that seems as though the object of their cultish affection is somehow spiritual or sacred.

The word itself is derived from the Latin *cultus*, meaning 'worship', and the French *culte*, 'care' or 'cultivate' (Oxford, 2008). Both are applicable: while some cult audiences actively 'worship' their object of textual devotion, other cultists work to cultivate or care for their texts, bringing it to the forefront, taking it from anti-mainstream to mainstream status, or even preserving its popularity. In this chapter, I'll discuss the different types of cult audience, while also providing insight into the construct of the audience, the fan, and the cultish enthusiast in order to create a more contemporary understanding of the modern 'cult' audience.

Conceptualising Fandom

In order to understand the cult audience, we must first understand the fan: fan mentality, fan engagement, the meaning and scope of the term as a defining label with cult behaviour as characteristic of certain type of audience. The term 'fan' is stubbornly difficult to define, as different conceptions of fan and fandom exist today. The word first appeared in 1889 as an Americanism derived from the Victorian-era use of the word 'fancy' (Oxford, 2008). Several negative terms are associated with the word 'fan', notably 'fanatic', a word that often represents the behaviour of the insane. In *Fan Cultures*, Matt Hills states, 'everybody knows what a "fan" is. It's somebody who is obsessed with a particular star, celebrity, film, TV programme, band; somebody who can produce reams of information on their object of fandom, and can quote their favourite lines or lyrics, chapter and verse' (2002, ix). Hills' use of the term 'obsessed' lends to the common understanding that fans are commonly perceived as existing outside of the norm, a person consumed with the act of fandom and textual engagement. The obsessed or cult fan is the one whom *Star Trek*'s Captain Kirk, actor William Shatner, advised to 'get a life' during a 1986 *Saturday Night Live* sketch; fan-knowledge is perceived as a deficit and not as a beneficial contribution to society.

But fans *do* contribute to a specific type of society, complete with a social hierarchy and systems of belonging: the fan culture. According to fan theorist Darshana Jayemanne, fans and fandoms generate fan *communities*, individual societies based upon and

> around the reception and remediation of cultural texts, [with a developed] complex system of belonging. Fandom is variegated, not only along the obvious lines of which texts are appreciated and appropriated by a particular group, but also by the medium in which the text is expressed, the specificities of translation, the location of the fans, the engagement with or collection of peripheral merchandise and the particular historical narratives and self-imaginings of the group in question. (2003)

Jayemanne's distinction certainly places the fan within a social context, as a participant within a subject-specific microcosm, a sort of textual ambassador who reveres the source text through interpretation and analysis. This construct places the fan within an almost academic-like environment, complete with textual immersion and a system of belonging, and yet still harkens to the concept of the 'cult', specifically in the associated behaviours of indoctrination, immersion, and ritual that occurs within fandom communities.

As an extension of the concept of the fan as textual ambassador, a more developed theory comes from the work of psychologists and audience theorists Nick Abercrombie and Brian Longhurst, who 'treat fans and enthusiasts as a form of skilled audience' (1998, 121). The 'skilled audience' refers to an audience that not only is knowledgeable about the fan product but also 'studies' the object of fandom as if it were a readable text. To grasp this concept fully, one must consider that Abercrombie and Longhurst consider the fan as a 'consumer' of their fan-object. For the television fans, this means that their favourite series, its cast, crew, and even the network broadcasting it are key components of the fan text and are items available for the audience to consume or digest, a concept that I relate to as 'patronage'. The audience, thus, is considered a patron of the television text. To serve as bona-fide patron, the fan must engage with the text on a regular, even ritual, basis.

For further elucidation, consider a fan of the American television series *Desperate Housewives*. The base-level of fan patronage would be the weekly viewing of new episodes. Further acts may entail recording the series for repeated viewing, watching online episodes, purchasing digital copies of episodes, buying licensed merchandise (DVD Series, soundtracks, official books, etc.), or buying third-party merchandise (a periodical featuring news about the series, a fan guide). Patronage is a consumptive process that requires the individual's desire to prolong and sustain active textual involvement on an individual level. The more the viewer watches and engages with the series text, the more they identify with the text of the series and perceive themselves as a fan. As their engagement intensifies, this helps the fan develop from a cultist (or ritual viewer), to an enthusiast.

Borrowing the model of 'enthusiast' from the work of psychologists Hogget and Bishop, Abercrombie and Longhurst argue that fans and enthusiasts differ in terms of the level of fan affect and media usage. Specifically, they identify the enthusiast as the fan 'expert', the viewer who can relate the arc of a series from its first pilot episode and intimately knows the details of the cast and crew. They are regular consumers of the text and operate with a high level of patronage, purchasing and accessing both official and unofficial merchandise to further promote their social status within the fandom as experts. As Abercrombie and Longhust view the fan as 'people who become particularly attached to certain programmes or stars within the context of relatively heavy mass media use' (138), this understanding defines the fan as a regular 'appointment-viewer': an individual who schedules his/her life around specific television programs. On this level, the fan is an individual who always tunes into the series but more than likely does not do more than purchase the DVD series for re-viewing. One step up from the fan is the 'cultist', the individual who forms 'explicit attachments' to source texts and engages in media usage that 'revolves around certain defined and refined tastes' (139). The cultists are more socially organised than the fan in that they form informal social networks as a result of shared interests. Unlike a fan or cultist, an 'enthusiast' is primarily focused upon the activities relational to his/ her media interest and participates heavily in clubs or organises events based around the media text. They also engage in a more specific form of media use limited to the cult object, such as official publications or events.

These different distinctions of audience and fan affect provide suitable groundwork to initiate discussion into my understanding of the fan and fandom as descriptors that are multi-layered and complex, with psychological and sociological impacts. Several theorists have attempted to create a distinct labelling and categorisation system of audience engagement and affect; I consider all of these viewers as 'fans', just on a sliding scale of engagement. Similarly, I consider the 'cultists' as fans who are both regular patrons of their object of fandom as well as engage in regular discourse with others about their favourite television series. These individuals often engage in the active process of soliciting or recruiting interest in their series. This discourse level may begin with water-cooler discussions about the series, the visiting of and posting upon internet message boards, or the organising of viewing parties. Consider the fans of the HBO series *Sex and the City*, a series chronicling the lives of four

New York City singles who divulge their experiences in their professions, their relationships, and their close friendships. Four years after the conclusion of the series, a film was released (aptly entitled *Sex and the City: The Movie* – 2008) with a tremendous response from its patron-fans. Once only regular viewers, these patron fans organised viewing parties to celebrate the release of the film across the country, promoting the movie release on internet websites and in their social circles. Abercrombie and Longhurst would view the behaviours of these women as 'enthusiasts' due to the social aspect of their engagement.

However, I see this as a prime example of the discourse-status of the fan – one that encourages social networking of others in order to promote the fan-object. Once the fan reaches this level of engagement, their interaction with the text shifts from an individual to collective processes, further insuring textual patronage and, in effect, impacting the continuity of the fandom. In the incidence of the *Sex and the City* feature release, the female fans helped to raise a respected $55 million in ticket sales on the film's opening weekend, knocking the previous-week winner and blockbuster *Indiana Jones and the Kingdom of the Crystal Skull* (Steven Spielberg, US, 2008) from its number one place in the ratings (Pandyah, 2008). This win was more than respectable, considering that the film had an 'R' rating, which often results in less than stellar box office performance. The film's success was immediately attributed to its strong fan base of women, with 'millions of loyal fans leading to brisk advance ticket sales, especially for opening day. This was an event film for female moviegoers and the numbers soared above even the loftiest of pre-release forecasts' (Pandyah, 2008). The rich and integrated social network of *Sex and the City* fans facilitated the film's success, reflecting the purchasing power of a well-developed and strong fan community.

Seeking out and creating a social environment for the discussion of the fan-text creates fandom communities, a central location for the 'skilled audience' of cult fans – those who are patrons and celebrants of the fandom. This concept of fan as 'skilled audience' is further reflected in Hill's *Fan Cultures*, with a working definition of fandom as

> not simply a 'thing' that can be picked over analytically. It is ... always performative; by which I mean that it is an identity which is (dis) claimed, and which performs cultural work.... Fandom, then, is never a neutral 'expression' or singular 'referent'; its status and its performance shifts across cultural sites. (2002: xii)

Here, the fan is a cultural *performer* who forms an identity within specific fandoms based upon and around the source text. In a 2005 article (contained in a special issue of *American Behavioral Scientist* on fandom) entitled 'Patterns of Surprise: The 'Aleatory Object' in Psychoanalytic Ethnography and Cyclical Fandom', Hills discusses what it means to become a fan, expanding on the static definition of an individual who is 'part of an interpretive community and a socially organised group of fellow fans' (2005a: 801). This characterisation of the fan reflects the sophistication in Hills' understanding of fandom and the fan affect. In *Fan Cultures*, Hills discusses the concept of performance within fandom, in a cultural sense. And here, the expansion of that very idea is reflected in the evolution of the fan as part of a community formed because of – and around – a particular fandom. This view is largely in concert with my own understanding of the cult fan and modern fandom as a whole – it is an activity largely motivated by the fan affect and the cultural action and designation of that affect. Consider again the example of the *Sex and the City* fans. These fans could easily be referred to as 'cultish' in nature, after all, fans came in droves to frequent theatres the weekend of its film release. One film reviewer described the *Sex and the City* fan audience as an 'estrogen brigade', a categorical comment that, although not openly negative, has a less-than-positive connotation about the nature of the *Sex and the City* fan audience. These fans tout the experience of drinking Cosmopolitans (*Sex and the City* protagonist Carrie Bradshaw's favourite drink) and eating cupcakes (also popularised by the series). Not only that, they can also relate the series' main characters' views about their physical body flaws in trivia, or what the name of the first wife of Carrie's long-term love interest and eventual fiancé 'Mr. Big' was. These women – a mix of mothers, college graduates, and professional women – all have formed an understanding of their own identity as fans of the series, based upon either an identification with or fascination of the women that the television series chronicled. This self-identification led them to integrate within a social community of other fans and thus to feel they 'fit' within their fandom, that they are part of an ingrained social network of like-minded women who in all likelihood are less similar than they perceive.

This example of the *Sex and the City* fandom is unique in that it is far removed from the typical understanding of the 'cult' fan. Cult, once negative, has become mainstream. Being a fan is becoming not just normal, it's cool. What's more, today's fans act within a social pattern that has been established by the hardship of those once-maligned fans of the past: those who paved the way to make fan engagement something to be celebrated instead of frowned upon. This concept is further clarified by Hills, who presents the idea of 'cyclical fandom', which 'appears to presuppose a level of self-reflexivity (and nonreflexivity) in relation to serialized fan engagements' (2005a: 803), where

> fan identity … is open to multiple revision and rewriting without prior
> fan objects necessarily being viewed as embarrassing, inauthentic,
> or deficient. This leads to the emergence of patterns of (routinized)
> surprise in iterated media consumption and fandom. (804)

Here, being a 'fan' is a type of evolutionary process. It supposes that we can all look back on that first text that we identified with as a 'fan' and then view each sequential fan experience that followed as part of a 'transmedia consumption as a matter of course', according to media scholar Richard Campbell, where individuals engage in a process of investigating and seeking fan texts in a ritualised process to derive pleasure, a type of 'modern autonomous imaginative hedonism' (1995: 77). It implies that the first pleasure we received as fans – say that first Saturday morning cartoon that we ritually viewed on a weekly basis, or the first prepubescent crush on a television-series character – is one we seek to recapture and build upon. What once gave us joy from the mere act of viewing alone changes as we age, develop, and mature, and we find that we need more to sustain that same hedonistic rush – thus encouraging us to bring others to our fandom, to buy merchandise, or to seek out internet sites and message boards.

Similarly, this understanding divorces us from the previous concept of the cult fan as married to only one genre of television series. Now, we're free to love a variety of series and to express our fan status for each and with different levels of engagement. In this sense, just because some individuals are fans of *Battlestar Galactica,* they need not be fans of every single science-fiction series – they can legitimately also be an equal fan of a series far removed from the deep-space, drama-filled quest of *Battlestar* – even a series such as *Sex and the City.*

These findings go beyond the static organisation of 'hardcore' or obsessive fan engagement that is often not at all cyclical and is indeterminately focused on one specific source text or genre. Similarly, the 'mainstream' fan often follows trends perceived as popular in a shifting, passive manner. If we establish that the modern audience has not only a penchant for developing at least a patron-fan based identity for texts, especially television texts, then we can also consider that the modern fan audience is equally susceptible to popular trends. An excellent example would be the amazing mainstream success of *Dancing with the Stars*. What premiered as a summer series catapulted into a ratings darling, a surprise considering that the series is based upon 'has-been' (and even never really were) media stars paired with ballroom dancers in a weekly competition showcasing their developing dancing skills. The series has expanded to a biannual run of new seasons, with fans who are so rabid that it has led to a weekly featurette on *Good Morning America* and mass-enrolment in ballroom dance classes around America. In an attempt to capitalise upon this fan frenzy, in 2008, networks such as *Bravo* premiered similar dancing series (*Shut up and Dance)* with a lukewarm audience response. Later that same year, MTV released a series entitled *America's Next Dance Crew,* revising the general format of 'People learning how to dance and judges telling them what went wrong' as made popular in the copycat series of *Dancing with the Stars.* The series became an MTV ratings boon, earning in the upwards of 20 million viewers for the first and second series finale episodes. These examples support Hill's idea that fans have evolved from being tied to one genre or nature of series, and that they are subject to the whims of what is perceived as popular or what could be, in terms of entertainment, a refreshing change of pace.

Fandom and Academia

Fandom, then, along with society's perception of being a fan, has certainly changed. These changes were largely ushered in by the work of a host of early fandom scholars, those who reflected the fan experience in a positive light and furthered contemporary discourse about what it means to be a fan. In 1992, two book-length publications about fan culture, Henry Jenkins' *Textual Poachers* and Camille Bacon-Smith's *Enterprising Women: Television Fandom and the Creation of Popular Myth,* initiated academic examination of both fans and fan culture. Jenkins' text is the first to address fandom from a theoretical perspective, combining participant research and ethnography to paint a portrait of interactions between fans and a source text. Jenkins' *Textual Poachers* is based upon an article written in response to a *Newsweek* feature on the twentieth anniversary of the television series *Star Trek* and its fandom entitled '*Star Trek*: Rerun, Reread, Rewritten.' Jenkins discusses the portrayal of fans during that time in American society, when fans were 'like cultural scavengers ... [they] reclaim works that others regard as "worthless" trash' (1988: 19). This 'reclaiming' process results in 'poaching', a concept developed by Michel de Certeau, an 'impertinent "raid" on the literary "preserve" that takes away only those things that seem useful or pleasurable to the reader', a kind of reading experience that 'becomes a type of play' (19). This 'play' includes taking aspects of the source text and creatively manipulating them, resulting in a derivative product that is symbolic of the reader's affective status as 'fan.' Fan videos, fanfiction, and role-playing are all examples of 'poaching' activities that are used to derive meaning from the text.

I prefer to refer to these 'poaching' activities as a function within the construct of patronage and discourse, primarily as a reflection on the individual's ability to interact with their fan-text in a creative or derivative capacity through written discourses (such as fan essays), academic research and scholarship on their object of fandom, or through visual art and musical compositions, a creative component of the fan experience reflected by and through the creation of cultural capital. Creativity serves as the performative element of fandom presented by Hills and is concurrent with Kurt Lancaster's research that presents the fan as a type of 'textual performer' where fans 'try to capture – through participation and immersion – the original cathartic moment felt during the first viewing of the text' (2001: 155). An excellent example of the interpretive, performative, and creative dimension of the fan experience is the writing of fanfiction. The source text – the television series – acts as a foundation for these derivative creative works, further fostering (and exemplifying) the depth of the relationship between the fully engaged cult fan and the text. In some respects, this creative element of cult fandom can be more critical and discursive than even an academic essay on the source text, where fans can express their displeasure over a character arc or episode by simply rewriting the text.

Cornel Sandvoss hypothesises that fanfiction is a result of technological advances, where the contemporary viewing audience has an increasing ability to control the boundaries of a test, which 'results in an ever-greater number of readings', and that 'readers select given parts while disregarding others' resulting in an 'erosion of the signification value in the reading of the show' (2005: 829.) Essentially, Sandvoss argues that as fans read the source text, they invariably begin to create and derive meanings that are separate but congruent to the canonical work. Fandom theorist Shennag Pugh illustrates the purpose of both writing fanfiction and the canonical 'editing' of the source text by fanfiction writers: 'people [write] fanfic because they [want] either "more of" their source text or "more from it"' (2004). Sometimes the purpose was to revise the wrongs of the writers, adding depth to the characters or to character development, or revealing more about a scene. As Pugh illustrates,

> Some fans, often female, wanted the action to slow down enough to give the characters and relationships time to evolve; they wanted more overt emotion and personal interaction than the scriptwriters were giving them. They wanted vulnerability in the characters too, so that they could feel with and for them. (2004)

Fanfiction writers, then are often using the source texts as a platform to provide more emotional resonance (and thus payoff) for the fan. Yet an interesting – and somewhat contrary – argument about this type of creative poaching has a far more political connotation. One of the key arguments in '*Star Trek:* Rerun, Reread, Rewritten', as well as in *Textual Poachers,* is that fans are a sort of renegade cultural task force battling against capitalist control of texts by mass-media conglomerates. Jenkins likens the textual poaching performed by these fans to the peasant revolts in Europe during the eighteenth and nineteenth centuries. These behaviours manifested by those in revolt – reactions to a 'moral economy' of implied standards and norms of behaviour – are approximate to the actions of the fans that he studied, where fans act as 'loyalists, rescuing essential elements of the primary text as misused by those who seek copyright control over the program materials' (41).

Jenkins' concept of an audience or fan 'revolt' presents an interesting modern-day example that adequately supports his argument. On 5 November 2007, the Writers Guild of America East and West initiated a strike against the Alliance of Motion Picture and Television Producers as a result of failed contractual negotiations for what television and film writers deem fair compensation for 'new media' (internet and other technology-based media). At the time of the contract negotiation, there was no agreement providing compensation for internet, streaming video, or digital-based media content. The strike effectively put a hold on the production of all network television shows and film scripts.

217

This strike is similar to the one held by the Writers Guild of America in 1988, which resulted in a loss of nearly $500 million to the American Entertainment Industry; the 21-week strike focused on the 'new media' of videocassette tape sales and distribution; at that time, the production alliance felt the media was 'unproven' and thus did not warrant a negotiation. The guild held strong and eventually won rights to residual profits based on VHS sales.

Unlike the strikes of yesteryear, today's guild is backed by the adoring fan audience that supports the television series forced on hiatus. This is a further example of how today's audience – and today's fans – see the creative powers-that-be behind their series as figures worth veneration, celebration, and the utmost of respect. This may be due in part to the changing nature of the audience, and how the audience feels that they owe a series' writers and creators because of the feelings that they have derived from watching, experiencing, and engaging with their favourite texts. In the 2007 strike, fans supported an innovative pencil-sending campaign (entitled 'Pencils 2 Media Mogels') that sent over 500,000 pencils to the producers behind the television series *Battlestar Galactica, Lost, Jericho, Smallville, Army Wives,* and *Criminal Minds,* and in an interesting twist, some were sent by fans on behalf of writer, director, and producer Joss Whedon, so that he could continue work on the series *Dollhouse* (Anon, 2007d). Fans purchased boxes of 12 pencils for $1 in support of individual series, and the first delivery occurred the week of Christmas outside the major network studio offices in Burbank California. While the corporations refused to accept the deliveries, the campaign reflected fan support of the strike on behalf of the writing teams (Stelter, 2007). Fans joined in the effort, bringing their favourite writers food and showing support by carrying signs and marching alongside them outside of the media studios.

Today's modern audience is more engaged with their televisual texts than the audiences of the past, partially a response to a changing social perception of what it means to be a fan. As television as a medium developed, the viewing audience has also grown along with it, getting more involved and becoming a part of the shows they venerate, indeed, playing a part in cultivating a series' success. To the television writer, there's no greater fan than the cult viewer, the one you can rely on to tell his/her friends and family about the series, watch on a regular basis, spend money on licensed and unofficial merchandise, or develop a fan website.

Fandom and the Internet

Some of the earliest fan research stemmed from the field of computer-mediated communication, where the earliest questions of internet-based 'communities' and virtual societies were initially asked. The contemporary television viewer, whether a fan, cultist, or enthusiast, is more than likely an internet user. The internet has impacted not only upon the social output and interaction of fans, but also upon the way that we view television. The major American networks – ABC, NBC, CBS, and FOX – utilise the internet as a primary source for viewer interaction and television series information, and as a conduit for media products (from previews of forthcoming episodes and series to less ad-interrupted streaming video of previously aired shows).

In essence, the internet creates the ultimate form of access for current and prospective viewers, providing a wealth of content, most of which is free or relatively inexpensive. Entire season passes of series are available for purchase and download from iTunes, easily transported from a home or office computer to the compact media of an iPod. Hulu, an iTunes competitor, offers visitors free viewings of both contemporary and classic series, encouraging fans to branch out into new fandoms with a click of a button. And the explosive popularity of YouTube, where users can capture and upload any media products they wish (even licensed content until it's reported and removed) has helped revolutionise the way that we access and make use of media.

These broad and sweeping changes have also affected the way that we communicate about our fandom. Thirty years ago, if you missed an episode you had to hope for a repeat. Now, an aired episode is available online within 24 hours. Can't afford to pay iTunes rate? There are cyber-'pirates' who have captured and uploaded the series on torrent websites for free-use. In essence, the technology works like this: using a computer and a digital video-recording device, the pirate 'steals' the copywritten material illegally. Then, the video file is encrypted into a file that is reduced in size and then uploaded to a peer-to-peer file-sharing website, known as a peer-to-peer (p2p) network. The 'torrent' – or quick transfer of the file over the internet – is then downloaded and shared amongst future viewers. Although illegal, this subterranean way of spreading media content has become more popular as more and more internet- and technology-savvy viewers find ways to get their content quickly. This immediacy is also evident in the way we talk about series – fans can chat about the shows online on official sites as they air, offering their views and thoughts with each frame, or can post to message boards their questions about a scene, character, or a piece of dialogue accidentally missed. The next day watercooler discussions are becoming the way of the dinosaur as fans find that they can discuss – in real time – their thoughts and feelings about a series' development or plot twists.[1]

Not only does the internet produce the immediacy of access, it also provides an interesting dichotomy when it comes to the storage of such content. Fansites built in honour of a series may or may not last the test of time like the fan-produced 'fanzines' of the 1970s, 1980s, and 1990s but certainly do house far more information than their paper counterparts. Fan 'wiki's' – Wikipedia-like, open source websites – are becoming more mainstream ways to convey current news releases, series developments, and detailed blow-by-blows of content. This type of content is provided by the most dedicated of fans yet, as fan interest wanes or as a series goes off-air, these websites often fall victim to increasing disinterest, resulting in the closure of fansites that once provided access to thousands of facts, volumes of fanfiction, and a catalogue of fan videos and art. The temporal nature of the internet – coupled with the short-term interest of some fan engagement – results in a loss of what was once valuable textual gold within online fandom.

What initiated this change in the societal expectation of fandom is evolutionary and yet somewhat predictable. Television, as the medium developed, has always asked its viewers to join and participate, from in-studio audiences providing realistic audience responses to everything from sitcoms to talk shows to the dial-in voting system of *American Idol* and its contemporaries. Today's audience is invited to 'go interactive' by logging online to chat mid-episode to their favourite dramas, to join a weight loss or lifestyle change campaign to lose weight or get involved in a fitness regimen. Ten years ago, cult series were identified by their small, anti-mainstream audience. Today, a cult audience is praised by the media and the cult series has gone mainstream – *Lost* is a prime example, with millions of viewers worldwide puzzling over the series' enigmas, its mysteries and meaning. It's easy to see that today's 'cult' audience is the one that the media moguls want watching their shows, the more viewers, the merrier – and the more lucrative a series' franchise becomes.

Once labelled as socially unacceptable, the cult audience is, in all actuality, today's mainstream. They tune in and watch each episode of their favourite series with relish, frequent official and unofficial websites, and speculate on the next week's and season's turn of events. They are the viewers the networks prize and promote to, the ones who will spend a few extra dollars on *Entertainment Weekly*, enrol in a season pass on TiVO and gleefully watch reruns. Behaviours once categorised as strange, odd, or obsessive are today socially acceptable. Today's cult, in essence, is a reflection of our modern television-viewing culture.

Recommended Reading

Abercrombie, Nick, and Brian Longhurst (1998) *Audiences: A Sociological Theory of Performance and Imagination.* London: Sage.

Hills, Matt (2002) *Fan Cultures.* London: Routledge.

Jenkins, Henry (1992) *Textual Poachers: Television Fans and Participatory Cultures.* London: Routledge.

Da Ali G Show
(Channel 4, 2000–2002/HBO, 2002–2004)
Hillary Robson

Sasha Baron Cohen's *Da Ali G Show* originally aired on the United Kingdom's Channel 4 for two series in 2000 before gaining a series run on the United State's Home Box Office in 2002 through 2004. The comedy sketch program followed the character of Ali G, a notorious rapper-style 'voice of da youth' who interviewed various political statesmen and cultural figures, including mainstream media journalists such as ABC's newscaster Sam Donelson. Cohen's other characters – Borat, a reporter from Kazakhstan, and Bruno, a gay Austrian – similarly conducted interviews of unsuspecting political, media, and cultural figures.

The character of Ali G, with his thick accent of a mix of dialects from Caribbean to UK slang, speaks in a unique lexicon (with terms such as 'babylons' for breasts, or misconstructions such as 'Chocolate Orange' for *Clockwork Orange*) that often befuddles his interviewees. His inane questions usually reflect his lack of awareness and ignorance of modern social or political issues and generally result in his subject leaving the interview in disgust or clear confusion.

The success of the characters on the *Ali G Show* hinge on two fundamental precepts: one, that the viewing audience gets the joke, and second, that Cohen's victims are ignorant to the fact that they are indeed being played. With Ali G's questions – asking if people believed in 'mahogany' instead of 'monogamy', referring to the 'grassy knoll' before asking 'who shot JR' – the jokes were contingent on an educated audience that understands not only American history and culture but also American popular culture.

In the premiere episode of the second season, Ali G made his trademark opening monologue. Standing in front of the illuminated word 'Respek', he reminds viewers that the central theme of his program, indeed, his life's mission, is focused on imbuing *respek*, but yet, it has so lost its meaning for society that 'if you look up the word behind me in the dictionary, you'll find it's been taken out.' And perhaps that's the reason that Cohen's characters attract such an enthusiastic cult following, because of respect. In order to be funny,

Cohen tramples on social constructions of propriety, pushes the envelopes, threatens cultural understandings, blasphemes icons and religions, mocks relationships, and satires race, gender and politics, all to show that indeed we've all lost a sense of 'respect' for one another. And that loss of common human decency and understanding is, in a word, funny.

But, the *Da Ali G Show's* cult following in the United Kingdom and the United States, marked by a relatively small viewing audience, was successful only as long as it remained in the underground. The series material became fodder for a 2002 film *Ali G Indahouse,* a release that gained little critical or social acclaim. Its 2004 release in the United States was a straight-to-DVD failure and HBO elected to not pursue a renewal of the critically acclaimed series. Many thought that Sasha Baron Cohen's comedic interviewing series would be permanently retired after a few seasons of brilliant – if not respectful – comedy.

While Ali G may have been the headliner, the secondary character of Borat proved the most successful of Cohen's characters. The 2006 film *Borat: Cultural Learnings of America for Make Benefit Glorious Nation of Kazakhstan* (Larry Charles, US) created such a mainstream splash that Cohen's Borat had to be retired. Despite the several years that it took to get the film's $18-million budget approved and to get the backing of studio support – the film opened to a blockbuster weekend in November 2006. In the United States alone, the film grossed more than $128 million. This mainstream, popular success resulted in the relatively quick death of Borat. With millions of dollars in the box office came instant recognition. What made the film funny – indeed, what made the character funny – was the fact that the people he interacted with believed him. They believed he was from a small town in Kazakhstan, that his society had an annual 'running of the Jew', that he carried a chicken in his bag, and that his laughable – but lovable – nature was genuine. When the film hit and had popular success (even gaining a few Oscar nods), the lawsuits started rolling in. Although Cohen's team had every 'character' appearing in the film sign a release, several filed suit. None of the lawsuits stuck (Davis, 2006).

What made Borat such a cult success – albeit a controversial one – is the way it became a true-life social satire, revealing individuals who came off looking like fools, jerks, or worse – misogynists, gay bashers, and racists. The movie is not unlike a messy and tragic car accident: terrible and horrifying, and yet unable to look away from. The *Electronic Journal of Communication,* looking at the movie in a series of issues entitled 'Misreading *Borat:* The

Risks of Irony in a Digital Age', asks the pointed question 'If provocative satire is designed to have a salutary impact (exposing and reducing the appeal of bigotry), can misrepresentations be harmful?' (Lewis, 2008). Although part of the movie works for audiences because of its shock value (the 'I can't believe he said that' or 'There's no way this could happen in my America'), there's also the added dimension of watching people humiliated by their own narrow-minded views of the world. This, in turn, produces a change in the social consciousness, a shift that Boston College's Paul Lewis argues is aided by the use of humour in order to act as a catalyst in 'inter-personal communication and in the maintenance of reform of accepted ideologies' (2008: 3). Although the audience may think of the worst 'characters' in the film as just that – characters – they are real human beings who live in the same world as the audience. It's not any particular group or class either – Borat shows us individuals from all walks of life who reveal their own dark and perverse ways of viewing the 'other' – that is, anyone other than themselves. And Cohen – through Borat – ridicules these unsavoury individuals, mocking them to reveal the 'levels of hateful ideation and contempt lurking below the veneer of American civilization' (Lewis, 3).

Cohen's Borat may now be retired, but the comic's mission of revealing societal ills is not. Bruno – the third and perhaps least popular of Cohen's characters – is the star of the film *Bruno* (Larry Charles, U.S., 2009). While Cohen's comedy has relied upon his audience's gullibility, Bruno's antics have been followed on various fan websites, including *The Ultimate Bruno, Borat,* and *+ Ali G* websites (http://www.boyakasha.co.uk/). The film exposes more cultural misunderstandings and the frank and often violent responses of those who feel scorned by Cohen's comedic stunts, this time striking fear in heartland America with the flamboyantly gay antics of Bruno.

What Cohen and his characters successfully reflect in terms of cult is that the cult audience is one played – and influenced – by emotion. As Lewis argues, 'the imperfect world [Cohen] seeks to reform is inhabited by imperfect human beings in need of correction. If some of these imperfect ones fail to see ... the character [as] not only foolish but woefully ignorant, sexist, and bigoted, if they laugh with rather than at him and his disgraced interlocutors, then they demonstrate just how urgently they need what Sacha Baron Cohen provides' (2008: 4). Although the intention may be to create humour, the message is clear: the deeper, subversive, and often hateful underbellies of society and culture are those that need the most exposition; sometimes, laughter may be the best medicine.

223

Notes

1. See Will Brooker (2009) for a case study of the interactive online fan practises of *Lost* fans.

23 The Cult of Cult TV?

Dick Fiddy

For the last two decades at the BFI Southbank (formerly the National Film Theatre or NFT) in London, regular screenings of TV material have sat happily alongside the screenings of the world's greatest movies. This is due to the British Film Institute's charge to champion and preserve the culture of Britain's television as well as film. To aid the process, I was brought in as a consultant to help advise on screenings and to work with an in-house programmer to formulate ways to best showcase TV. My route into this business was not straightforward, my interest in television had started merely as a hobby and I had no plans to try and pursue a career as an archivist or TV consultant – rather I thought my future might lay in writing comedy for television as I had had some success in the field by then (the 1980s). However, a meeting of other enthusiasts at a TV screening at the Scala Cinema in London had unexpected consequences. After the screening, the organisers invited some of us to a meeting at the British Film Institute to discuss further ways to exploit television – an area the Scala programmer thought was currently under-explored.[1] At the meeting, it was decided to use the money accrued from the successful Scala TV screenings to launch a TV magazine which would treat television to the same critical overview enjoyed by film.[2] I was one of the editorial and writing team on the magazine which did achieve something of a cult success, that is, it had a limited print-run, was eagerly devoured by like-minded enthusiasts, and is now treated as a collectors item. The editors of the magazine were contacted by the BFI, who were then setting up the Museum of the Moving Image, and they enquired as to whether we would be willing to write a partial 'History of British Television' for MOMI. However, most of the other members of the editorial border were too busy (most already had jobs in the media), so I was left as the one with time to fulfil a year-long contract. That assignment got me within the BFI and later (1990s), when they were intending to run regular TV screenings at the NFT, I was brought in as a consultant. Thus my hobby became a job (a phenomenon much more common these days as the internet has proven a quick-track for some enthusiasts to turn their interests into careers). I hadn't come from an academic background but just possessed one of those minds that retained a lot of trivial information about the media. As I wrote and researched more, it may have made me analyse and think about television in an academic way but this was developing through the job not vice versa. That process became even more intense when the regular consultancy began. The in-house programmer was Veronica Taylor, who had come from a more formal academic background than me and had already been at the BFI for some years in various departments. She had not studied TV per se but had a solid grounding as an impassioned viewer and our areas of knowledge neatly dovetailed; Ms Taylor was *au fait* with the Arts, documentaries, serious dramas and classics of the small screen, whilst I brought to the table a knowledge of the more esoteric areas of the medium, the flotsam and jetsam of series drama, comedy, genre programming, and the rapidly disappearing world of Variety – areas sometimes referred to as 'cult'.

Very quickly we attracted a core TV audience who were coming out to see the small screen on the big screen and reacquaint themselves with programmes (then) unrepeated and not available on video or DVD. Some sessions proved more popular than others: comedy, SF, ghost stories all attracted good audiences while documentaries, soap opera, natural history programmes – despite their large home audience ratings – fared less well in the cinema. Particularly popular titles included John Byrne's *Tutti Frutti*[3], Galton and Simpson's wonderful *Hancock's Half Hour*, and long-form classics such as *An Age of Kings*.[4] It became obvious that there was a big difference between the type of TV fan who would watch a show at home and the type who would go out and pay to watch it in a cinema. Oddly, some of the less popular genres on TV (ballet, Arts programming, children's shows) went down extremely well with our audiences and provided good houses. Had we stumbled on a vein of cult TV? Did 'cult TV' mean programmes of limited appeal which had a fanatical following absent from the more popular genres? Sadly not. Our audiences came to us because they had no other way of seeing these particular programmes. In those days, apart from rare exceptions, 'repeat' referred to a programme repeated within some months of its original broadcast whilst still under contract. The notion of retrospective repeats (i.e., programmes from a previous generation) was something that really happened only on special anniversaries (such as the BBC TV's 50th Celebrations in 1986). Thus without channels and DVD releases to exploit past programming, fans had few – if any – chances to assess or re-assess older programmes. Not so with films, which, ironically, regularly enjoyed resurrection on television.

Later, when repeat channels, greater DVD publishing, and an increased regard for vintage television programming *did* result in far greater access to the material, we found we still had our audiences and realised that part of the appeal was the shared experience of seeing the material. Comedy especially benefits from this treatment. In a way, that desire to watch a show in an auditorium with other 'fans' could be described as a 'cult' practice and perhaps gives us a clue to the modern idea of what cult TV really is. Post the DVD revolution (and even more so with PVR technology[5]), it also became noticeable that fans were consuming TV in a different way. Box sets inspired binge-viewing with punters happy to watch several hours of a series in a row; in the case of an intense, serialised title such as *24* or *State of Play,* it becomes a far less frustrating way to view. This acceptance of long-form absorption has allowed us to programme such marathons at BFI Southbank and we have been rewarded with avid audiences happy to spend a whole day or weekend with other like-minded individuals. This may also be a clue to a new cultish way of devouring programming (or certain programming) but it's only a part of the phenomenon of cult TV.

Some years ago, I found myself as a guest at a weekend event billed as a cult TV convention.[6] A lot of fans paid a tidy sum to book into a hotel for a few days and visit various events, interviews, screenings, workshops, and discussions. What amazed me was the breadth of TV output covered; alongside the traditional fan-friendly SF shows, comedies, and action/adventure dramas, the schedule also included interviews with veteran weather girls, a lecture about the development of ITV logos, a look at the history of colour broadcasting, a discussion about regional news shows, a look at the upcoming U.S. TV season, a presentation of obscure theme tunes, silent film footage of location shooting, the memories of a continuity announcer, and other such flotsam and jetsam from the world of the small screen. It seemed to me that, for the cult TV organisers, the word 'cult' encompassed all of TV past and present, a definition which, on the surface, seems to fly in the face of the accepted meaning of the term. But on further reflection I realised that was wrong. 'Cult' in this case referred to the way television was watched and obsessed-over by these people. It was the fact that they were equally interested in the nitty gritty of all aspects of the small screen that united them and in that sense they did make a cult. This was a different use of the word (and phrase) to the one that I had understood in the past.

It's unlikely that the term ever referred to 'a programme of limited popularity that engendered a small but obsessive fan following', which I believe is an interpretation it might suggest to an outsider not so captivated by the medium. The first uses of cult TV I came across (in magazines or from friends) referred to programmes that were actually very popular but spawned in their wake an intensive fan following. With their huge viewing figures, series such as *Doctor Who, The Prisoner,* or *Star Trek* aren't cult programmes per se, but they were the earliest shows that attracted a cult following. Unless the shows are very long running (like *Doctor Who*), these fan bases usually sprang up once the series was over, thus 'cult' in this case referred to a group of fans who gave the show an afterlife of discussion, argument, and analysis. In the days before the net, for such fans to congregate they had to find each other by forming a fan club or by going to gatherings of some sort. These gatherings might be conventions where cast and crew of a certain show are on hand to discuss it directly with fans, or screenings at, for instance, The Scala or the NFT, or – more informally – meetings in a pub or other such large rooms where fans themselves have arranged to meet up.

It was in the latter half of the 1960s that this form of cult TV came into being. Certainly, in the 1950s, people might have discussed programmes that had touched a particular chord (*1984*, The *Quatermass* serials, for example; see Catherine Johnson on the *Quatermass* serials in this volume) but a response to recent broadcasting (shown the evening or a couple of evenings before) is not a cult response. Thus water-cooler chats poring over the latest instalment of *Lost* or *Doctor Who* aren't examples of cult TV, just examples of popular TV having an impact. Coming together specifically to discuss those programmes – either the following evening or months/years later – would be considered an example of cult TV viewing and reaction.

So cult TV never referred to programming but to the response to certain programmes. In the late 1960s and the early 1970s – as previously mentioned – cult groups would usually emerge after a programme had ended its run[7] (with a couple of notable exceptions, *The Man from UNCLE*[8] being one). But by the late 1970s and the 1980s, there was a faster reaction to (genre) series which meant groups were formed whilst the programme was still on, one such group was Horizon the *Blake's 7* fan club formed in 1980 when *Blake's 7* was still on the air . These groups formed the basis of the public perception of cult TV fans: a minority of obsessives who seemed to expend an awful amount of energy on something that non-believers found trivial. This meant that cult TV fans – in the eyes of the general public – became tarred with the same brush as trainspotters and birdwatchers, considered as eccentric but harmless and possibly in need of something better to do with their time. Also – as with the other pastimes – the TV groups were predominantly male, though there was evidence that the male/female balance was changing towards the end of the 1980s.

This whole process accelerated manifold with the emergence and spread of the internet. Fan clubs and fan forums became global, which meant that discussions could be international; in extreme cases, some forum topics started immediately after an episode ended or whilst it was still mid-broadcast. So the cult of cult TV viewing and response was suddenly connected together and the accessibility of the technology and the fan sites meant that a whole new fan base – who in the past may not have been moved to share their views – suddenly came on board. A lot of the fans were now female and proved equally obsessive in their desire to pick over the minutiae of their favourite programmes. These fan sites also proved financially lucrative to the marketers of spin-off merchandise of favourite shows, with books, CDs, posters, pictures, T Shirts, and DVDs all being offered via the website and being snapped up by the fans. Cult TV took on a new and important place in the broadcasting environment, even allowing fans to interact directly with show personnel.

So the definition of a cult TV fan may not have changed but the response to the definition has. A cult TV fan could still be described as 'someone who obsesses over a particular programme or TV star' but whereas in the 1970s this would conjure up an image of some 'anorakked saddo' by the late 1990s that same definition could apply to someone able to interact with programme makers, meet like-minded members of the opposite sex, write fan fiction, and fuel a huge industry of spin-off merchandising. Not so sad, not so lonely. And rather than being ignored by programme makers, such cult fans are now sought after, as are their views and ideas. Cult fans wield a lot of power these days. It is unlikely that *Star Trek* would have ever returned to TV and movies if it wasn't for the manic Trekkers (and/or Trekkies) who kept the flame burning for the original 1960s series. The same is probably true for *Doctor Who*, although that revival neatly demonstrates another consequence of cult TV: that of a fan becoming a 'name' in the industry and then resurrecting his/her favourite programme – or programme type – of the past. By the 1990s, some of the teenage cult TV fans of the 1970s from both sides of the Atlantic were working in the broadcast industry and had an instinctive feeling that certain aspects of the 1970s schedules were absent from the modern schedules. There was a gap in the market that needed filling. Cult TV fans had grown up, the internet had turned them into a global force and those working within the industry were able to return to themes and programmes from the past to fill that gap. Hence *Doctor Who, Life on Mars, Primeval, Torchwood, Spooks,* and other such serials in the United Kingdom and shows such as *Alias, Buffy, Smallville, Chuck,* and *The X-Files* in the United States were all driven by show-runners who were self-confessed cult TV fans.[9]

Although the internet has enabled the phenomenon to expand and progress, the basic elements still apply. Analysis plays an important part in the process, some fans will obsess over the most obscure subtexts within a show, others will project storylines beyond the parameters of the programme. But analysis and obsession alone do not make a cult. Look at football, a game that has enjoyed a stunning rebirth since the launch of the Premiership in England and a new streamlined EUFA Champions League competition. The game is worth billions and is truly global. Football fans obsess and analyse but can hardly be called a 'cult'. Why? I think one of the key reasons is that when football is shown on TV or listened to on radio, the broadcasters provide their own instant analysis. Often, these days, the pundits providing the analysis are ex football players themselves and, therefore, can provide a succinct reading of the game albeit one that may come in a verbal package devoid of some of the more subtle nuances of the language ('the boy done brilliant'). Nevertheless their use of the game's own unique terms and phrases (nutmegging, an 'agricultural' clearance, a hospital ball etc.) imbue their commentary with an air of authenticity and also bring these words and phrases into the scope of the everyday football fan. Thus, because of this immediate shared analysis, anybody with a passing interest in the game becomes privy to the finer tactics and terms, and the language ceases to become something unique to the players and obsessive fans and is shared by all – thus preventing the after-match pub discussions becoming a 'cult' practice. One of the key things in keeping a cult a cult is the specialist language that allows like-minded fanatics to use shorthand in their conversations. For instance, every self-respecting cult fan of *Buffy* understands what is meant by the term Buffyverse and can appreciate the usages of Giles-isms. Casual fans may struggle with these ideas. Cult fans of *Star Trek* will know at least some Klingon phrases, others perhaps not. Any fan of *The Man from UNCLE* will know that UNCLE stands for the United Network Command for Law and Enforcement but only extreme fans will know that UNCLE's arch enemy THRUSH is an acronym for The Technological Hierarchy for the Removal of Undesirables and the Subjugation of Humanity.[10]

However, new approaches to the marketing of TV and films have begun to bring in some on-screen analysis of the programme almost akin to football punditry. Hence DVD extras such as director commentaries, behind-the-scenes featurettes, and cast and crew interviews are much welcomed by fans who can never get enough of their favourite shows. Also there is increasing use of after-show analysis and discussion on the TV itself, possibly beginning with the United Kingdom's BBC3 post-show discussion series focussing on *24* (*Pure 24*) and later E4's *Lost* (*Lost in Lost*) and more recently championed by such tie-in programming as *Doctor Who Confidential, Torchwood Declassified,* and *Heroes Unmasked.* If such immediate analysis becomes the norm for general programming, it may lead to certain shows having their 'cult' status diminished as the obsession would be shared too thinly. Part of the joy of being in a cult is the exclusivity of language and ideas, when shows become too popular and discussions open out to a wider congregation, some lament the loss of the specialism that inevitably follows.

So, at present, the term cult TV would seem to refer to the method of watching and reacting to certain TV shows rather than referring to the shows themselves. One person's mainstream is another person's cult. The cult itself is fuelled by obsession crossed with enthusiasm, analysis, discussion, and projection. In essence then, the cult operates similarly to the world of academia. Academics (and I am masquerading as one for the purposes of this chapter) also use terminology baffling to non-academics (descriptors, contextualisation, plenary) and equally obsess over their chosen subjects, analysing and postulating to unusual – some would say absurd – lengths. But if one can appreciate the position and worth of academia then one can also understand the current value – and meaning – of cult TV.

Notes

1. Steve Woolley, who would go on to become a successful feature film producer.
2. *Primetime – The Television Magazine*, edited by WTVA (Wider Television Access) launched in 1981.

3. *Tutti Frutti* (BBC 1987), a five-part musical comedy/drama starring Emma Thompson and Robbie Coltrane.
4. *An Age of Kings* (BBC 1960), a series of 15 TV dramas based on Shakespeare's history plays.
5. Personal video recorders such as Sky Plus or TIVO
6. The 8th Annual Cult TV Convention, Liverpool 2001, for further information see http://www.cult.tv/
7. *The Prisoner* fan club Six of One, for instance, was started a decade after the show's initial U.K. run.
8. In the 1960s, the UNCLE TV show had an officially organised fan club with members getting their own UNCLE ID card, newsletter, and other such memorabilia. It was strictly a one-way street though with no mechanism for the fan's to feed back to the organisers.
9. Russell T. Davies in the United Kingdom was a huge *Doctor Who* fan and fought for the chance to revive the series. Likewise Ashley Pharoh, co-creator of *Life on Mars,* was inspired by previous TV shows. In the United States, Chris Carter (*X Files*), J. J. Abrams (*Alias, Lost*), Gouch and Miller (*Smallville*), Joss Whedon (*Buffy, Firefly*), and Josh Schwarz (*Chuck, The OC, Gossip Girl*) are all on record as fans of genre TV.
10. As revealed in *The Man from UNCLE* spin-off paperback title *The Dagger Affair* (1966) by David McDaniel.

24 Subcultural Celebrity

Matt Hills

One of the attributes which has characterised cult TV is that its dedicated and vocal fan audiences tend to amass considerable knowledge of those both behind, and in front of, the camera (Hunt 2003). Cult TV fans, who keenly value their favoured shows, ascribe 'artistic' and 'authored' status to these television programmes, sometimes in line with TV industry discourses of authorship and quality, sometimes in the absence of such discourses. To take one example, the original series of *Doctor Who* was not promoted by the BBC as 'authored' or 'quality' TV, but its fans nevertheless built up immensely detailed knowledge of what they perceived as signatures of quality linked to specific producers, such as Philip Hinchcliffe, and script-editors/writers, such as Robert Holmes. For cult TV fans, then, the names and faces of production staff are often just as well-known as those of star actors: celebrity is not at all restricted to those receiving wider recognition.

By the time of *Doctor Who*'s return – it having been off the air as a regular TV series since the late eighties – the show was widely publicised in relation to its new executive producer and lead writer, Russell T. Davies, and was industrially positioned as 'authored' TV. But even here, fans developed distinctive and highly detailed forms of knowledge about the show's production staff, not just responding to the new version of *Who* as authored by Davies but also looking for the production 'signatures' of designers, such as Edward Thomas, directors, such as Joe Ahearne and Euros Lyn, and other writers, such as Paul Cornell and Steven Moffat. The work of all these production personnel (and many more) is celebrated and analysed by fans, whose interpretations typically take a resolutely multi-authored and egalitarian approach rather than 'reading' the new *Doctor Who* simply as the work of its showrunner Russell T. Davies. And these cult fan interpretations are now increasingly reinforced and mirrored by industry practices such as DVD commentaries and podcasts which feature a range of actors and media producers discussing their work, often in relatively informal registers which imply that fans are symbolically 'watching with' these official producers. And these commentaries involve not just showrunners or executive producers, but also a wide range of production personnel from special effects creators through to music composers, suggesting that the TV industry is very much aware of fans' focus on texts as multi-authored (Hills 2007). In some cases, fans' detailed awareness of the work of specific producers can result in criticism of their creative labour, as Derek Johnson has demonstrated in the case of *Star Trek* fans and their eventual dislike of the franchise decisions and directions taken by the likes of Rick Berman and Brannon Braga, especially on *Star Trek: Enterprise* (see Johnson 2007: 75).

Cult fans also engage, creatively and intently, with the leading characters of the narrative worlds they appreciate. As a result, actors and fictional personae may be blended together into semiotic amalgams by fan audiences, though some scholars have argued that it is the characters who are primary for cult TV fans – specific actors just happen to embody those figures, for example, Lucy Lawless appearing as Xena, Warrior Princess, or Patrick Stewart providing the visage and expressivity of Jean-Luc Picard (see Gwenllian-Jones 2000; Pearson 2004). However, actor and character may become so tightly interwoven for some fans that any change in actor is greeted with dismay and deemed to be 'inauthentic' or a character violation (see Black 2004 on the curious case of 'Uma Peel').

By responding to cult TV in a way that stresses and sometimes critiques the creative input of a wide range of production staff – as well as by focusing on the acting performances of regulars, guest stars, and bit-part players alike – cult TV fans generate shared and communal knowledge of the many people involved in making 'their' beloved television shows. This means that industry figures who are not widely known become extremely well-known to fans of cult TV who celebrate such TV as a form of art or criticise it for failing to live up to this potential, such as *Doctor Who* fans' disparagement of John Nathan-Turner and the latter phase of his 1980s tenure as producer. In turn, this creates a situation where many industry insiders become celebrities, of a kind, to their cult fans. They can be thought of as celebrities, rather than merely as behind-the-scenes media workers, because although the (sometimes very sizeable) fan audience is able to sustain a sense of 'knowing' these media producers – recognising them in photos, following their careers, perhaps even meeting them at organised fan conventions – the individuals inspiring this attention cannot and do not (generally) reciprocate it. For them, the audience remains largely imagined.

However, although the 'non-reciprocal intimacy at a distance' typical of fan–celebrity relations (Thompson 1995) is present here, these cult TV industry insiders are often not what might be called 'household names'. That is, their celebrity is not generalised or ubiquitous and may instead be restricted to the fanbases for the specific cult shows they have worked on. In this situation, the term 'subcultural celebrity' has been coined to describe the type of celebrity often linked, and limited, to cult television:

> 'subcultural celebrities' [are] mediated figures who are treated as famous only by and for their fan audiences. Although some previous work on celebrity has considered how audience subcultures interpret

and recognise their idols in distinctive ways, such work has still tended to focus on culturally ubiquitous celebrities who are read differently by audience subcultures. Academic work to date has not focused significantly on the *restricted celebrity status* that might be created by audience subcultures. Cult TV and its fan cultures offer one cultural site where this type of celebrity is generated and sustained. (Hills 2003a: 61)

Such 'restricted' rather than 'general' celebrity status can mean that the mediated figures involved are not widely known, but it also relates to what might be termed 'post-fame' celebrities – those who were perhaps widely known and recognised earlier in their careers but are now perhaps only marginally involved in the TV industry, for example, Paul Darrow and Gareth Thomas, the former stars of *Blake's 7*. Nevertheless, these formerly famous TV celebs may continue to be celebrated by fans of now-defunct TV programmes at conventions, within Appreciation Societies, on message boards, and other such forums.

This specific type of cult TV subcultural celebrity has been affectionately represented in Hollywood comedies such as *Galaxy Quest* (Dear Parisot, US, 1999) and in the UK TV movie *Cruise of the Gods,* starring Rob Brydon, Steve Coogan, and David Walliams (Declan Lowney, UK, 2002). As its name suggests, *Galaxy Quest* concerns itself with a fictional *Star Trek*-like cult TV show whose actors have not gone on to sustain TV careers but retain loyal fans who still celebrate them at conventions. By contrast, *Cruise of the Gods* imagines a British cult TV show, 'The Children of Castor', which resembles *Survivors* and *Blake's 7,* Terry Nation's actual cult Brit series. Again, its fictional stars have not all gone on to achieve further fame but are still embraced in an egalitarian spirit by the diegetic 'Castor' fans. These representations testify to the fact that fans of cult TV shows often display 'enduring fandom' (Kuhn 2002) which continues long beyond the cancellation or conclusion of the programmes concerned. And it is the durability of this fandom which underpins the post-fame mode of subcultural celebrity possessed by some cult TV actors.

Subcultural celebrities can be said to possess a quality of imagined 'closeness through distance' for their fans, by which I mean that these celebrities, just like more generalised or ubiquitous examples, exist as objects of knowledge for fandom largely through their mediated performances and promotional/publicity materials such as published interviews. 'Closeness through distance' thus indicates fans' imagined and desired proximity to their favoured celebs which occurs in relation to the 'distancing' of mass and niche media images. However, subcultural celebrity status is not exclusively managed and presented in this way. Unlike generalised or ubiquitous celebrities, subcultural celebrities are far more likely, at some point, to have embodied, social interactions with their fans, meeting them at conventions, doing planned 'signing sessions' to promote niche products, perhaps even sharing the dance floor with them at a convention disco, or going on organised cruise trips such as the *Star Trek*-themed CruiseTrek (see Hills and Williams 2005; http://www.cruisetrek.com/). It can also be argued that the web has allowed for a greater sense and experience of closeness to these celebrities as writers/directors can take part in online discussions or respond to fans' questions through weblogs, for example, Ron Moore's Sci-Fi Channel blog promoting the re-imagined version of *Battlestar Galactica*. (See http://blog.scifi.com/battlestar/). Indeed, Moore has also taken part in podcast commentaries in which he cultivates and presents a 'back-stage' persona for the benefit of fans (http://www.scifi.com/battlestar/downloads/podcast/season04/). Given all these possible scenarios for subcultural celebrity-fan interaction, it can be argued that in these instances, 'distance through closeness' is more characteristic of the social relationship, that is, interactions between fans and celebrities are not always purely mediated here, but the privacy of the celebrity still has to be respected, and the social encounter variously managed. Very, very few fans may, of course, move entirely beyond 'para-social' and relatively stage-managed exchanges, becoming fan club presidents and the like, and hence working alongside cult celebrities in a supportive role. But through conventions or cruises aimed at their cult TV fandom, fans can move partly beyond pure 'para-social' relations, and into the cultural space of 'distance through closeness', wherein the privacy of the subcultural celebrity still has to be respected, despite – and because of – the potential for embodied, social interaction. Though cult TV fans can get 'up close and personal' with their favoured subcultural celebrities, such as the actor James Marsters who has appeared in US and UK cult TV shows like *Buffy the Vampire Slayer* and *Torchwood*, it doesn't inherently follow that they can or will achieve any greater 'access' to the 'authentic' selves of such celebrities (Hills and Williams 2005). What this does mean, however, is that binaries based on 'mediated' and one-way interaction versus 'embodied' and two-way social interaction are at least partly blurred and muddied by the phenomenon of subcultural celebrity. To give one example, Chris Rojek in his sociological study *Celebrity* (2001) argues that celebrity belongs to the former, mediated, and one-way cultural terrain, whereas people who are celebrated within our social networks garner 'renown' rather than celebrity. Though subcultural celebrity is typically (though not inevitably) initiated by 'mediated', one-way interaction, it can lead to the temporary integration of the celebrity into a fan's social circle at assorted conventions, gatherings, and charity events and can begin to involve temporal shifts between moments of celebrity-fan social networking and periods of celebrity-fan social distance. Clearly separating out mediated 'celebrity' and embodied 'renown' makes much less sense here than in the past where film and TV celebrities may have existed for fans only in their mediated guises and textual personae (Hills 2003a; Hills and Williams 2005).

As well as striking at this binary of what might be termed 'para-social' versus 'proper social' interaction, the notion of subcultural celebrity also threatens to more radically deconstruct the conceptual separation of 'fan' and 'celebrity'. For those who would usually be thought of as 'fans' can also become subcultural celebrities in their own right: individuals celebrated within a fandom who are known and recognised by many, many more participants than they are able to reciprocate recognition towards. The fact that subcultures have their own niche media partly helps to facilitate this; somebody may write for a fan-targeted professional magazine, and hence their work and face and name might all become recognisable to others whom they don't actually 'know' in person. Or fans may become subcultural celebrities by producing fanzines or by posting regularly to specific message boards and articulating especially memorable, idiosyncratic versions of fan identity. Alternatively, some may be especially adroit at expressing widely shared fan viewpoints and value systems (see Hills 2006b). Science fiction fandom has long had these types of 'Big Name Fans' or 'Secret Masters of Fandom' (BNFs/SMoFs), but equivalents have also come to exist within cult TV fan cultures. These sorts of subcultural celebrities acquire high status within the hierarchies of fandom, occupying positions of symbolic and subcultural power which can, under some circumstances, be translated into 'professionalized fandom' whereby a living is made, at least partly, out of fan-based, subcultural forms of knowledge and expertise (see Hills 2006b:111–116). Fan-cultural magazine editors, archivists and TV historians, cultural producers of multi-platform online content, or other niche products, may all share backgrounds in cult TV fandom. Indeed, it may now even be possible to analyse cult TV fandom as a type of 'career path' for at least some participants, although where fans do 'turn pro' this may not always have been a conscious aim. Making such a transition typically also demands that fans possess 'official' skills/literacies and cultural competencies outside of (and in addition to) their amassed fan knowledge.

Assorted TV professionals like to flaunt their fan credentials and represent themselves as 'one of the fans', in touch with the feelings and experiences of their subcultural audiences, for instance, Ron Moore working on the re-imagined *Battlestar Galactica* in the United States, or Russell T. Davies spearheading the re-imagined *Doctor Who* in the United Kingdom. The roles of 'fan' and 'celebrity' can thus be hybridised and re-combined in a series of ways, sometimes as a result of cult TV shows being reinvented, and this means that the latest producers either need or want to engage with the concerns of established long-term cult TV fans (Hills 2006b).

Graeme Turner has argued that 'discourses of celebrity invade all kinds of [cultural] sites today' (2004:15). The subcultural celebrity of all manner of production, staff and actors who have worked on cult TV shows, along with the subcultural celebrity of Big Name Fans – and associated blurrings of 'fan' and 'celebrity' – all suggest that where cult television is concerned, Turner is absolutely right to highlight the extension of celebrity discourses. Cult TV and its fans have both helped to generate celebrities who are specifically recognised *by* their subcultures and those who are specifically known for actions and cultural productions *within* these subcultures. In each of these cases, the notion of 'generalised' or ubiquitous celebrity is of relatively little use to media and cultural analysis. 'Subcultural celebrity', as a concept, offers a way into understanding the distinctive practices and interpretations of cult TV's dedicated fan audiences, as well as illuminating the distinct temporalities of cult TV fans' appreciations. These can become life-long passions, at odds with the sometimes short-term-ism of 'fashionable' TV shows, and the sometimes much shorter-term industry commitments of producers and actors. Subcultural celebrity thus emerges out of the specific production-history knowledge and textual expertise of cult TV fans, frequently dismissed as 'trivia' by non-fans (Hunt 2003), and out of the 'enduring fandom' that tends to surround cult television programmes.

Recommended Reading

Hills, Matt (2003) 'Recognition in the Eyes of the Relevant Beholder: Representing "Subcultural Celebrity" and Cult TV Fan Cultures', *Mediactive*, 2: 59–73.

Hills, Matt and Williams, Rebecca (2005) ' "It's All My Interpretation": Reading Spike through the Subcultural Celebrity of James Marsters', *European Journal of Cultural Studies* 8:3, 345–365.

25 *Sapphire & Steel*
(ITV, 1979–1982)

Sergio Angelini

All irregularities will be handled by the forces controlling each dimension.
Transuranic heavy elements may not be used where there is life. Medium
atomic weights are available: Gold, Lead, Copper, Jet, Diamond, Radium,
Sapphire, Silver, and Steel. Sapphire and Steel have been assigned.

This narration began each episode of P.J. Hammond's *Sapphire & Steel*, a dense and often deliberately obscure and enigmatic drama serial that has serious claim to being the most frightening series ever screened by ITV before the 9 o'clock watershed. Hammond was a writer best known for his work on such adult police dramas as *Z Cars* and *The Sweeney,* but after contributing scripts to such children's programmes as *Ace of Wands*, and the supernatural anthology show *Shadows*, he decided to create his own series for younger viewers. Initially known as 'The Time Menders', it featured agents from another dimension who help two children in distress when their parents mysteriously vanish from their isolated country house filled with dozens of clocks that suddenly stop ticking. Hammond's conception soon became too dark and frightening for a tea-time slot; what eventually emerged, with its sophisticated and enigmatic storytelling and emphasis on an atmosphere of fear, was a show clearly aimed at older audiences. The first story (none have individual titles) was broadcast at 7 o'clock across six evenings on Tuesdays and Thursdays in July 1979. It still contains seeds of Hammond's original approach, the initial viewpoint largely being that of two young children. Subsequent serials would be much more clearly made for adults, featuring as they do violent deaths and disfigurement, attempted suicides, monstrous shape-shifting creatures, and much more besides.

In *Sapphire & Steel* time itself is the enemy, often seen as a malevolent force that aims to disrupt the space-time continuum by finding a weakness in the fabric that shields the present and breaking through from other dimensions to cause death and destruction. In Hammond's words, the protagonists had to stop the break and 'seal the time fabric to restore the Earth's equilibrium' (Hammond, 1992: 4). The six serials and 34 half-hour episodes have an almost palpable air of menace quite unlike any of its contemporaries, and its heroes as mysterious as the enemies they face. The titular agents, elementals with special powers including the ability to communicate telepathically, are played by David McCallum and Joanna Lumley and much of the series' strength derived from the sexual energy in the interplay between them. The air of intimacy their performances generated was further emphasised by the stories' confined settings, such as deserted railway stations, garages, or even junk shops, and enhanced in two serials by the appearance of the flirtatious Silver (David Collings).

The appeal of the show also lies in its handsome production values. Apart from some stock footage in the second serial and a few scenes on a rooftop in the third, the series was made entirely on video in the studio using sets designed by Stanley Mills and lit remarkably darkly, a style little used at the time not least due to the limitations of the camera equipment and resistance by the cameramen of the time. The programme has a distinctively claustrophobic feel, combining limbo sets (many sequences take place against a black background seemingly out of time and space), atmospheric lighting, and clever use of minimalist music and augmented audio effects in a powerful if decidedly anti-naturalistic style. The imaginative use of sound and discreet special effects is well in evidence in the fourth story in which people are trapped inside photographs, featuring a faceless monster inspired by the work of surrealist painters Magritte and Dali.

The series is probably best remembered by its fans for its second story, set in a train station, and for its sixth and final serial, both of which reached stunning conclusions that would have been impossible in the likes of *Star Trek* or *Doctor Who* for their darkness, emotional violence, and sheer ambiguity. The second story climaxes with a chilling and cruel finale in which innocent and blameless ghosthunter Tully (sensitively played by Gerald James), hitherto little more than a comic sidekick, is sacrificed by Steel without the slightest hesitation. With its emphasis on nursery rhymes and games and people's fascination with historical artefacts as triggers for time to burst through into the present, the show used easy nostalgia and the seeming innocence of recollected youth and the trappings of science fiction and fantasy for an unusually thoughtful and troubling experiment in genre splicing. Gothic themes and elements of the occult were combined with space ships, time travel, and, on one memorable occasion, a pro-vegetarian parable couched as a 'return of the repressed' narrative.

In both look and atmosphere, with its studio-bound style and strong design, the series comes across as a succession of stage plays presented in half-hour chunks, but done with a confidence and panache not usually attempted for a show in the SF/fantasy genre, especially not one making so few concessions to narrative clarity or straightforward character development. Hammond seems to have been influenced as much by the absurdist works of Pinter and Ionesco as by more predictable sources as H.G. Wells' and

J.B. Priestley's popular time plays such as 'Dangerous Corner' and 'An Inspector Calls'. Ironically, Priestley's influence is particularly noticeable in the only *Sapphire & Steel* story not actually written by Hammond. The fifth serial, by Don Houghton and Anthony Read, is set in a contemporary country house where a 1930s-style party is being held. In a neat metaphysical reversal of a typical Agatha Christie plot, the guests start being bumped off one by one before vanishing out of existence. Sapphire and Steel eventually realise that they are there not to stop a crime but rather to ensure that a murder actually does take place.

   Sapphire & Steel has never garnered the level of fan appreciation or even critical support that one associates with the likes of *Star Trek*, *Doctor Who,* or *The Prisoner,* for instance, but has nonetheless maintained a crucial place in cult circles for the originality of its conception and for the seriousness with which it was produced. This was never truer than in the case of the climactic concluding story, in which a little more information about the characters was finally revealed but within a story that was often impenetrable, the unpeeling of multiple layers of ambiguity all leading to more confusion. We learn that Sapphire and Steel are 'Operators' while Silver is a 'Technician' and they are all working to safeguard the present on earth, but in this final story it seems that they have now fallen foul of those who work above them as they are envious of their success, calling on 'transient beings' from the past to destroy our heroes. The two protagonists are trapped in a window in space, left to wander in time for eternity ('This place is nowhere and it's forever'). Although Hammond had planned a story to follow it, the devastating and dark conclusion of what proved to be the final serial, in which the villains succeed and our protagonists are seemingly defeated in a dramatic but frustratingly open ending, has consolidated the show's cult status and has led to subsequent attempts to find a resolution and extend the narrative in the form of fan fiction and in a continuing series of audio adventures in which David Warner and Susannah Harker took over the principal roles but with Collings returning as Silver.

26 Gen, Slash, OT3s, and Crossover – The Varieties of Fan Fiction

Roz Kaveney

One of the consequences of the internet has been a vast expansion in the amount of fan fiction out in the public domain; putting together a photocopied or duplicated zine full of such material was always something of an undertaking, whereas finding the other writers with shared interests who are always going to be a significant part of one's audience is now easy as a mouse-click. Though there is a lot of fan fiction based on material from comics, film, books, and celebrity journalism, it was television that produced the first major wave of fanzine fan fiction and that has been the core of fan fiction's subject matter on the internet. It is also television which has had the closest reciprocal relationship with fan fiction – sometimes being influenced by the view of relationships taken by fan writers in later canonical episodes of the show, and sometimes, almost certainly, playing consciously with the expectations of an audience that includes fan writers and their readers.

In the first place fan fiction derives from our love of stories, both the specific stories of the shows and films that the fan fiction refers to, and the general process of story-telling, the desire of both audience and creator to find out what happens next and how it feels as it happens. When we get to the end of an episode, or a season, or even come to the hiatuses that are a part of the rhythm of the American television year, we are both fascinated and concerned by the gap in the story and feel a desire to fill it. That desire has to do both with the specifics of our caring about Buffy, or Xena, or the Winchester twins, and with the love of story itself. The closer our imitation of the character idiolects and plot twists of the show in whose fandom we are writing, the closer our attention to the show's accumulation of continuity,[1] the more pleasurable our experience as writer of something for which we are ourselves one of our own assumed ideal readership. The existence of such an assumed ideal readership is one of the things which makes fan fiction a genre – the core relation between authors and readership of science fiction and crime fiction is also predicated on the existence of such an assumed ideal readership, who know the tropes and appreciate the dance of ideas.

The knowledge that fan fiction is being written for an assumed ideal reader of which its author is one, but not the only one, brings out another important aspect of the fan fiction culture, the fact that it is built on what anthropologists and sociologists such as Titmus call a 'gift relationship', on the at times quasi-erotic assumption that pleasure received for free is best repaid by the free offer of pleasure given. This is why, for example, in the subculture surrounding SF fanzines, the letter of comment page is so important, and letters of comment are one of the currencies in which those fans not currently producing fanzines of their own stay recipients in good standing of the fanzines on which they comment.

Much fanfiction is written to commission – people will ask for a particular sort of story, or for erotic fiction featuring a particular partnership, often as an online birthday present – or in exchange for ficathon challenges where likely contributors post cues for a story they would like to see and scan the challenges for something that they would enjoy writing. These are often seasonal in nature – there is a proliferation of them in many fandoms in the weeks leading up to Christmas. Sometimes they are more specifically part of a directly friendly relationship – during my period of intense *Buffy the Vampire Slayer* fanfiction writing, I wrote my Joyce/Jenny Calendar story 'Not an Earring' as a birthday present to Pam who curated a Joyce Summers site and requested that particular pairing.

Fan fiction is one currency – intelligent commentary is another – through which a group of people who share a taste for a particular show or medium evolve into a community. People trade stories, commentaries, and ideas – and other fannish modes of expression such as vids (clips from shows recut as the visuals for appropriate music) – and this exchange makes fan communities more than mere groups of casual online friends, groups with internal hierarchies of prestige – Big Name Fans – occasional meetings and conventions and also, alas!, feuds.

Fan fiction is often a way in which we comment on the shows and films that they relate to express our dissent from particular directions that they took, creating alternate universes to the mainline of the shows' plotting in order to do so. Many *Buffy* fans were critical of the decision to make the redemption of Spike contingent on his acquisition of a new soul and preferred to explore through fiction the possibility of his redemption through love alone while still demonic. This is a significant enough subset of *Buffy* fanfiction for its writers and advocates to be known as 'redemptionistas'.

Much of the urge to write fiction which crosses over material from one fandom to another is purely ludic – to write, as people have, crossovers between Buffy and Father Ted that are true to both shows is both a source of endless comic invention and fascinating technical problems. A lot of the time such crossovers are done for the sake of sheer virtuoso performance – the crossover site 'Twisting the Hellmouth' crosses the Buffy universe with other media as unlikely as the Travis McGee novels of John D. McDonald or the British situation comedy *Father Ted*. Occasionally it is possible to find a combination of shows or films that is more than just amusing – setting Almodovar side by side with Harry Potter allows one to criticise the implicit pederasty of much Potter fanfiction and the sometimes near-mawkish nostalgia that pervades the Spaniard's work.[2]

This desire to critique aspects of shows and of the surrounding culture of which they are a product finds one of its major expressions in slash fiction, both that dealing with gay relationships between male characters and that creating lesbian interactions, femslash. One of the driving forces behind slash and femslash is the pervading heterosexism of commercial media – if television will not give us the due proportion of same-sex eroticism we are entitled to expect, then we will make it for ourselves. This is particularly the case when shows hint, or can be read as hinting, at suppressed same-sex desire between characters.

Sometimes fanfiction gets written as an implicit rebuke to media which impute strict heterosexuality in milieu where bisexuality would be a more probable norm. My 'Burning Down the House' was a reaction to the film *The Banger Sisters* (Bob Dolman, US, 2002) in which Susan Sarandon and Goldie Hawn played former groupies who had allegedly never been persuaded by tired rock stars to have sex for their delectation.

A lot of male slash fiction is written by heterosexual women for whom eroticisation of intertwined male bodies is erotic in and of itself and also as an expression of utopian desire for a fulfilled egalitarian sexuality. It is a way of expressing discontent with the level of equality available to the women who write it in the heterosexual relations they prefer; it is also a way of doubling the number of objects of erotic consideration. It is a form of pastoral, sometimes estranged from actual consideration of the implications of male homosexuality in a sexist society and sometimes demonising the female characters who might stand between the male bodies in this dream. In her piece on male slash, Joanna Russ suggests[3] that the attraction of it for lesbian women is that it is 'more noble', that in a society which undervalues female sexuality, writing about male homosexuality is more validated (1985); significantly, Russ was writing in a period before *Xena: Warrior Princess*, *Buffy,* and the other female-centred and female-positive shows that featured modern action heroines shifted the interest of lesbian writers of fanfiction to femslash. It is important to stress the emergence of femslash as a significant, though still minority, part of fan fiction since much academic writing has focussed on male-centred slash as if it were the only variety.

A lot of both male slash and femslash is less about sexual acts than about the process of relationships, plots that are intended to bring characters together. Often these are to a greater or lesser degree coming out stories – the stories of how characters accepted gay or lesbian identities through falling in love, or by having sex as a consequence of one's acting as carer to the other's woes or physical injuries. This latter topos is sufficiently common that it is known by the genre tag 'hurt/comfort'. Other slash is more purely about the sex and is known as PWP or 'Plot? What Plot?'; as a general but not exclusive rule, fiction that is about the growth of relationships is more likely also to be concerned with close imitation of character idiolects than stories in which characters from shows are the flesh puppets of erotic imagination.

One of the negative aspects of all fanfiction is its tendency in inexperienced or incompetent hands to produce what are known as 'Mary Sues'. A Mary Sue is typically a character invented for the occasion, a character whose purpose is to place an idealised version of the author in the fictional world they most desire to inhabit. Mary Sues standardly possess particular gifts of physical skill, outstanding moral character, and infinite lovableness that enable them to sort out all of the problems of a selection of the inhabitants of that universe in almost no time at all Other writers and readers standardly mock Mary Sues as a too overt piece of wish-fulfilment and as making the writer's job too easy.

However, there is an element of Mary Suing both in many shows and in much good fanfiction – the Companions in *Doctor Who* have always been to some degree identification figures for the audience particularly in the hands of the team who took over the revived show, authors most of whom had pre-existing identities as devoted fans of the show. Russell T. Davies has been criticised for this in particular, but his creations – Rose and then Jack Harkness, Martha, and Donna – are something more, simply because they have to make the hard moral and other choices that go with true protagony. A lot of good fanfiction derives from writers finding particular characters in shows sympathetic because in a sense they are personal totems, aspects of oneself with which one wishes to engage and think through by writing. (In my own fan fiction, I have paid much attention to Cordelia Chase and to Dawn Summers from *Buffy* – as a transsexual woman, I found myself identifying with the self-consciousness of both characters and their search for authenticity. In particular, in my story 'Dawn in Rome' I was fascinated by Dawn's insecurity about having an artefactual identity, and in having a version of Dawn work those issues through.)

The case made against fanfiction by those who detest it has in part to do with belief in the supreme virtue of originality – a cultural obsession of Western art since the Romantics – and hence the claim by writers such as Megan Lindholm that fanfiction is never more than a set of training wheels which people with talent have failed to outgrow. I would argue on the contrary that the sheer technical challenge involved in taking fanfiction and making it work is a serious school of talent, just as it was when every poet wrote versions of Horace or when the subject of poetry was the Arthurian or Greek mythoi. Fan fiction provides technical challenges as well as a vehicle for personal artistic expression.

246

There is a perfectly reasonable criticism of fanfiction that some writers do not like people trespassing on their material – the general feeling in the fan fiction community has always been that this should be respected, which is why writers who have expressed this view have generally not had to back it up with legal sanctions. There is also the fact that many writers of fan fiction are young and inexperienced and learning their trade – much fan fiction is execrably bad. Quite a lot of it is not, and the community of interest and dedication – most people participate in more than one fandom – that produces both the best and the worst is one to which it is stimulating to belong.

Notes

1. Continuity consists primarily of 'canon', which is to say things that actually happen on screen in the course of episodes, secondarily of 'fanon', which is those things or interpretations of things which fan discussion of shows assumes as an explanation for what we have seen. Some fanon is definitively confuted by later events on screen – this is known as 'being Jossed' in homage to Joss Whedon – and some is retrospectively confirmed. When Faith first appeared in Season 3 of *Buffy the Vampire Slayer* (*BtVS*), fan writers interpreted some of her behaviour as deriving from sexual interest in Buffy. Whedon has said that this was not his original thought but was a part of what he then started to write, while retaining a fair amount of ambiguity in the actual writing. Subsequently, in Season 4, he showed Faith as picking up almost instantly on Willow's relationship with Tara, and, in Season 1 of *Angel*, as flirting with Lilah Morgan. In Season 7 of *BtVS*, the First Evil, presenting as Faith's former patron, the Mayor, tells Faith that 'she'll never love you' in an attempt to bring her back to the dark side. At this point, when Faith's love for Buffy is actually mentioned on screen, fanon metamorphoses into canon, and, moreover, does so retrospectively.
2. My own story 'Five Disillusions'. All my stories referred to in this text are at www. glamourousrags.dymphna.net.
3. In the essay on fan fiction in her collection *Magic Mommas, Trembling Sisters, Puritans and Perverts* (1985).

Works Cited

Abbott, Stacey (ed.) (2005a) *Reading Angel: The TV Spin-off with a Soul*, London and New York: I.B.Tauris.

—— (2005b) 'Kicking Ass and Singing "Mandy": A Vampire in LA', in Stacey Abbott (ed.) *Reading Angel: The TV Spin-off with a Soul*, London and New York: I.B.Tauris, 1–13.

—— (2005c) 'From Madman in the Basement to Self-sacrificing Champion: The Multiple Faces of Spike', *European Journal of Cultural Studies* 8:3, 329–344.

—— (2009) ' "It's a Little Outside the Box": How *Angel* Breaks the Rules', in Stacey Abbott (ed.) *Angel,* Detroit: Wayne State University Press, 83–103.

Abbott, Stacey, and Simon Brown (2007) ' "Serious Spy Stuff": The Cult Pleasures of *Alias*', in Stacey Abbott and Simon Brown (eds) *Investigating Alias: Secrets and Spies*, London and New York: I.B.Tauris, 1–8.

Abercrombie, Nick, and Brian Longhurst (1998) *Audiences: A Sociological Theory of Performance and Imagination*, London: Sage.

Adalian, Josef (2007) 'Showtime Renews *Californication*', *Variety Online* no. 6 (September). Available at: http://www.variety.com/article/VR1117971522.html? categoryid=1238&cs=1&query=californication. Accessed 12 January 2008.

Adams, Michael (2003) *Slayer Slang: A Buffy the Vampire Slayer Lexicon*, Oxford: Oxford University Press.

Ain't It Cool (2007) 'HEROES Ends Early This Season!! ORIGINS to Air after the HEROES Season Finale in April!!', 21 June. Available at: http://www.aintitcool. com/node/33110. Accessed 27 November 2008.

Alvarez, Rafael (2004) *The Wire: Truth Be Told*, New York: Pocket Books.

Andrae, Thomas (1996) 'Television's First Feminist: *The Avengers* and Female Spectatorship', *Discourse* 18:3, 112–136.

Anon (2001) 'Viewers for Quality Television Closes Shop'. Available at: http:// tv.zap2it.com/tveditorial/tve_main/1,1002,271%7C64819%7C1%7C,00.html. Accessed 29 November 2008.

—— (2005) '*Alias* ends mission with fifth season', *The Hollywood Reporter*, 29 November.

—— (2006a) '*Lost* ratings fall with Sky debut'. Available at: http://news.bbc. co.uk/1/hi/entertainment/6165448.stm. Accessed 27 November 2008

—— (2006b) '*Dexter* Slays Showtime Records', 20 December. Available at: http://www.tv.com/tracking/viewer.html?tid=98737&ref_id=62683&ref_ type=101&tag=story_list;title; 7. Accessed 31 October 2007.

—— (2007a) 'It's GO TIME for Showtime', 16 July. Available at: http://www. multichannel.com/article/CA6460196.html. Accessed 31 October 2007.

—— (2007b) '*Dexter* Season Finale Does in Showtime Ratings Mark', 18 December. Available at: http://www.multichannel.com/article/CA6513773. html. Accessed 16 March 2008.

—— (2007c) '*Dexter* Sets Showtime Ratings Record'. Available at: http://www. ew.com/ew/article/0,,20161845,00.html. Accessed 16 March 2008.

Anon (2007d) 'Stop the Presses: The First Delivery Has Occurred', *Pencils 2Media Mogels.* 12 December. Available at: http://www.pencils2mediamoguls.com/. Accessed 27 November 2008.

Apple – iTunes – iTunes Store – TV Shows. Available at: http://www.apple.com/itunes/store/tvshows.html. Accessed week of 15–22 July 2008.

Armstrong, Jennifer (2005) 'Love, Labor, Lost', *Entertainment Weekly* no. 838/839, 9 September, 30.

Arnold, Thomas K. (2006) 'Sony's Universal Media Disc Facing Last Rites', *Reuters* 30 March. Available at: http://www.rss-feed.org/644294_Sony-S-Universal-Media-Disc-facing-last-rites-Reuters.htm. Accessed 30 August 2007.

Associated Press (2007) 'ABC's Grey's Anatomy Rebukes Star for Slur' 22 January. *MSNBC Online*. Available at: http://www.msnbc.msn.com/id/16696521/. Accessed 8 November 2008.

Bacon-Smith, Camille (1992) *Enterprising Women: Television Fandom and the Creation of Popular Myth*, Philadelphia: University of Pennsylvania Press.

Baker, Roy Ward (2000) *The Director's Cut*, London: Reynolds and Hearn.

Balio, Tino (1998) ' "A Major Presence in All of the World's Important Markets": The Globalization of Hollywood in the 1990s', in Steve Neale and Murray Smith (eds) *Contemporary Hollywood Cinema*, London and New York: Routledge, 58–73.

Barnouw, Erik (1990) *Tube of Plenty: The Evolution of American Television*, 2nd revised edn, New York: Oxford University Press.

Battis, Jes (2005) *Chosen Families in Buffy the Vampire Slayer and Angel*, Jefferson, NC: McFarland.

—— (2007) *Investigating Farscape: Uncharted Territories of Sex and Science Fiction*, London: I.B.Tauris.

Battlestar Galactica (2003) *Battlestar Galactica: The Resistance (Web series) – TV.com*. Available at: http://www.tv.com/battlestar-galactica-2003/battlestar-galactica-the-resistance-web-series/episode/828222/summary.html. Accessed 28 August 2007.

Baudrillard, Jean (1988) 'Simulacra and Simulations', in Mark Poster (ed.) *Selected Writings*, Stanford: Stanford University Press, 166–184.

'BBC Annual Report and Accounts 2006/7 Part Two: The BBC Executive's review and assessment', *BBC – Annual Reports and Accounts 2006/2007*. Available at: http://www.bbc.co.uk/annualreport. Accessed 30 August 2007.

BBC – Doctor Who – The Official Site. Available at: http://www.bbc.co.uk/doctorwho. Accessed 28 August 2007.

Benjamin, Walter (1969) 'The Work of Art in the Age of Mechanical Reproduction', W. Benjamin *Illuminations*, trans. Harry Zohn, ed and intro. Hannah Arendt, New York: Schocken, 217–252.

Berkvist, Robert (1968) 'Vampires are Voluptuous', *The New York Times* Sunday, 29 December, 17.

Bernardi, Daniel Leonard (1998) *Star Trek and History: Race-ing toward a White Future*, New Brunswick, NJ: Rutgers University Press.

Black, David A. (2004) 'Character; or, The Strange Case of Uma Peel', in Sara Gwenllian-Jones and Roberta E. Pearson (eds) *Cult Television,* Minneapolis: University of Minnesota Press, 99–114.

Boddy, William (2004) *New Media and Popular Imagination: Launching Radio, Television, and Digital Media in the United States*, Oxford: Oxford University Press, 2004.

Bourdieu, Pierre (1984) *Distinction: A Social Critique of the Judgement of Taste*, translated by Richard Nice, London: Routledge.

Briscoe, Desmond, and Roy Curtis-Bramwell (1983) *The Radiophonic Workshop – The first 25 Years*, London: BBC Books.

Brooker, Will (2009) 'Television Out of Time: Watching Cult Shows on Download', in Roberta Pearson (ed.) *Reading Lost*, London and New York: I.B.Tauris, 53–78.

Brown, Dan (2004) '*Trailer Park Boys* Returns', *CBC News Online*, 6 April. Available at: http://www.cbc.ca/arts/features/trailerpark/. Accessed 25 November 2008.

Brown, Les (1998) 'The American Networks', in Anthony Smith (ed.) *Television: An International History*, 2nd edn, Oxford: Oxford University Press, 147–161.

Buckingham, David, Hannah Davies, Ken Jones, and Peter Kelly (1999) *Children's Television in Britain*, London: BFI.

Butler, Judith (2000) Interview: 'Changing the Subject: Judith Butler's Politics of Radical Resignification', in Gary A. Olsen and Lynn Worsham (eds) *JAC* 20:4, 727–763.

Caldwell, John Thornton (1995) *Televisuality*, New Brunswick, NJ: Rutgers University Press.

Campbell, Lisa (2005) 'Brace Yourselves', *Broadcast*, 5 August, 21.

Campbell, Richard (1995) 'Conspicuous Confusion: A Critique of Veblen's *Conspicuous Consumption*', *Sociological Theory* 13:1, 37–47.

Caughie, John (2000) *Television Drama: Realism, Modernism, and British Culture*, Oxford: Oxford University Press.

Chapman, James (2002a) *Saints and Avengers: British Adventure Series of the 1960s*, London and New York: I.B.Tauris.

—— (2002b) 'Is There Honey Still for Tea? *The Avengers*', in J. Chapman (ed.) *Saints and Avengers: British Adventure Series of the 1960s*, 52–99.

Clark, Anthony (2008) '*The Avengers* 1961–69', *Screenonline*. Available at: http://www.screenonline.org.uk/tv/id/473728/. Accessed 6 November 2008.

Collins, Jim (1992) 'Television and Postmodernism', in Allen, Robert C. (ed.) *Channels of Discourse, Reassembled: Television and Contemporary Criticism*, Chapel Hill: University of North Carolina Press, 327–349.

Cooke, Lez (2003) *British Television Drama: A History*, London: BFI.

Cotta Vaz, Mark (2005) *The Lost Chronicles: The Official Companion Book*, London, Transworld Publishers.

Crissell, Andrew (1997) *An Introductory History of British Broadcasting*, London: Routledge.

Daley, Steve (1986) 'The Chemistry Is Right for *Moonlighting*' *Chicago Tribune* 6 April. Available at: http://www.davidandmaddie.com/chemistry-chicagotribune86.htm. Accessed 22 August 2008.

Davis, Erik (2006) 'Borat: The Hilarious Aftermath', 10 November *Cinematical*. Available at: http://www.cinematical.com/2006/11/10/borat-the-hilarious-aftermath/. Accessed 10 April 2008.

Davis, Glyn (2004) ' "Saying It Out Loud": Revealing Television's Queer Teens', in Glyn Davis and Kay Dickinson (eds) *Teen TV*, London: BFI, 127–140.

Digital Television (DTV) 'Tomorrow's Television Today!' Available at: http://www. dtv.gov. Accessed 25 August 2007.

Downey, Kevin (2007) 'Say Good-bye to the Serialized Drama', *Media Life*, 14 May, reproduced in *The Rash Report*. Available at: http://www.rashreport.com/pdfs/ presspass/medialife_goodbye_051407.pdf. Accessed 29 November 2008.

Dr Blog Bot (2008) 'Exclusive: Jed Whedon and Maurissa Tancharoen Interview' (19 July 2008). Available at: http://doctorhorrible.net/exclusive-jed-whedon-maurissa-tancharoen/151/. Accessed 22 July 2008.

Dr. Horrible's Sing-along Blog (2008) http://doctorhorrible.net. Accessed 22 July 2008.

Dr. Horrible (2008) Available at: http://drhorrible.com. Accessed 22 July 2008.

Durbin, Jonathan (2003) 'Gals Loving Boys: Women Seem to Love *Trailer Park Boys*', *McLean's*, 24 November 24. Available at: http://www. encyclopediecanadienne.ca/index.cfm?PgNm=TCE&Params=M1ARTM0012 539. Accessed 9 July 2008.

Eco, Umberto (1987) '*Casablanca*: Cult Movies and Intertextual Collage', in U. Eco *Travels in Hyperreality*, trans. William Weaver, London: Picador, 197–211.

Edwards, Richard (2008) 'Red Alert [News: Above and Beyond] – As Seen on TV', *SFX* 169, May, 24.

Elber, Lynn (2007) 'Will 'Lost' Ratings Plunge Doom Series?' 16 February. Available at: http://abcnews.go.com/Entertainment/wireStory?id=2882578. Accessed 16 June 2007.

Elliott, Stuart (2007) 'In a Time of High Anxiety, A Sedative of the Occult', *The New York Times on the Web,* 21 May, reproduced in *The Rash Report.* Available at: http://www.rashreport.com/pdfs/presspass/nytimes_sedative_052107.pdf. Accessed 27 November 2008.

Ellis, John (1992) *Visible Fictions: Cinema, Television, Video*, London: Routledge.

epguides.com. Available at: http://epguides.com. Accessed 28 August 2007.

Federal Communications Commission (FCC) Home Page. Available at: http:// www.fcc.gov. Accessed 25 August 2007.

Feuer, Jane, Paul Kerr, and Tise Vahimagi (eds) (1984) *MTM 'Quality Television'*, London: BFI.

Fiske, John (1992) 'The Cultural Economy of Fandom', in Lewis, Lisa A. (ed.) *The Adoring Audience: Fan Culture and Popular Media*, London: Routledge.

Fiske, John, and John Hartley (1978) *Reading Television*, London: Methuen.

Gee, James Paul (2003) *What Video Games Have to Teach Us about Learning and Literacy,* New York: Palgrave MacMillan.

Gelineau, Mark (2008) 'Coyote in the Black: The Evolution of Malcolm Reynolds as Trickster Shaman', *Slayage: The Online International Journal of Buffy Studies* 7:1. Available at: http://slayageonline.com.

Geraghty, Lincoln (2007) *Living with Star Trek: American Culture and the Star Trek Universe*. London and New York: I.B.Tauris.

Gitlin, Todd (1983) *Inside Prime Time*, London and New York: Routledge.

Gomery, Douglas, and Luke Hockley (eds) (2006) *Television Industries*, London: BFI.

Gough, Paul J. (2007) '*Lost* Won't End with a Blackout', *Hollywood Reporter* 14 June. Available at: http://www.hollywoodreporter.com. Accessed 15 June 2007.

Grainge, Paul (2009) '*Lost* Logos: Channel 4 and the Branding of American Event Television', in Roberta Pearson (ed.) *Reading Lost*, London and New York: I.B. Tauris, 101–124.

Griffiths, Alan (2003) *Digital Television Strategies: Business Challenges and Opportunities*, Basingstoke: Palgrave MacMillan.

Griffiths, John (2007) 'What Lies Beneath', *Emmy* 29:3, 126–135

Gwenllian-Jones, Sara (2000) 'Starring Lucy Lawless?', *Continuum: Journal of Media and Cultural Studies* 14:1, 9–22.

—— (2003) 'Web Wars: Resistance, Online Fandom and Studio Censorship', in Mark Jancovich and James Lyons (eds) *Quality Popular Television,* London: BFI, 163–177.

Gwenllian-Jones, Sara, and Roberta E. Pearson (eds) (2004a) *Cult Television,* Minneapolis: University of Minnesota Press.

Gwenllian-Jones, Sara, and Roberta E. Pearson (2004b) 'Introduction', in S. Gwenllian-Jones and R.E. Pearson (eds) *Cult Television*, Minneapolis: University of Minnesota Press, ix–xx.

Halfyard, Janet K. (2001) 'Love, Death, Curses and Reverses (in F Minor): Music, Gender, and Identity in *Buffy the Vampire Slayer*', *Slayage: The Online International Journal of Buffy Studies* 1:4. Available at: http://slayageonline.com.

—— (2006) 'Screen Playing: Cinematic Representations of Classical Music Performance and European Identity', in Miguel Mera and David Burnand (eds), *European Film Music*, Aldershot: Ashgate, 73–85.

Hammond, P.J. (1992) *Sapphire and Steel*, 2nd edn, London: Virgin Books.

Haraway, Donna (1991) 'A Manifesto for Cyborgs: Science, Technology, and Socialist-Feminism in the Late Twentieth Century', in D. Haraway *Simians, Cyborgs and Women: The Reinvention of Nature,* New York: Routledge, 149–181.

Harris, Paul (2006) 'America's TV Genius Strikes Gold Again', *The Observer*, 24 September.

Hayles, N. Katherine (1999) *How We Became Posthuman: Virtual Bodies in Cybernetics, Literature and Informatics*, Chicago: University of Chicago Press.

Helford, Elyce Rae (2000) 'Feminism, Queer Studies, and the Sexual Politics of *Xena: Warrior Princess*', in Elyce Rae Helford (ed.) *Fantasy Girls: Gender in the New Universe of Science Fiction and Fantasy Television*, Lanham: Rowman & Littlefield, 135–162.

Heroes TV Show on NBC. 'Webisodes'. Available at: http://www.nbc.com/Heroes/Webisodes/. Accessed 1 August 2008.

Higgins, John M., and Allison Romano (2004) 'The Family Business', *Broadcasting and Cable*, 1 March, 1, 6, 31.

Hight, Craig (2005) 'Making-of Documentaries on DVD: *The Lord of the Rings* Trilogy and Special Editions', *The Velvet Light Trap*, 56:3, 4–17.

Hill, John (1991) 'Television and Pop: The Case of the 1950s', in John Corner (ed.) *Popular Television in Britain*, London: BFI.

Hills, Matt (2000) 'Media Fandom, Neoreligiosity, and (Cult)ural Studies' *The Velvet Light Trap: A Critical Journal of Film and Television* 2:1, 73–84.

—— (2001) 'Interview with Henry Jenkins' *Intensities* 2. Available at: http://www.cult-media.com/issue2/CMRjenk.htm. Accessed 10 April 2005.

—— (2002) *Fan Cultures*, London and New York: Routledge.

—— (2003a) 'Recognition in the Eyes of the Relevant Beholder: Representing "Subcultural Celebrity" and Cult TV fan Cultures', in *Mediactive* 2, 59–73.

—— (2003b) '*Star Wars* in Fandom, Film Theory, and the Museum: The Cultural Status of the Cult Blockbuster', in Julian Stringer (ed.) *Movie Blockbusters,* London and New York: Routledge, 178–189.

—— (2004a) '*Dawson's Creek*: "Quality Teen TV" and "Mainstream Cult?"', in Glyn Davis and Kay Dickinson (eds) *Teen TV*, London: BFI, 54–67.

—— (2004b) '*Star Trek*', in Glen Creeber (ed.) *Fifty Key Television Programmes*, London: Arnold, 193–197.

—— (2005a) 'Patterns of Surprise: The "Aleatory Object" in Psychoanalytic Ethnography and Cyclical Fandom', *American Behavioral Scientist* 48:7, 853–894.

—— (2005b) 'Cult TV, Quality and the Role of the Episode/Programme Guide', in Michael Hammond and Lucy Mazdon (eds) *The Contemporary Television Series*, Edinburgh: Edinburgh University Press, 190–206.

—— (2006a) 'Realising the Cult Blockbuster: *The Lord of the Rings* Fandom and Residual/Emergent Cult Status in "the Mainstream"', in Ernest Mathijs (ed.) *The Lord of the Rings: Popular Culture in Global Context*, London and New York: Wallflower Press, 160–171.

—— (2006b) 'Not Just Another Powerless Elite? When Media Fans Become Subcultural Celebrities', in Su Holmes and Sean Redmond (eds) *Framing Celebrity: New Directions in Celebrity Culture*, London and New York: Routledge, 101–118.

—— (2007) 'From the Box in the Corner to the Box Set on the Shelf: "TV III" and the Cultural/Textual Valorisations of DVD', *New Review of Film and Television Studies* 5:1, 41–60.

Hills, Matt, and Rebecca Williams (2005) '"It's All My Interpretation": Reading Spike through the Subcultural Celebrity of James Marsters', *European Journal of Cultural Studies* 8:3, 345–365.

Hollows, Joanne (2003) 'The Masculinity of Cult', in Mark Jancovich, Antonio Lázaro Reboll, Julian Stringer, and Andy Willis (eds) *Defining Cult Movies,* Manchester: Manchester University Press, 35–53.

Home, Anna (1993) *Into the Box of Delights,* London: BBC Books.

Hunt, Nathan (2003) 'The Importance of Trivia: Ownership, Exclusion and Authority in Science Fiction Fandom', in Mark Jancovich, Antonio Lázaro Reboll, Julian Stringer and Andy Willis (eds) *Defining Cult Movies*, Manchester: University of Manchester Press, 185–201.

Jacobs, Jason (2000) *The Intimate Screen: Early British Television Drama*, Oxford: Oxford University Press.

Jancovich, Mark, and Nathan Hunt (2004) 'The Mainstream, Distinction, and Cult TV', in Sara Gwenllian-Jones and Roberta E. Pearson (eds) *Cult Television*, Minneapolis: University of Minnesota Press, 27–44.

Jaramillo, Deborah L. (2002) 'The Family Racket: AOL Time Warner, HBO, *The Sopranos* and the Construction of a Quality Brand', *Journal of Communication Inquiry* 26, January, 62.

Jayemanne, Darshana (2004) 'Microstatecraft: Belonging and Difference in Imagined Communities', *Refractory* 3:1. Available at: http://blogs.arts.unimelb.edu.au/refractory/category/browse-past-volumes-3/. Accessed 12 February 2006.

Jenkins, Henry (1988) '*Star Trek* Rerun, Reread, Rewritten: Fan Writing as Textual Poaching', *Critical Studies in Mass Communication* 5:2, 85–107

—— (1992a) *Textual Poachers: Television Fans and Participatory Cultures*, New York and London: Routledge.

——(1992b) ' "Strangers No More, We Sing": Filking and the Social Construction of the Science Fiction Fan Community', in Lisa A. Lewis (ed.) *The Adoring Audience: Fan Culture and Popular Media*, London: Routledge, 209–236.

—— (2002) 'Interactive Audiences?', in Dan Harries (ed.) *The New Media Book*, London: BFI, 157–170.

——(2006) *Convergence Culture: Where Old and New Media Collide*, New York and London: New York University Press.

Jenkins, Henry and John Tulloch (1995). *Science Fiction Audiences: Watching Doctor Who and Star Trek*. London: Routledge.

Johnson, Brian D. (2006) 'Sexing Up *Trailer Park Boys*', *McLean's* 9 October. Available at: http://www.encyclopediecanadienne.ca/index.cfm?PgNm=TCE&Params=M1ARTM0012981. Accessed 9 July 2008.

Johnson, Catherine (2005a) *Telefantasy*, London: BFI.

—— (2005b) 'Quality/Cult Television: *The X-Files* and Television History', in Michael Hammond and Lucy Mazdon (eds) *The Contemporary Television Series*, Edinburgh: Edinburgh University Press, 57–71.

Johnson, Catherine (2007) 'Tele-branding in TVIII: The Network as Brand and the Programme as Brand', *New Review of Film and Television Studies* 5:1, 5–24.

Johnson, Derek (2007) 'Inviting Audiences In: The Spatial Reorganization of Production and Consumption in "TV III" ', *New Review of Film and Television Studies* 5:1, 61–80.

Johnson-Smith, Jan (2005) *American Science Fiction TV* , London and New York: I.B.Tauris.

Jowett, Lorna (2005) *Sex and the Slayer: A Gender Studies Primer for the Buffy Fan*. Middletown, CT: Wesleyan University Press.

—— (forthcoming 2009) 'Hybridities: Genre, Technology, Science and Magic in *Angel*', in Lincoln Geraghty (ed.) *Future Visions*, Lanham, MD: Scarecrow Press.

Kassabian, Anahid (2001) *Hearing Film: Tracking Identifications in Contemporary Hollywood Cinema*, New York and London: Routledge.

Kerr, Paul (1984) 'Drama at MTM: *Lou Grant* and *Hill Street Blues*', in Jane Feuer, Paul Kerr and Tise Vahimagi (eds) *MTM: 'Quality Television'*, London: BFI.

Kinsey, Tammy A. (2005) 'Transitions and Time: The Cinematic Language of *Angel*' in Abbott (ed.) *Reading Angel,* 44–56.

Kohlberg, Lawrence (1981) *The Philosophy of Moral Development*. San Francisco: Harper.

Kuhn, Annette (2002) *An Everyday Magic: Cinema and Cultural Memory*, London and New York: I.B.Tauris, London.

Kuppers, Petra (2004) 'Quality Science Fiction: *Babylon Five*'s Metatextual Universe', in Gwenllian-Jones and Pearson (eds) *Cult Television,* 45–59.

Lavery, David, (1995) 'The Semiotics of Cobbler: *Twin Peaks*' Interpretive Community', in D. Lavery (ed.) *Full of Secrets: Critical Approaches to Twin Peaks*, Detroit: Wayne State University Press, 1–26.

Lemish, Dafna (2007) *Children and Television, a Global Perspective,* London: Blackwell.

Lewis, Paul (2008) '(Mis)reading Borat: The Risks of Irony in the Digital Age', *The Electronic Journal of Communication* 18:2, 1–5.

Littleton, Cynthia, and Liz Miller (2008) 'Screenwriters Strike Back: Dr. Horrible Leads Web Charge', *Variety* 18 July. Available at: http://www.variety.com/article/VR1117989200.html?categoryId=2522&cs=1. Accessed 22 July 2008.

Lost – Missing Pieces Home. Available at: http://abc.go.com/primetime/lost/missingpieces. Accessed 01 August 2008.

Lyon, J. Shaun (2005) *Back to the Vortex: The Unofficial and Unauthorised Guide to Doctor Who 2005,* Tolworth, UK: Telos Publishing.

Macnee, Patrick, with Dave Rogers (1997) *The Avengers and Me*, London: Titan.

Maio, Barbara (2008) 'Between Past and Future: Hybrid Design Style in *Firefly* and *Serenity*', in Rhonda V. Wilcox and Tanya R. Cochran (eds) *Investigating Firefly and Serenity: Science Fiction on the Frontier*, London, New York: I.B.Tauris.

Manovich, Lev (2001) *The Language of New Media*, Cambridge, MA: MIT Press.

Mark Lawson Talks to Russell T. Davies, prod./dir. Partridge, Helen, BBC Four: 16 January 2008.

Mathijs, Ernest, and Xavier Mendik (2008) 'Introduction: What Is Cult Film?', in E. Mathjs and X. Mendik (eds) *The Cult Film Reader*, Maidenhead, UK: Open University Press, 1–11.

McAdams, Deborah (1999) 'Franchise Programming', *Broadcasting and Cable* 11 October, 24–25.

McCabe, Janet (2000) 'Diagnosing the Alien: Producing Identities, US "Quality" Drama & British TV Culture in the '90s', in Bruce Carson and Margaret Llewellyn Jones (eds) *Frames and Fictions on Television: The Politics of Identities within Drama*, Exeter: Intellect, 141–154.

McCabe, Janet, and Kim Akass (2005) *Reading Six Feet Under: TV to Die For*, London and New York: I.B.Tauris.

——(2007) *Quality TV: Contemporary American Television and Beyond*, London and New York: I.B.Tauris.

Mendik, Xavier, and Graham Harper (eds) (2000) *Unruly Pleasures: The Cult Film and Its Critics*, Guildford: FAB Press.

Messenger Davies, Maire, and Roberta Pearson (2007) 'The Little Program That Could: The Relationship between NBC and *Star Trek*', in Michele Hilmes (ed.) *NBC: America's Network*, Berkeley: University of California Press, 209–223.

Meyer, Michaela D. (2005) 'From Rogue in the 'Hood to Suave in a Suit: Black Masculinity and the Transformation of Charles Gunn', in Abbott (ed.) *Reading Angel*, 176–188.

Miller, Toby (1997) *The Avengers*, London: BFI.

Moravec, Hans (1990) *Mind Children: The Future of Robot and Human Intelligence*, Boston: Harvard University Press.

Morse, Margaret (1998) 'What Do Cyborgs Eat?: Oral Logic in an Information Society', in M. Morse (ed.) *Virtualities: Television, Media Art and Cyberspace*, Bloomington and Indianapolis: Indiana University Press, 125–154.

Murray, James (1998) '*The Avengers*', *Cinefantastique*, 30:3, 32–57.

Murray, Janet H. (1997) *Hamlet on the Holodeck*. Cambridge, MA: MIT Press.

Nazzaro, Joe (2002) *Writing Science Fiction and Fantasy Television,* London: Titan Books.

Nelson, Robin (2007a) 'HBO Premium: Channelling Distinction through TVIII', *New Review of Film and Television Studies* 5:1, 25–40

Nelson, Robin (2007b) *State of Play: Contemporary 'High-end' TV Drama*, Manchester: Manchester University Press.

Newcomb, Horace (1974) *TV: The Most Popular Art*. New York: Anchor.

——(1997) 'From Old Frontier to New Frontier', in Lynn Spigel and Michael Curtin (eds) *The Revolution Wasn't Televised: Sixties Television and Social Conflict*, London: Routledge.

Nordyke, Kimberly (2007) '*Dexter* Dips in Ratings, Still Bloody Good'. *Reuters* 10 October. Available at: http://uk.reuters.com/article/televisionNews/idUKN1046649820071010. Accessed 16 March 2008.

Ornebring, Henrik (2007) 'The Show Must Go On…And On: Narrative and Seriality in *Alias*', in Abbott and Brown (eds), *Investigating Alias: Secrets and Spies*, London and New York: I.B.Tauris, 11–26.

Oxford English Dictionary Online (2008) Oxford: Oxford University Press.

Page, Adrian (2001) 'Postmodern Drama', in Glen Creeber (ed.) *The Television Genre Book*, London: BFI, 43–46.

Pandya, Giitesh (2008) 'Box Office Guru Wrapup: Fans Power *Sex* to the Top Spot: Sex Appeal Rules the Box Office', *Rotten Tomatoes* News 2 June. Available at: http://www.rottentomatoes.com/m/sex_and_the_city_the_movie/news/1731859/. Accessed 2 June 2008.

Paramount/UPN press release (2005) 2 February.

Pearson, Roberta E. (2003) 'Kings of Infinite Space: Cult Television Characters and Narrative Possibilities', *Scope: An Online Journal of Film and Television Studies*. Available at: http://www.scope.nottingham.ac.uk/article.php?issue=nov2003&id=262&section=article&q=pearson.

——(2004) '"Bright Particular Star": Patrick Stewart, Jean-Luc Picard, and Cult Television', in Sara Gwenllian-Jones and Roberta E. Pearson (eds) *Cult Television*, 61–80.

—— (2007) '*Lost* in Transition: From Post-network to Post-television', in Janet McCabe and Kim Akass (eds) *American Quality Television*, 239–256.

Penley, Constance (1997) *Nasa/Trek,* London: Verso.

Perren, Alisa (2003) 'New US Networks in the 1990s', in Michele Hilmes (ed.) *The Television History Book*, London: BFI.

Perryman, Neil (2008) '*Doctor Who* and the Convergence of Media: A Case Study in 'Transmedia Storytelling', *Convergence: The International Journal of Research into New Media Technologies* 14:1, 21–39

Poniewozik, James (2005) 'Best of 2005: Television'. *Time Magazine*, 16 December. Available at: http://www.time.com/time/arts/article/0,8599,1141640,00.html. Accessed 27 November 2008.

Porter, Rick (2007) '"Heroes" Expands Universe with "Origins": Stand-alone episodes will help NBC cut down on repeats', 14 May. Available at: http://www.zap2it.com/tv/news/zap-nbcupfronts-heroesorigins,0,5536579.story. Accessed 27 November 2008.

Postgate, Oliver (2002) *Seeing Things*, Sidgewick & Jackson, London.

—— (2003) *Does Children's Television Matter?* Available at: http://www.oliverpostgate.co.uk/archive1.html. Accessed 18 November 2008.

Potter, Tiffany, and C.W. Marshall (eds) (2007) *Cylons in America: Critical Studies in Battlestar Galactica*, New York and London: Continuum.

Pounds, Michael C. (1999) *Race in Space: The Representation of Ethnicity in Star Trek and Star Trek: The Next Generation*, Lanham, MD: Scarecrow Press.

Pugh, Sheenagh (2004) 'The Democratic Genre: Fan Fiction in a Literary Context' *Refractory* 5. Available at: http://www.refractory.unimelb.edu. Accessed 1 April 2005.

Pullen, Kirsten (2000) 'I-Love-Xena.com: Creating Online Fan Communities', in David Gauntlett (ed.) *web.studies*, London: Arnold, 52–61.

Rackham, Jane (2004) 'Face of the Week: Rob Lowe', *Radio Times* 26 June–2 July, 57

RapidShare: Easy Filehosting. Available at: http://rapidshare.com. Accessed 22 July 2008.

The Rash Report, email to R. Pearson, 20 August 2007.

Reeves, Jimmie L., Mark C. Rogers, and Michael Epstein (1996) 'Rewriting Popularity: The Cult Files', in David Lavery, Angela Hague, and Marla Cartwright (eds), *"Deny All Knowledge": Reading The X-Files*, Syracuse, NY: Syracuse University Press, 22–35.

——(2007) 'Quality Control: *The Daily Show*, the Peabody and Brand Discipline', in Janet McCabe and Kim Akass (eds) *Quality TV: Contemporary American Television and Beyond*, London: I.B.Tauris, 79–97.

Richards, Denzell (2007) '*Alias* DVD: Re-packaging American "Quality" and "Cult" Television Series' in Stacey Abbott and Simon Brown (eds) *Investigating Alias: Secrets and Spies*, London and New York: I.B.Tauris, 186–199

Richardson, Michael (1990) 'Under the Influence of *The Avengers*', *Primetime* 16, 28–33.

Riess, Jana (2004) *What Would Buffy Do: The Vampire Slayer as Spiritual Guide*, San Francisco: Jossey-Bass.

Rogers, Adam (2006) 'Captain's Log: Want to Understand *Battlestar Galactica*? Eavesdrop on its Writers', *Slate* 29 November. Available at: http://www.slate.com. Accessed 20 July 2008.

Rogers, Mark C., Michael Epstein, and Jimmie L. Reeves (2002) '*The Sopranos* as HBO Brand Equity: The Art of Commerce in the Age of Digital Reproduction', in David Lavery (ed.) *This Thing of Ours: Investigating The Sopranos*, London: Wallflower, 42–57.

Rojek, Chris (2001) *Celebrity,* London: Reaktion Books.

Romano, Allison (2002) 'Can *The Shield* Fix FX?', *Broadcasting and Cable*, 11 March, 16–17.

—— (2004) 'Showtime's New Chief has Emmy Envy', *Broadcasting and Cable*, 19 January, 30.

—— (2007) "'Showtime: Getting Hip to Success', *Broadcasting and Cable*, 10 September, 23.

Rose, Jacqueline (1984) *Peter Pan, or the Impossibility of Children's Fiction*, London: MacMillan.

Roy, Sanjoy (2008) 'Dr Horrible Is the Start … of something' *The Guardian* 21 July 2008. Available at: http://blogs.guardian.co.uk/tv/2008/07/dr_horrible_is_the_start_of_so.html. Accessed 22 July 2008.

Russ, Joanna (1985) *Magic Mommas, Trembling Sisters, Puritans and Perverts,* Cross Press.

SanctuaryForAll. Available at: http://www.sanctuaryforall.com/social/. Accessed 22 July 2008.

Sandvoss, Cornell (2005) *Fans: The Mirror of Consumption,* London: Polity Press.

Saxey, Esther (2001) 'Staking a Claim: The Series and Its Fan Fiction', in Roz Kaveney (ed.) *Reading the Vampire Slayer*, London and New York: I.B.Tauris,187–210.

SCIFI.COM | Battlestar Galactica. Available at: http://www.scifi.com/battlestar. Accessed 28 August 2007.

Sconce, Jeffrey (1995) '"Trashing" the Academy: Taste, Excess, and an Emerging Politics of Cinematic Style', *Screen* 36:4, 371–393.

—— (2003) 'Dickens, Selznick, and *Southpark*', in John Glavin (ed.) *Dickens on Screen*, Cambridge: Cambridge University Press, 171–187.

Sherman, Jay (2005) 'Disney Transformed: Other Media Companies Expected to Follow Technology Trail', *Television Week*, 17 October, 26.

Smith, David *'The Avengers* Forever'. Available at: http://theavengers.tv/forever/welcome.htm. Accessed 6 November 2008.

Snopes (2006) '*Battlestar Galactica* Suicide', *Snopes.Com* 3 March. Available at: http://msgboard.snopes.com/message/ultimatebb.php?/ubb/get_topic/f/30/t/002609/p/1.html. Accessed 27 November 2008.

Solow, Herb (2005) Interview with Maire Messenger Davies and Roberta Pearson, April 2005.

Stambler, Lyndon (2005) 'Risk and Reward', *Emmy* 27:5, 54–59.

Stelter, Brian (2007) 'Hollywood Strike: The Pencil Angle', *The New York Times: TV Decoder* 12 December. Available at: http://tvdecoder.blogs.nytimes.com/2007/12/12/hollywood-strike-the-pencil-angle/. Accessed 12 December 2007.

Supernatural Video. Available at: http://www.cwtv.com/cw-video/supernatural. Accessed 01 August 2008.

Thomas, Deborah (2006) 'Reading *Buffy*' *Close Up 01*, London: Wallflower Press, 167–244.

Thomas, Mike (1996) 'The Unsolved Mystery of *The X Files*', *TV Zone Special* 21, 8–13

Thompson, John B. (1995) *Media and Modernity*, Cambridge: Polity Press.

Thompson, Robert J. (1996) *Television's Second Golden Age*, Syracuse, NY: Syracuse University Press.

Tulloch, John, and Henry Jenkins (1995) *Science Fiction Audiences: Watching Doctor Who and Star Trek*, London: Routledge.

Turnock, Rob (2007) *Television and Culture, Britain and the Transformation of Modernity,* London and New York: I.B.Tauris.

Van Dusen, Chris, and Stacy McKee (2006) *Grey's Anatomy: Notes from the Nurses Station*, New York: Hyperion.

Wall, Brian and Michael Zryd (2001) 'Vampire Dialectics', in Roz Kaveney (ed.) *Reading the Vampire Slayer*, London and New York: I.B.Tauris, 53–77.

Wax, Roberta G. (2005) 'Labors of Love: Morality Play', *Emmy* 27:5, 17.

Whedon, Joss (2001) 'A.V. Club Interview', *The Onion*, 5 September, 5. Available at: http://www.avclub.com/articles/joss-whedon,13730/

—— (2005) 'The Final Season' DVD featurette, *Angel: The Complete DVD Collection* Region 2, Twentieth Century Fox.

Whedonesque: Joss Whedon weblog. Available at: http://whedonesque.com. Accessed 28 August 2007.

Whitfield, Stephen E., and Gene Roddenberry (1991) *The Making of Star Trek*, London: Titan Books.

Wilcox, Rhonda V. (1993) ' "In Your Dreams, Fleischman" ': Dr. Flesh and the Dream of the Spirit in *Northern Exposure*', *Studies in Popular Culture* 15:2, 1–13. Rpt. In *Critical Studies in Television: Scholarly Studies in Small Screen Fictions* 1:2 (Autumn 2006), 6–18.

——(2005) *Why Buffy Matters: The Art of Buffy the Vampire Slayer*, London and New York: I.B.Tauris.

Wilcox, Rhonda V., and David Lavery (2005) 'The Depths of *Angel* and the Birth of *Angel* Studies', in Stacey Abbott *Reading Angel*, 221–229.

Wilcox, Rhonda V., and Tanya R. Cochran (2008) ' "Good Myth": Joss Whedon's Further Worlds', in R.V. Wilcox and T.R. Cochran (eds) *Investigating Firefly and Serenity: Science Fiction on the Frontier*, London and New York: I.B.Tauris, 1–11.

Williams, Linda Ruth (2005) 'Twin Peaks: David Lynch and the Serial-Thriller Soap', in Michael Hammond and Lucy Mazdon (eds) *The Contemporary Television Series*, Edinburgh: Edinburgh University Press.

Williams, Raymond (1974) *Television: Technology and Cultural Form*, London: Fontana.

Wilson, Leah (ed.) (2008) *Grey's Anatomy 101*: Seattle Grace, Unauthorized, Dallas: Benbella.

Wood, Tat, and Lawrence Miles (2004–2007) *About Time: The UnAuthorised Guide to Doctor Who*, Six Volumes, Des Moines: Mad Norwegian Press.

YouTube – Broadcast Yourself. Available at: http://www.youtube.com. Accessed 30 August 2007.

Zicree, Marc Scott (1982) *The Twilight Zone Companion,* New York: Bantam.

Zicree, Marc Scott (1992) *The Twilight Zone Companion*, Los Angeles: Silman-James Press.

Zinder, Paul (2007) 'Sydney Bristow's "Full Disclosure": Mythic Structure and the Fear of Motherhood', in Abbott and Brown (eds), *Investigating Alias: Secrets and Spies*, London and New York: I.B.Tauris, 40–53.

Television and Film Guide

Television

24 (Fox, 2001–)
30 Rock (NBC, 2006–)
1984 (BBC, 1954)
4400, The (Paramount Network Television, 2004–2007)

Ace of Wands (ITV, 1970–1972)
Adams Family, The (ABC, 1964–1966)
Adventures of Robin Hood, The (ATV 1955–1957)
Alias (ABC, 2001–2006)
Alien Autopsy: (Fact of Fiction?) (Fox, 1995)
All in the Family (1971–1979)
Ally McBeal (Fox, 1997–2002)
American Gothic (CBS, 1995–1996)
America's Next Dance Crew (MTV, 2008)
An Age of Kings (BBC, 1960)
Andy Pandy (BBC, 1950)
Angel (WB, 1999–2004)
Army Wives (ABC, 2007–2008)
Avengers, The (ITV, 1961–1966)

Babylon 5 (PTEN, 1994–1997; TNT 1998)
Bagpuss (BBC, 1974)
Battlestar Galactica (NBC, 1978–1979)
Battlestar Galactica (Sci-Fi, 2004–2009)
Battlestar Galactica: Razor (Sci-Fi, 2007)
Beauty and the Beast (CBS, 1987–1990)
Beavis and Butthead (MTV, 1993–1997)
Beverley Hillbillies, The (CBS, 1962–1971)
Beverley Hills 90210 (Fox, 1990–2000)
Bewitched (ABC, 1964–1972)
Big Brother (C4, 1999–)
Bill, The (ITV, 1984–)
Black Adder (1983–1999)
Blake's 7 (BBC, 1978–1981)
Bleak House (BBC, 2005)
Blue Peter (BBC, 1958–)
Bonanza (NBC, 1959–1973)

Boris the Bold (BBC, 1972)
Buffy the Vampire Slayer (WB, 1997–2001; UPN, 2001–2003)

Cagney and Lacey (CBS, 1982–1988)
Californication (Showtime, 2007–).
Carnivale (HBO, 2003–2005)
Charmed (WB, 1998–2006)
Chuck (NBC, 2007–)
Clangers, The (BBC, 1969)
Commish, The (ABC, 1991–1995)
Corner, The (HBO, 2000)
Criminal Minds (CBS, 2005–)
Cruise of the Gods (BBC, 2002)
Crystal Tipps and Alistair. (BBC/Q3, 1972)
CSI (CBS, 2000–)
Curb Your Enthusiasm (HBO, 2000–)

Da Ali G Show (C4, 2000–2002, HBO, 2002–2004)
Daily Show, The (Comedy Central, 1996–)
Dark Shadows (ABC, 1966–1971)
Dancing with the Stars (ABC, 2005–)
Danger Man (US title *Secret Agent*) (ITV, 1960–1961, 1964–1967)
Danger Mouse (ITV, 1981–1992)
Dark Angel (Fox, 2000–2002),
Davy Crockett (ABC, 1954–1955)
Dawson's Creek (WB, 1998–2003)
Dead Famous (Living TV, 2004–2006)
Deadwood (HBO, 2004–2006)
Desperate Housewives (ABC, 2004–)
Dexter (Showtime, 2006–)
Doctor Who (BBC 1963–1989; 2005–)
Dollhouse (FOX, 2009–)
Dragnet (NBC, 1951–1959)
Dr. Horrible's Sing-Along Blog (online, 2008)

Eli Stone (ABC, 2008–)
Ellen (ABC, 1994–1998)
Enterprise (UPN, 2001–2005)
ER (NBC, 1994–2009)
Extras (BBC, 2005–2007)

Family Guy (FOX, 1999–2002, 2005–).
Father Ted (C4, 1995–1998)

Farscape (Sci-Fi, 1999–2003)
Fear Itself (NBC, 2008–)
Femme Nikita, La (USA Network, 1997–2001)
Fingerbobs (BBC/Q3, 1973)
Firefly (FOX, 2002)
Flintstones, The (ABC, 1960–1966)
Flower Pot Men (BBC 1952)
Friday Night Lights (NBC, 2006–)
Friends (NBC, 1994–2004)
The Fresh Prince of Bel Air (NBC, 1990–1996)
Fringe (Fox, 2008–)

Gangsters (BBC, 1975–1978)
Gargoyles (Buena Vista Television, 1994–1996)
Ghost Whisperer (CBS, 2005–)
Gilmore Girls (WB/CW, 2000–2007)
Good Times (CBS, 1974–1979)
Gossip Girl (CW, 2007–)
Grey's Anatomy (ABC, 2005–)

Hancock's Half Hour (BBC, 1956–1960)
Hercules: the Legendary Journeys (Universal, 1995–1999)
Heroes (NBC, 2006–)
Highlander (Syndicated, 1992–1998)
Hill Street Blues (NBC, 1981–1987)
Homicide: Life on the Street (1993–2000)
Homicide: Second Shift (1997–2000)
The Honeymooners (CBS, 1955–1956)

I Love Lucy (CBS, 1951–1957)
I Spy (NBC, 1965–1968)
In The Night Garden (BBC, 2007)
Into the Labyrinth (HTV, 1980–1982)
Invasion (ABC, 2005–2006)
Ivor the Engine (A-R, 1959, BBC, 1975)

Jericho (CBS, 2006–2008)
Jerry Springer Show, The (Syndicated, 1991–)
The Jeffersons (CBS, 1975–1985)
Joan of Arcadia (CBS, 2003–2005)

Kidnapped (NBC, 2006)
Kolchak: The Night Stalker (ABC, 1974)

The L Word (Showtime, 2004–)
Larry Sanders Show. The (HBO, 1992–1998)
Lou Grant (CBS, 1977–1982)
Life (NBC, 2007–)
Life on Mars (BBC, 2006–2007)
Ludwig (BBC/Q3, 1975)
Lost (ABC, 2004–)
Lyon's Den, The (NBC, 2003)

Mad Men (AMC, 2007–)
Magic Roundabout, The (BBC 1965–1969, 1972–1975)
Magnum P.I. (CBS, 1980–1988)
Man from UNCLE, The (NBC, 1964–1968)
Man in a Suitcase (ITV, 1967–1968)
Mary Tyler Moore Show, The (CBS, 1970–1977)
MASH (CBS, 1972–1983)
Medium (NBC, 2005–)
Miami Vice (NBC, 1984–1989)
Monty Python's Flying Circus (BBC, 1969–1974)
Most Haunted (Living TV, 2002–)
Moon Stallion, The (BBC, 1978)
Moonlighting (ABC, 1985–1989)
Muffin the Mule (BBC, 1946)
My So-Called Life (ABC, 1994–1995)
Mystery Science Theater 3000 (Comedy Central/Sci-Fi Channel, 1988–1999)

New Avengers, The (ITV, 1976–1977)
Newsnight (BBC, 1980–)
Night Gallery (NBC, 1970–1973)
Nine, The (ABC, 2006)
Nip/Tuck (FX, 2003–)
Northern Exposure (CBS, 1990–1995)
NYPD Blue (ABC 1993–2005)

O.C., The (Fox, 2003–2007)
Office, The (BBC, 2001–2003)
Outer Limits, The (ABC, 1963–1965; Showtime 1995–2002).
Over There (FX, 2005)
Owl Service, The (Granada, 1969)

Panorama (BBC, 1953–)
Patterns (NBC, 1955)
Picket Fences (CBS, 1992–1996).

Play School (BBC2 1964–1988)
Pogles, The (BBC 1965)
Police Surgeon (ITV, 1960)
Practice, The (ABC, 1997–2004)
Primeval (ITV, 2007–)
Prison Break (Fox, 2005–)
Prisoner, The (ITV, 1967–1968)
Professionals, The (ITV, 1977–1983)
Pushing Daisies (ABC, 2007–2009)

Quantum Leap (NBC, 1989–1993)
Quatermass (BBC, 1979)
Quatermass Experiment (BBC, 1953)
Quatermass Experiment (BBC, 2005)
Quatermass II (BBC, 1955)
Quatermass and the Pit (BBC, 1958–1959)
Queer as Folk UK (Channel 4, 1999)
Queer as Folk US (Showtime, 2000–2005)
Question Time (BBC, 1979–)

Red Dwarf (BBC, 1988–)
Remington Steele (NBC, 1982–1987)
Requiem for a Heavyweight (CBS, 1956)
Rescue Me (FX, 2004)
Roobarb (BBC, 1975)
Robinson Crusoe (BBC, 1965)
Roseanne (ABC, 1988–1997)
Roswell (WB, 1999–2002)
Rowan and Martin's Laugh-In (NBC, 1968–1973)

Saga of Noggin the Nog, The (BBC, 1964–1971)
Saint, The (ITV, 1962–1969)
Sanctuary (online, 2007) (Sci-Fi, 2008–)
Sapphire & Steel (ITV, 1979–1982)
Saturday Night Live (NBC, 1975–)
Seinfeld (NBC, 1990–1998)
Sesame Street (CTW, 1969–)
Sex and the City (HBO, 1998–2004)
Shadows (ITV, 1975–1978)
Shield, The (FX, 2002–2008)
Shut up and Dance (Bravo, 2008)
Simpsons, The (Fox, 1989–)
Singing Ringing Tree, The (UFA, 1955)

Six Feet Under (HBO, 2001–2005)
Smallville (WB/CW, 2001–)
Soap (ABC, 1977–1981)
Sopranos, The (HBO, 1999–2007)
South Park (Comedy Central, 1997–)
Spin City (ABC, 1996–2002)
Spooks (BBC, 2002–)
SpungeBob SquarePants (Nickelodeon, 1999–)
St. Elsewhere (NBC, 1982–1988)
Stargate SG–1 (Showtime, 1997–2002, Sci-Fi, 2002–2006)
Star Trek (NBC, 1966–1969)
Star Trek: The Next Generation [Syndicated; 1987–1994]
Star Trek: Deep Space Nine (Paramount Pictures, 1993–1999)
Star Trek: Voyager (UPN, 1995–2001)
Starved (FX, 2005)
State of Play (BBC, 2003)
Supernatural (WB/CW, 2005–)
Survivors (BBC, 1975–1977)
Sweeney, The (ITV, 1975–1978)

Teletubbies (BBC, 1997–2001)
Terminator: The Sarah Connor Chronicles (Fox, 2008–2009)
Thirtysomething (ABC, 1987–1991)
Thunderbirds (ATV, 1965–1966)
Tomorrow People, The (ITV, 1973–1979)
Tonight (BBC, 1957)
Torchwood (BBC, 2006–)
Trailer Park Boys (Paramount Comedy, 2001–)
Tru Calling (Fox, 2003–2005)
Tudors, The (BBC, 2007)
Tutti Frutti (BBC, 1973)
Twilight Zone, The (CBS, 1959–1965)
Twin Peaks (ABC, 1990–1991)

Vanished (Fox, 2006)
Veronica Mars (UPN/CW, 2004–2007)

Wagon Train (NBC, 1957–1962, ABC, 1962–1965)
Waltons, The (CBS, 1972–1981)
War Game, The (BBC, 1965)
Weeds (Showtime, 2005–)
West Wing, The (NBC, 1999–2006)

Wild Palms (ABC, 1993)
Will and Grace (NBC, 1998–2006)
Wire, The (HBO, 2002–2008)
Wishbone (PBS, 1995–1998)
Wonderfalls (FOX, 2004)

X-Factor, The (ITV, 2004–)
X-Files, The (FOX, 1993–2002),
Xena: Warrior Princess (Syndicated, 1995–2001)

Yak (Yorkshire, 1972)

Z Cars (BBC, 1962–1965, 1967–1978)
Zoo Time (Granada 1956–1968)

Film

21 grams (Alejandro González Iñárritu, US, 2003)

Alien vs Predator (Paul W.S. Anderson, US, 2004)
Ali G in Da House (Mark Mylod, UK, 2002)
American Beauty (Sam Mendes, US, 1999)
Asphalt Jungle, The (John Huston, US, 1950)
Avengers, The (Jeremiah Chechik, GB, 1998)

Banger Sisters, The (Bob Dolman, US, 2002)
Blade Runner (Ridley Scott, US, 1982)
Blair Witch Project, The (Daniel Myrick and Eduardo Sánchez, US, 1999)
Borat: Cultural Learnings of America for Make Benefit Glorious Nation of Kazakhstan (Larry Charles, US, 2006)

Carrie (Brian DePalma, US, 1976)
Casablanca (Michael Curtiz, US, 1943)
Citizen Kane (Orson Welles, US, 1941)
Clash of the Titans (Desmond Davis, US, 1981)
Close Encounters of the Third Kind (Steven Spielberg, US, 1977)
Cloverfield (Matt Reeves, US, 2008)

Diary of the Dead (George Romero, US, 2008)
Double Indemnity (Billy Wilder, US, 1944)

Galaxy Quest (Dean Parisot, US, 1999)
Golden Compass, The (Chris Weitz, US, 2007)
Goldfinger (Guy Hamilton, GB, 1964)
Groundhog Day (Harold Ramis, US, 1993)

Hellboy (Guillermo del Toro, US, 2004)

Indiana Jones and the Kingdom of the Crystal Skull (Steven Spielberg, US, 2008)
Jason and the Argonauts (Don Chaffey, UK/US, 1963)

Murder My Sweet (Edward Dmytryk, US, 1944)

On Her Majesty's Secret Service (Peter R. Hunt, GB, 1969)

Pirates of the Caribbean: The Curse of the Black Pearl, The (Gore Verbinski, US, 2003)
Planet of the Apes (Franklin J. Shaffner,US, 1968)
Postman Always Rings Twice, The (Tay Garnett, US, 1946)

Quatermass Conclusion, The (Piers Haggard, UK, 1979)

Rashomon (Akira Kurosawa, JP, 1950)
[Rec] (Jaume Balagueró and Paco Plaza, Sp, 2007)
River's Edge (Tim Hunter, US, 1986)
Riviere du hibou, La (Robert Henrico, Fr, 1962)
Rocketeer, The (Joe Johnston, US, 1991)
Rocky Horror Picture Show, The (Jim Sharman, UK/US, 1975)

Sex and the City: The Movie (Michael Patrick King, US, 2008)
South Park: Bigger, Longer and Uncut (Matt Parker and Trey Stone, 1999)
Star Trek: The Motion Picture (Robert Wise, US, 1979)
Star Trek XI (J.J. Abrams, US, 2009)
Star Wars (George Lucas, US, 1977)

Touch of Evil (Orson Welles, US, 1958)
Trailer Park Boys: The Movie (Clattenburg, CA, 2006)
Twin Peaks: Fire Walk with Me (David Lynch, US, 1992)

Index